LETTERS OF
JOHN HENRY NEWMAN

Other books by the editors

By Muriel Spark and Derek Stanford (jointly)
>Tribute to Wordsworth: a symposium
>My Best Mary (Letters of Mary Shelley)
>Emily Brontë: her life and work

By Muriel Spark
>Child of Light: a reassessment of
>Mary Shelley
>John Masefield: a study
>Selected Poems of Emily Brontë
>Letters of the Brontës
>The Comforters (a novel)

By Derek Stanford
>The Freedom of Poetry (essays)
>Christopher Fry: an appreciation
>Dylan Thomas: a literary study
>Fénelon's Letters to Men and
>Women: a selection

LETTERS

of

JOHN HENRY NEWMAN

———≈))))))◆((((((≈———

A Selection
edited and introduced by
Derek Stanford
and
Muriel Spark

THE NEWMAN PRESS
Westminster, Maryland
1957

Nihil obstat Andreas J. Moore, L.C.L.
                                Censor deputatus.

Imprimatur E. Morrogh Bernard. *Vic. Gen.*

Westmonasterii, die 13a Martii, 1957.

PRINTED IN GREAT BRITAIN BY
JOHN BUCKLE (PRINTERS) LIMITED
THEATRE PLAIN, GREAT YARMOUTH
NORFOLK
MCMLVII

CONTENTS

CONTENTS

CONTENTS

PART II

Newman as Catholic

THE LETTERS (*continued*)   *page*

EDITORIAL NOTE

Our editorial bias is to some extent dictated by the selections of letters and extracts already made by others from Newman's vast correspondence.

Apart from two unpublished letters, those in this book have appeared in the following works: *Letters and Correspondence of John Henry Newman during his Life in the English Church* edited by Anne Mozley (1891), *Correspondence of John Henry Newman with John Keble and Others 1839—1845* edited at the Birmingham Oratory (1917), *Cardinal Newman and William Froude, F.R.S., a Correspondence* by Gordon Huntington Harper (1933), *The Life of John Henry Cardinal Newman* by Wilfrid Ward (1912), *Catholic Life and Letters of Cardinal Newman* by John Oldcastle (1885), *Life of Cardinal Manning* by Edmund Sheridan Purcell (1895) and *Letters and Notices* (1891).

For permission to use all letters published here we wish to thank the Birmingham Oratory and to acknowledge the kindness accorded to us by Father Stephen Dessain of the Oratory.

We are also greatly indebted to Father Philip Caraman, S.J. who most generously made available to us for purposes of study a collection of Newman's manuscript letters to the Jesuit Fathers, two of which are included in this selection.

D.S.

30th November, 1956   M.S.

For
ROBIN SPARK
with love

PART I

NEWMAN AS ANGLICAN

BY

DEREK STANFORD

I

The Apologia versus the Letters

When Anne Mozley's edition of John Henry Newman's *Letters and Correspondence* "during his Life in the English Church" appeared, it was greeted by the poet-critic Lionel Johnson with the following words of ovation. "There are," he wrote in his review for *The Anti-Jacobin* (Jan. 31, 1891),[1] "pages in these volumes which for exquisite refinement of analysis might have been written by one or two great living Frenchmen; minute accounts of mental and physical states, displaying a very genius for psychological work. There are curious passages of self-description, telling us how conscious he was of his own irony, or shyness, or vehemence, and of their effects upon other people. There are passages of nature description, full of magical touches, and illustrating his susceptibility to the influence of season and place. An admirable judge of wine; an excellent violinist; a man of rare feeling for perfection in beauty material or spiritual."

This is a handsome panegyric, and one which the most summary recollection of Newman's many and versatile talents will fully be seen to justify. Of one side of Newman it presents a fair report: of the other it says little or nothing. In his admirable rhetoric of praise, Johnson would seem to have viewed the letters in the light of Newman's other writings ("the slightest and most occasional note" of which, he tells us, was better known to him than "anything else in literature"). The virtues, so readily apparent, in Newman's formal compositions, Johnson appears to have appropriated to the private Newman of the correspondence. This error in the perspective of attention is common enough among Newman admirers. Nor is its origin hard to locate. The recognition of the nation at large, attending the appearance of the *Apologia*, necessarily makes that book a

[1] Included in *Post Liminium: Essays and Critical Papers* by Lionel Johnson (1912).

focal-point for Newman readers. In a way it is natural that this should be so. By its publication, Newman obtained the restitution of his good name among a great number of minds who had previously been unsympathetic. All the blandishment, appeal, and pathos which his rare personality possessed is present in this masterly story:[1] all the acrimony, stiffness, and prejudice of his complex disposition is omitted. For, indeed, in this matter, there are two distinct Newmans: the serene lucid stylist of the *Apologia,* writing from a standpoint of assured retrospection; and the restless, ambitious, seeking spirit, sometimes arrogant, not seldom pettish, who was the unquiet author of the letters.

I think the mistake by which we establish the *Apologia* not only as the central canon in Newman literature, but as the best authentic source-book for information on the author's life and thought, comes about in the following manner—a manner which must lead us, if there is error, to convict ourselves and not Newman of it. First, we assume that the *Apologia* is strictly an autobiography both in formal purpose and correctness as to fact. But these presuppositions are open to question, and it can be queried whether the book is really Newman's most accurate attempt to meet the demands of such a form of writing.

In the sub-title to the first edition, and in the first sentence to the edition of 1865, Newman speaks of the *Apologia* as A History of His Religious Opinions. The chapter-headings endorse this idea, Chapter One being styled "History of My Religious Opinions up to 1833," Chapter Two "History of My Religious Opinions from 1833 to 1839," and so forth up to Chapter Five which is described as "Position of My Mind since 1845." The essential nature of the work is suggested in the words of the Advertisement to the first popular edition contributed by Father Neville of the Oratory, Birmingham, Newman's literary executor. "The book," he reminds us, "was written throughout *currente*

---

[1] " There is," wrote Lionel Johnson in *The Academy* (Nov. 8, 1890), " one biography in our language, and Boswell wrote it; the one autobiography Newman has written." (v. *Post Liminium*). But is the *Apologia* most correctly thought of as an autobiography in the fullest sense? This question I have attempted to elucidate.

calamo as an answer to an attack by Charles Kingsley; its separate parts being sent to press, sometimes before being completed, in order to fulfil the conditions of publication, i.e. an unfailing appearance on Thursday in consecutive weeks." "These hurrying circumstances," explains Father Neville, "necessarily confined its author to such materials as he had close to hand." In other words, however diligent the soul-searching which Newman practised, a full inspection of documents which might well have prompted or corrected an already ageing memory (Newman was then sixty-three) proved impossible. Controversy recollected in tranquility might serve as an epithet for the more valuable matter of the *Apologia,* such matter being considered, not as the debate with Kingsley, but rather as the remembered conflict in Newman's own mind and person between Anglican and Roman claims. Proper to its origin, subject, and treatment, the book offers only a partial account of its author. A man's defence of himself in a police-court cannot be taken as his life-story, its purpose being something more immediate than this. It is true that the defendant must swear to tell the truth, yet let him attempt a minute retrospection and the magistrate will soon recall him to matters more pertinently to hand. Newman's *Apologia* is the literary equivalent of that portion of a man's life story which he might offer as defence in court, and if we take it as something else the fault lies not with Newman but with us.

Further, the most cursory research in Newman bibliography reveals that other documents, relevant to the issue, have long existed. The two-volume *Letters and Correspondence of John Henry Newman during his life in the English Church,* published in 1891, carried "a brief autobiography"[1] running to a hundred pages. The same work also contained extracts from Newman's private diaries.[2] That these sources are not better known is probably due to the comparative difficulty of procuring copies

---

[1] & [2]   These two sources, together with Newman's memoir of his illness in Sicily, along with other private writings not included in the *Letters and Correspondence* have at length been published under the editorship of Fathers Tristram and Dessain of the Oratory, Birmingham, as *John Henry Newman: Autobiographical Writings* (1956).

of the *Letters* to-day. The *Apologia*, on the other hand, has been reprinted at frequent intervals.

Not only has a numerous class of readers taken the *Apologia* as an essential life story rather than as an *ad hoc* defence. It has also chosen to ignore the nature and constituents of that defence and of the parties engaged in controversy dealt with in the book's lucid pages. Illustrative of this class is Oscar Wilde who wrote on Newman in his dialogue *The Critic as Artist*. The character Gilbert, a young aesthete, who pronounces upon the *Apologia*, is not interested in the author's overt subject. "The mode of thought that Cardinal Newman represented," he tells his companion and disciple Ernest, "—if that can be called a mode of thought which seeks to solve intellectual problems by a denial of the supremacy of the intellect—may not, cannot, I think, survive. But the world will never weary of watching that troubled soul in its progress from darkness to darkness. The lonely church at Littlemore, where the breath of the morning is damp, and the worshippers are few, will always be dear to it, and whenever men see the yellow snapdragon blossoming on the wall at Trinity they will think of that gracious undergraduate who saw in the flower's sure recurrence a prophecy that he would abide for ever with the Benign Mother of his days—a prophecy that Faith, in her wisdom or her folly, suffered not to be fulfilled."

Newman himself was of the opinion that "The true life of a man is in his letters," and if we approach his correspondence as a postscript to his *Apologia* or to the entire body of his work, we are inverting a natural procedure. I have remarked how Lionel Johnson appropriated to Newman's letters many of the virtues of his formal compositions. To do so is to lose the image of the private correspondent in the full-dress public figure. It is to find in the correspondence merits of style and character which, properly speaking, do not exist there in their refined and separated state. It is to ignore the inevitable detritus of moral and spiritual endeavour; to view all attributes of thought and conduct as perfected and accomplished in their growth when, actually, they have not been segregated from the adhering error and wrong. It is possible, if we believe in Newman's cause for canonisation, to view the correspondence as a record of a saint in the making. What is not possible is to regard it as the account of a substantially achieved sainthood. I am, of course, referring here to the letters which Newman wrote while in the English Church. The tale they tell increasingly is one of a traveller in a dark wood. Like Dante, the traveller finds himself there "In the midway of this our mortal life." The light darkens as he proceeds, perspective and possibilities diminish. The journey is long, his adversaries many, and in the murk which closes round him, it is not surprising that their faces seem distorted, and their acts and gestures at times daemonic.

Such was Newman's adventure in the wood of Anglicanism, a happening not without irony, since—as self-appointed woodsman on that site—he had planted saplings there himself and had hoped to fell a deal of timber which none the less outlasted him. Newman's mind was neither disinterested nor factual. There was no calm ground to it, no serenity in approaching knowledge. Rather was it innately dramatic, presenting to itself new events, fresh ideas, as factors in a perpetual engagement of forces. The resultant restlessness, excitement, and mobility are recorded faithfully in these letters. And if they can seldom be said to testify to peace of spirit, they bear indisputable witness to an intense activity of mind.

II

In Search of Self

John Henry Newman was born on February 21, 1801, in Old Bond Street in the City of London. His father was a banker but in no big way of business, of easy disposition and few intellectual tastes. His mother, descended from Huguenot stock, was strictly religious, regular in church-going and inclining to standards of worship which we should now describe as Low Church. The question of Jewish blood in Newman's parents has often been raised inconclusively. Certainly it might, if proved, explain a number of colourful 'un-English' traits in their brilliant, so different son. One thinks, for instance, of his proneness to tears and of his night-long sobbing embrace of the body of his dead friend Ambrose St. John.

The young Newman early possessed a sense of the numinous. It is possible that the bare 'Low Church' service, which he and his family attended, did not constitute a locale favourable to the presences of the supernatural in terms of imaginative apprehension. The bare church walls proved poor conductors for the sensuous-minded boy.[1] Deterred from finding it in the precincts of worship, Newman discovered it manifested to him in his everyday life at home and at school. He experienced the sensation and fostered the notion that life might be a dream, or he an Angel, and all this world a deception, his fellow-angels by a playful device concealing themselves from him, and deceiving him with the semblance of a material world.[2] The shrewd but unsympathetic author of the *Analysis of Cardinal Newman's "Apologia pro Vita Sua,"* a fundamentalist Evangelical, has shown how this experience accorded with the neo-Platonic thought of the Alexandrian Fathers whom Newman later studied and praised. Although the author does not so observe, perhaps we may believe it was this Patristic thought which interpreted Newman's boyhood notion in ecclesiastical hierarchical terms. Newman's early numinous experience bears striking resemblance to that which Wordsworth knew as a boy, when frequently he found it necessary to touch or take up physical objects to convince himself of their materiality. Without his reading in Patristic literature, it is possible that Newman's belief in an Invisible Church, which had at the same time a Visible form and structure, would have remained a formal proposition to which he might have given only "notional"[3] assent. Because, in adulthood

[1] " The secret of the course of Dr. Newman's mind is this—it is sensuous."— *Analysis of Cardinal Newman's " Apologia pro Vitâ Suâ."* (the " anonymous " author is T. R. Grundy).

[2] The passage is quoted from the *Apologia* with only slight alterations.

[3] (and [1] & [2] opposite) These terms are taken from Newman's *Grammar of Assent.*

the Fathers provided an intellectual framework for a boyhood experience, Newman met with "real"[1] assent the "actual"[2] truth of the Church Invisible which is said to be the Visible Catholic Church. That his early "mistrust of the reality of material phenomena,"[3] taken by itself, had no essential connection with Christian doctrine is suggested by the subsequent direction of Wordsworth's mind, whose middle- and old-aged Anglicanism was never more than nominal.

Newman suffered from 'examination nerves' and attempting at Trinity College, Oxford, to take his B.A. with honours, he barely gained the pass degree. This misfortune he later reversed by obtaining a fellowship at Oriel, the intellectual hive of the University, in 1823. Ordination followed in 1824.

The prevailing spirit of the Oriel Common Room was rationalistic. Its leading members were sometimes referred to as the Noetics. They were, as Hugh Walker remarks, " the 'intelligent' of the Church, the men who laid emphasis on 'the intelligible,' the men to whom *credo quia impossible*—would itself have been impossible."[4] The first Noetic personalities belonged to no single section of the Church. Copleston and Hawkins were High Churchmen, Hampden was an Evangelical, Whatley and Thomas Arnold were what was later called Broad Church. The tone of this Common Room, to which the diffident sensitive Newman now found himself expected to contribute, was stringent and critical. Saintsbury has commented on Whatley's curiously English "sort of knock-me-down Johnsonian dogmatism,"[5] and the mental bias of the O.C.R. probably bore some resemblance to the temper of present-day Logical Positivists.

For a young man of Newman's conventional upbringing this was all a little frightening. But it was stimulating, also. "Much as I owe to Oriel," Newman wrote to Whatley in 1826,[6] "to none,

[3] *Apologia.*

[4] *The Literature of the Victorian Era.*

[5] *Nineteenth Century Literature.*

[6] *Letters and Correspondence of John Henry Newman during his Life in the English Church.* All further quotations in this essay, when not otherwise indicated, are taken from this source.

as I think, do I owe so much as to you. I know who it was who first gave me heart to look after my election, and taught me to think correctly, and—strange office for an instructor—to rely upon myself."

To Dr. Hawkins, Vicar of the University Church of St. Mary's, and afterwards Provost of Oriel, Newman also paid proper tribute. "He was the first," he wrote in the *Apologia*, "who taught me to weigh my words, and to be cautious in my statements."

For a while Newman studied with these masters, but their talk proved dangerously bracing. In truth, he appears to have experienced guilt for having dallied with these bold reasoners. "I was beginning to prefer intellectual excellence to moral," he tells us. "I was drifting in the direction of liberalism. I was rudely awakened from my dream at the end of 1827 by two great blows—illness and bereavement."[1]

Geoffrey Faber in his book *Oxford Apostles* has suggested that the base of Newman's religion (at whatever period of his life) was fear. This is not to deprecate his faith so much as to determine its kind. The basis of religion in some men is joy; in some, love or praise; in others, fear. "The fear of the Lord is the beginning of wisdom." There is certainly a good case for believing this to be so of Newman. In his later Anglican days, his attitude to post-Baptismal sin was gloomy and severe in the extreme. He even doubted whether the Atonement (with its emphasis on salvation) was a suitable theme for contemporary pulpits. The same, on occasion, could be argued of his attitude in the Roman Church.

However this may be, Newman revolted from the Noetics. A number of younger men, with different ideas, were conveniently to hand, offering for the old lamp of reason the new rushlight of tradition. From Hawkins, as Newman admits, he had already obtained one doctrine of Tradition, i.e. "that the sacred text was never intended to teach doctrine, but only to prove it, and that

[1] He was taken ill in November while examining in the schools. In January, Mary—his favourite sister—died.

if we would learn doctrine, we must have recourse to the formularies of the Church, for instance, to the Catechism and to the
Creeds."[1] But the free-play and masculine forwardness of thought,
with which this went accompanied among the Noetics, proved
too vast a liberty for Newman's sanction-seeking conscience. It is
possible, too, that the Oriel arguments appealed to a vein of
deep-sunk scepticism which Newman was unwilling to explore.
Influenced by Butler's *Analogy of Religion*, Newman's defence
of Christianity was grounded on the sum of possibilities—a mode
of reasoning which must always leave us with a margin of doubt.

What we do know is that the notion of tradition which
Newman learned from his new and younger friends—from Keble,
Hurrell Froude, and, later, from Pusey—was retrospective and
consolidatory. On the whole, its face was turned to the past: in
Keble's case to the Church of Laud and Herbert; in Hurrell
Froude's, to the Middle Ages; in Pusey's, to the Ancient Fathers.
All of them were seeking a return—even if a synthetic one—to
a condition or conditions of the past. Hurrell Froude talked of
the need for a "Second Reformation" to re-Catholicise the
English Church, and Keble and Pusey in their more moderate
fashion looked towards a similar end.

In addition, the tone of these young men differed from that of
the Oriel Noetics which was tough, logical, and dry with com-
mon-sense. Keble was saintly and poetic, a precocious and prodigious classical scholar who preferred a cure of village souls to
the round of academic honours. He none the less maintained
contact with Oxford, and through both his poetry and his
disposition exerted a strong influence on Newman. Keble's poem
The Christian Year is generally under-rated nowadays (Saintsbury, in the light of it, wrote of the poet as a "Christian
Horace"),[2] but to Newman, who was also a poet, it spoke with
an intimate charm and helped to engender that romantic atmosphere in which the Oxford Movement was suffused. To employ
Newman's own Greek, it probably did as much as anything to

[1] *Apologia.*

[2] *Nineteenth Century Literature.*

establish the θοsῆ (ethos) of the Movement, whose *enfant terrible* was the impetuous 'cross-country' theologian and amateur mediaevalist, Hurrell Froude. The relationship between him and Newman was of a close and tender nature, with the former inciting the latter to ever fresh commitments of the Catholic faith and ever more precipitate policy and action.

Pusey, the greatest scholar of the group, with a reputation for erudition in Biblical studies far beyond this limited circle, began by rather disturbing Newman's tremulous religious conscience. With that strain of affectation, which he was later to repudiate Newman noted down his impressions of Pusey in the May of 1824: "That Pusey is Thine, O Lord, how can I doubt? His deep views of the Pastoral Office, his high ideas of the spiritual rest of the Sabbath, his devotional spirit, his love of the Scriptures, his firmness and zeal, all testify to the operation of the Holy Ghost; yet I fear he is prejudiced against Thy children." This last sentiment was a reference to the Evangelical notion of the Chosen or Elect, among whom Newman counted himself when he was not, with spirits uneasy, sporting with the hardened Noetics. But Pusey, made suspect in Newman's eyes through contact with German scholarship, sloughed off the more dangerous skins of his seeming liberalism and entered into the work of the Movement one year after its inception.

In the December of 1832 Newman left with Hurrell Froude for a cruise and tour in the Mediterranean. Much has been made of his impressions of Rome, but it was Sicily which influenced him with a high sense of the numinous which he did not register in the capital of the Western Church. Along with Froude and his father, Newman had already visited the island. "Spring in Sicily!" he had written to his sister Jemima. "It is the nearest approach to Paradise of which sinful man is capable." Now, instead of making his way home, along with his friends across France, Newman returned south by himself. There, once more, in that land of Greek remains, amid the fallen theatres and temples, an intimation of innocence and peace visited his restless heart. Of Tairominium he confessed that he had never seen

"anything more enchanting than this spot." "I never knew that
nature could be so beautiful; and to see that view was the nearest
approach to seeing Eden. O happy I! It was worth coming all
the way, to endure sadness, loneliness, weariness, to see it. I felt,
for the first time in my life, that I should be a better, more
religious man if I lived there."

We are apt to forget in ecclesiastic Newman the lover of
classical literature. Recalling his life in the Roman Church, it is
easier to keep this image in mind, since his lectures *On the
Scope and Nature of University Education* pay so choice a tribute
to the study of humane letters and the culture of the ancients
from which they derive. In Newman the Anglican, it is the
propagandist, the controversial and illiberal critic who too often
fills the picture. This being so, his instinctive response to the
classical landscape of Sicily, in which the ghost of Virgil and the
locus dei seemed still to have some shadowy existence, is all the
more significant. "The hills recede," he wrote in a letter. "Etna
was magnificent . . I understood why the poets made the
abode of the gods on Mount Olympus."

But this experience of in-breaking beauty was followed by a
severe fever which at one stage looked to prove mortal. Geoffrey
Faber who speculates on Newman's "psychopathological" disposition[1] (today we should probably use the term 'psychosomatic')
believes there was a rhythm in Newman's life wherewith periods
of tranquility and ease were followed by periods of depression
and distress, as if some innate sense of guilt punished a state of
well-being with one of ill health or low-spirits. Suffice it to say
that Newman nearly died, that while he was nursed in his
delirium by an Italian servant he asserted he would live because
he had not sinned against the light, that he urged on his conva-
lescence by repeating to this simple servant that he had a work
to do in England. One year later he began an account headed
My Illness in Sicily, a reconstruction of this event to which he
occasionally added up to 1874. Of this remarkable paper a friend
wrote to Anne Mozley (Newman's sister-in-law): "There is a

[1] *Oxford Apostles* (1933).

great deal about his illness, and a good deal that goes into minutiae and special feelings in illness. But he so plainly always looked on the fever in all its features as a *crisis in his life,* partly judgment on past self-will, partly a sign of special electing and directing favour, that the prominence given to it is quite accounted for by those who knew him, and explains why all these strange pictures of fever are given."

Newman landed in England on July 9, 1833, and found there was indeed work to be done. "The following Sunday, July 14," as he notices in the *Apologia,* "Mr. Keble preached the Assize Sermon in the University Pulpit . . . I have ever considered and kept the day, as the start of the religious movement of 1833." What, briefly, was this movement which Keble's sermon so successfully touched off? It was a sort of churchmen's trade union, though its leaders did not think of it quite in those terms. Lord Liverpool, a previous Prime Minister, had told the Bishops to "put their house in order," failing which he would do it for them. Such was the general attitude of the Whigs towards ecclesiastical abuse. Plurality of livings and the absentee holding of benefices offended their strong economic sense. In Ireland, with its large Roman Catholic majority, and its Presbyterian minority in the north, the National Church throughout the land was something of an anomaly. The Whigs, with their budgeting eye for waste, decided to suppress ten Irish bishoprics, telling protesting Church members to be thankful things were not worse.

This was the rationalist pragmatic temper of the Government towards the Church which caused Keble to sound the alarm. In his sermon on "National Apostasy,"[1] he considered the symptoms which suggested that the country was "becoming alienated from God and Christ." People, it seemed, no longer doubted the virtue and good will of men who did not worship in the parish church, parents allowed their children to marry into families which were not C. of E., the authority of clergy was often borne impatiently. The situation was clearly a grave one.

That same July, in Oriel, a resolution was taken "to unite and

[1] *Sermons Academical and Occasional.*

associate in defence of the Church." At a later meeting, two points were agreed on: "to fight for the doctrine of the Apostolical Succession and for the integrity of the Prayer Book." From this decision there quickly followed the first *Tracts for the Times,* by which the Movement was provided with a theory and a *mystique.* If the Church resented the State's supremacy in matters of discipline, doctrine, and property, its best defence was to authenticate its independence in these matters. This the Movement endeavoured to do by appealing to the Apostolical Succession (the notion of an unbroken chain, effected by the act of consecration, between the Apostles and contemporary bishops). If the Church was not putting its house in order, at least it was energetically engaged in the compilation of title-deeds.

The various names by which members of the Movement were known indicate aspects of the alliance—the Tractarians, the Sacramentalists, the Oxford Apostolicals. Later, when Newman had left the Movement, they were referred to as the Puseyites after the sober learned figure who took over its leadership. One of the best short summaries of the Movement, though very critical of its aims, occurs in a review by Dr. Thomas Arnold, the pioneering headmaster of Rugby. Recalling the term bestowed upon Archbishop Laud and his followers for their persecution of the Puritans, he spoke of the Tractarians as "The Oxford Malignants."[1] Their "fanaticism," he maintained, was not only bigoted: it lacked authentic implementation. Followed his famous definition of the Movement: "A dress, a ritual, a name, a ceremony;—a technical phraseology; the superstition of the priesthood without its power;—the form of episcopal government, without its substance; a system imperfect and paralysed, not independent, not sovereign; afraid to cast off the subjection against which it is perpetually murmuring."[2] It is surprising how well this accords with many a Roman statement on the present Anglo-Catholic position.

[1] The implied comparison was not unjust. The Oxford Movement in its first phase wished to limit the scope and privileges of both Dissenters and Roman Catholics. Its attitude to other Christian Churches, in its early years, was fiercely anti-ecumenical.

[2] *Edinburgh Review* (Vol I. xiii, 1836).

In staking a claim for the English Church on antiquity, continuity of dogma, apostolic office and authority, Newman was foremost. The most fertile and frequent contributor to the *Tracts for the Times,* he published also two full-length works: *The Prophetical Office of the Church* in 1837 and *The Lectures on Justification by Faith* in 1838. The concluding wording to the title of the first—"viewed relatively to Romanism and Popular Protestantism"—suggests the tendency of the book, which was to establish the *via media* as a body of worship and doctrine midway between the opposite poles of Puritan and Roman religion. The second work can be said to offer both a moderate critique and defence of the popular Protestant belief in justification by faith alone.[1] Again, its endeavour is to strike a balance between Lutheran and Roman doctrines of salvation, the balance constituting the Anglican ideal as Newman represented it. In addition to these lectures and publications, in 1838 he assumed the editorship of the *British Critic,* the Movement's magazine. But by far the most influential part of his work were his sermons delivered at St. Mary's and published serially afterwards. The musical, searching, modulated tone; the limpid, choice, poetic language; and the earnestness of thought and delivery combined to make the preacher's appearance an occasion of memorable beauty. "Who could resist," wrote Matthew Arnold, recalling the Oxford of his youth, "the charm of that spiritual apparition, gliding in the dim afternoon light through the aisles of St. Mary's, rising into the pulpit, breaking the silence with words and thoughts which were a religious music—subtle, sweet, mournful?"[2] To the younger Arnold the aesthetic fascination of the spectacle was complete. To the same Arnold, later in life, it

---

[1] Popular opinion has generally considered the difference between Roman and Protestant doctrine on justification and salvation to turn upon the greater stress which Rome places on good works. This is largely erroneous. Père Bouyer, French Protestant pastor now become a Roman Catholic, has demonstrated how Luther's essential teaching was in pure accordance with early Catholic doctrine and with the contentions of St. Thomas Aquinas. He also indicates how later Protestant practice tended to divide this common unity. (v. *The Forms and Spirit of Protestantism,* 1956).

[2] *Discourses in America.*

seemed that the Cardinal had adopted "a solution which, to speak frankly, is impossible." Who could resist? Well, Arnold resisted; but remembered the experience all his life.

That Newman's words, in his Sermons, were his own, that he was sincere in uttering them, there can be no question. But whether the thoughts which they expressed were likewise innate and individual to him is a matter permitting of some doubt. Newman was wont to regard himself as the rhetorician of the Oxford Movement, as the literary orator who gave currency to the ideas of its "philosophers," Keble and Hurrell Froude. The fuller implication of this tendency of thought may be seen by considering a passage of Newman's memorandum *My Illness in Sicily*, written in 1834. "I seemed to see more and more my utter hollowness. I began to think of all my professed principles, and felt they were mere intellectual deductions from one or two admitted truths. I compared myself with Keble, and felt that I was merely developing his, not my, convictions. I know I had *very* clear thoughts about this then, and I believe in the main true ones. Indeed, this is how I look on myself; very much (as the illustration goes) as a pane of glass, which transmits heat, being cold itself. I have a vivid perception of the consequences of certain admitted principles, have a considerable intellectual capacity of drawing them out, have the refinement to admire them, and a rhetorical or histrionic power to represent them; and, having no great (i.e. no vivid) love of this world, whether riches, honours, or anything else, and some firmness and natural dignity of character, take the profession of them upon me, as I might sing a tune which I liked—loving the Truth, but not possessing it, for I believe myself at heart to be nearly hollow, i.e. with little love, little self-denial."

This is an intriguing admission, make what we will of it. One thing it might suggest, which would be false, is that Newman lacked the power of creative thought. His gift of thought was as obvious as his evident disinclination for it. It is this, I believe,

---

[1] To apply the term " philosopher " to Keble, as Newman does, seems curiously inept. Whatever else Keble was—poet, preacher, scholar, saint, or bigot—his was hardly the vocation of systematic or abstract thought.

which must account for the small element of metaphysical writing in the corpus of his work.[1] Unlike the ignorant man in the Wandering Scholar's song, Newman had small reason to

. . . fear the toss of the
Horns of philosophy,

yet it is possible he did fear these weapons, chiefly when wielded by himself. One redoubtable exception to this is the *Fifteen Sermons Preached before the University of Oxford*, between 1826 and 1843, towards a "Theory of Religious Belief." Lacking the persuasive embellishments, the affecting treatment of the *Parochial Sermons*, they attempt more nearly than any of his work to arrive at a statement of religious belief in terms of analytic truth.

In a footnote to the second of the *University Sermons*, Newman remarks that "The author was not acquainted at the time this was written with Mr. Coleridge's work, and a remarkable passage in his *Biographia Literaria* in which several portions of this Sermon are anticipated." Newman in his letters and writings makes several references to Coleridge, generally to the effect that his thought vaporises Church teaching by translating Christian dogma into transcendental terms. Metaphysically, there was a kinship between the ideas of the two men, but while Coleridge freely evolved his argument against a background of pro-Lutheran, anti-Laudian, individual High Churchmanship, Newman, committed by clerical ties, by classic formularies of the Faith, and by the Church's 'proofs of history,' was forced to rescind or cut his speculation more closely.

But Newman's approach to the Christian Church was, firstly, historical;[2] secondly, theological; thirdly, moral; and, only fourthly, philosophic. Prior to the start of the Movement proper, he had published an historical work on *The Arians of the Fourth Century*.[3] This was the first of a number of researches into the

---

[1] The author of the *Analysis of Cardinal Newman's " Apologia pro Vitâ Suâ "* makes a shrewd observation when he says that the predominating interest in Newman's mind up to 1845 was not Christ in relation to " truth " but Christ in relation to the contending claims of Canterbury and Rome.

[2] I mean that while in the English Church he sought to decide and authenticate the truth of the Christian Church primarily through historical inquiry.

[3] Newman had been at work on it since 1831. It appeared in 1833.

history of the Early Church which finally carried him over the Anglican border into Rome. Saintsbury maintained that Newman "was distinctly deficient in the historic sense."[1] The present writer possesses little means of verifying this verdict with any nicety. Suffice it to say that the man who could write that "the Church of Rome apostatised at Trent"[2] appears to be taking liberties with history.

What persuaded Newman in his doubts as to whether the English Church had the Catholic faith was a number of parallels which he discovered between early and present times. The doubts began in 1839 when he was studying the history of the Monophysite[3] controversy in the fifth century, were strengthened by an article which Cardinal Wiseman[4] had written on the Donatist Christians[5] in which he compared that heretical body to the Church of England in relation to orthodox Romanism, and were conclusively confirmed by his own study of St. Athanasius in his conflict with the Arians.[6] As he remarks in the *Apologia*, "The ancients supplied a text and the moderns provided it with a commentary." That resemblances existed is doubtless true: that Newman discovered "parallels" in lines of no final likeness is possible. But what indicates the subjective bias in his inter-

---

[1] *Nineteenth Century Literature.*

[2] Had he said that the Council of Trent was no General Council it would have been another question.

[3] Monophysites: " the name given to those who held the doctrine that Christ had but *one* composite *nature* " (*Encyc. Brit.*)

[4] *Dublin Review* (August, 1839).

[5] The Donatists were " a powerful sect which arose in the Christian Church of northern Africa at the beginning of the 4th century . . . The predisposing causes of the Donatist schism were the belief . . . that validity of all sacerdotal acts depended upon the personal character of the agent, and the question arising out of that belief, as to the eligibility for sacerdotal office of the *traditores*, or those who delivered up their copies of the Scriptures under the compulsion of the Diocletian persecution." (*Encyc. Brit.*)

[6] Arius, who died in 336 A.D., and whose writing gave rise to wide controversy, " wished to establish the unity and simplicity of the eternal God. However far the Son may surpass other created beings, he remains himself a created being, to whom the Father before all time gave an existence ' formed out of nothing.' Arius was quite unconscious that his monotheism was hardly to be distinguished from that of pagan philosophers, and that his Christ was a demi-god." (*Encyc. Brit.*). The great opponent of the Arians was Athanasius.

pretation of facts is that Newman afterwards confessed he was
unable to demonstrate in convincing detail the arguments which
had so persuaded him. Writing in 1844 from his "Anglican
death-bed" at Littlemore, he admits that the cogent exactitude
of these parallels escapes him. "I ought," he says, in the rough
draft of a letter,[1] "to illustrate all this—but I do not know how
to do justice to my reasonings and impressions. They are just not
present—the impression remains, but the process of argument is
like a scaffolding taken down when the building is completed.
I could not recollect all the items which went to make up my
convictions, nor could I represent it to another with that force
with which it came to my own mind. Corroborations too are
generally coincidences—resulting from distinct courses of thought
or from the bodies of fact which require a certain frame of mind
to appreciate." This is honest, but surely it goes perilously near
to implying, with Kierkegaard, that "truth is subjectivity"—a
formulation which Newman would have been the first to
repudiate.[2]

Outward events also played a part in weaning him from the
English Church, the most prominent of these being the affair of
the Jerusalem Bishopric A politic arrangement had been made
between England and Prussia by which an English archbishop
was to consecrate a bishop to minister to the Protestants in
Palestine, the Bishops of Jerusalem to be, alternately, members
of the English and Prussian State Churches. The scheme actually
proved abortive; but here, for Newman, was heresy exalted,
heresy blessed by apostolic hands.

Other powerful reasons exist for positing the presence in
Newman's mind of a bias towards Catholicism in its pristine
Roman form. In the Low-Church environment of his parents'
home, he had as a child inscribed the cover of a simple exercise-
book with the design of a rosary and crucifix (a much more
audacious piece of doodling then than such an act would be

---

[1] The Editor of the *Correspondence of John Henry Newman with John Keble and others*
1839–1845 remarks in a foot-note that this was " Evidently intended to be an
Open Letter."

[2] v. his essay on *Private Judgment* written in 1841 (*Essays Critical and Historical*).

to-day). His attitude towards the episcopacy of the English Church more resembled that which the clerisy and laity of the Roman Church observe towards their hierarchy. He speaks, for example, of "that delicacy towards authorities which has been so painfully harassing to me." Anglican practice has tended to regard the bishops as justices-of-the-peace, as ecclesiastical magistrates, who, in times of harmony, are perhaps more seen than heard. Roman procedure, on the other hand, makes of the bishop a sort of administrator. One keeps a keen eye open for trouble: the other has trouble brought before him. From his own Bishop of Oxford, Newman frequently sought directives and corroboration. But the Bishop was unwilling to assume responsibility for what, he felt, should be Newman's own decisions. His only action, in time of disturbance, was gently and quietly to bind over the brilliant trouble-maker.[1]

Not only was Newman anxious to secure episcopal approval for his words and actions; he sought to obtain it from his friends and equals. Writing to C. R. Church, he speaks of looking on Pusey *as being in loco superioris.*" This way of looking at his colleague originated not with him but with Newman. The wording of a letter to Keble is also significant. In it he speaks of requesting from his friend not advice as to whether he should give up St. Mary's (whose vicar he had been since 1828), but rather "leave" to resign his living. Yet if he sought authority in the English Church it was in its aspect of support—support, that is, for his own schemes and wishes, rather than in obedience to dictation.

Mention has been made of Newman's foreign nature, of the possible mingling in his blood of Semitic and Latin elements, and of his emotionally expressive temperament, more oriental than Saxon-Norman. This is a field of unproven speculation, but the supposition of alien stock in Newman's subtle and exotic

[1] Newman was wont to represent action in the most dramatic fashion. He had, he complained left and right, " been silenced." On the other hand, he admitted that his position—without the Bishops' confirmation of it; indeed, with their express rebuttal of it, seemed to be that of " a sort of schematic or demagogue." Such was the necessary logic of his thought.

disposition could account for his misunderstanding of an institution so native, so natural, to the English as the English Church —for misunderstand it he certainly did. Since Newman's day there have been those who have intellectually accepted an historical defence of the Church of England; but to others it may seem that the C. of E. cannot be defended in that fashion, unless we substitute a providential for a sequential reading of history. One most honest defence, which I believe articulates a vast body of silent feeling in the Church of England, is that which the Rev. Frank Bennett[1] recently expressed. There is, he says, no theory of the Church of England any more than there is a theory of the Bible. The C. of E. is a Scriptural Church, though not in a fundamentalist sense. The Bible, he describes as a "tension book," as the record of a living tension or engagement between God and His people. In a like manner, he holds the C. of E. to be a "tension Church," concerned with the same kind of 'compass' relationship to God. Whether or no we approve this notion, it is clearly the sort of idea which Newman would neither have endorsed nor understood.

In 1841 the general alarm over the tendency of Newman's *Tract XC* made quite plain to all his direction.[2] It was evident now that the Church of England could not long contain his thought. By the following year over twelve thousand copies of the Tract had been sold, but this dissemination merely served to warn off his more moderate sympathisers. "I saw indeed," wrote Newman in the *Apologia*, "that my place in the Movement was lost; public confidence was at an end; my occupation was gone." Henceforth he was to be as much embarrassed as supported by his younger followers. This second wave of Tractarians was emotional and—though sometimes talented—hot-headed.

[1] *Theology* (July, 1956).

[2] In dedicating the second edition of his *Apologia* (1857) to Canon Flanagan, Newman says that *Tract XC* " was not a resolution of the 39 Articles into the Council of Trent, but an experimental inquiry *how far* they would approximate to it, under the notion that the Church of Rome would have *in her turn* to approximate to Protestants." He adds also that " the Tract had no wish to force a sense upon the 39 Articles, which they would not admit, but it considered them ' patient of a Catholic interpretation.' "

Some dropped away, others pressed on, arriving at the goal before their teacher. But whether relapsing or seeking fresh conversion, they proved a capricious and unruly handful.

Newman lay four years on his "Anglican death-bed" (as he termed his interregnum). This period was marked by his contracting out of academic and Anglican commitments. Early in 1842 he removed to Littlemore, establishing a sort of retreat-house there, and largely severing connection with Oxford. From Littlemore there issued, at intervals, as plangent a pulpit-music as ever this great preacher voiced. "The season is chill and dark, and the breath of the morning is damp, and worshippers are few; but all this befits those who are by their profession penitents and mourners, watchers and pilgrims. More dear to them that loneliness, more cheerful that severity, and more bright that gloom, than all those aids and appliances of luxury by which men nowadays attempt to make prayer less disagreeable. True faith does not covet comforts."[1]

In 1842 he resigned the living of the University Church of St. Mary's. On October 3, 1845 he wrote to Dr. Hawkins, Provost of Oriel, resigning his Fellowship; and was received into the Roman Faith by a Passionist Father five days later. So long a Catholic without knowing it, protesting so long against its recognition, Newman appears to me *anima naturaliter Catholica* The tale of his conversion is important not because it settles anything, but because it exhibits one man's endeavour outwardly to become what inwardly he is. We recall Spinoza's aphorism that the principle of every created being is to persist in its own identity. Newman's quest for the true Church was a quest for self-discovery and fulfilment.

III

Newman in his Letters

During the first thirty-eight years of his life, Newman's letters tend to earnestness. The best of them are high-spirited; the

[1] *Sermons on Subjects of the Day.*

worst, a little pompous or stiff. What we notice about the majority is their purposive tone and content. They are written to inform someone about something; and this aim gives them a unity which the letters of miscellaneous news and chatter lacks. The writer's strenuous unrelaxing mind is active in nearly all of them. Those objectives he held before him, and his approximation to them, are constantly noted and re-assessed. They are the records of a restless idealist, reminders and communiqués of one bent on self-improvement equally as on the improvement of others.

Newman was a perfectionist, but his notion of perfection and how to achieve it underwent considerable changes. In this sense, his letters offer the autobiography of a mind in its search for self-knowledge. In them, we follow those twists and turns, those divagations and doublings-back, those self-contradictions which accompany the growth of light in certain beings. Besides the purpose of self-discovery which these explorative movements aid, they serve to plot the activities of a subtle psychological tactician. Some are like dispatches from the front-line, some like orders from headquarters, others like notes from one commander to another, reciting the position or promising assistance. What the *Apologia,* in the name of harmony and unity, distorts, the letters delineate with faithful minuteness. Reading them, we possess the rough draft, the raw-material of a life-story.

Newman's earnest nature is early made evident. A certain religious precociousness is apparent in his fondness, at the age of sixteen, for William Beveridge's *Private Thoughts*—a seventeenth-century book of devotion. Two letters, about this time, to his late tutor, the Rev. W. Mayer, make both his religious interests and his moral scruples plain. Indeed, the behaviour of Oxford youth, particularly of the Gentlemen Commoners—a fast, unacademic, aristocratic body—scandalised Newman's unworldly sense. Commenting on such affairs, his letters contain a touch of priggishness. Late in attaining to a measure of self-knowledge, he was late, too, in learning to regard the garish scene with just detachment.

But the moral attention and earnestness which Newman unremittingly practised seems periodically to have produced reactions of weariness and strain. It is then that the assertive confident tone, the stringent veiled self-righteousness, the forward-looking course of the letters alter. Expressions of infirmity, self-pity, loneliness, or helplessness replace them. Writing to his mother from Trinity, Oxford, he tells her that inward examination caused him to shudder at himself. This self-doubt, or self-hatred (as Geoffrey Faber represents it), would appear to be of a different order to the Christian's candid admission of the fallen Adam in his nature. Regarded with affection and admiration by many, Newman could write in the following strain to Keble: "I think I am very cold and reserved to people, but I cannot ever realise to myself that any one loves me. I believe that is partly the reason, or I *dare* not realise it."

Newman's state of mind underwent cyclic changes. Of his enthusiastic cycles, one of the notes is aggressiveness—vehemence of statement and fierceness of attack. Of his depressed periods, the most striking note is pathos. "My days are gone like a shadow, and I am withered like grass," he laments in his last year at Littlemore. Nine years before, in 1836, he admits to his essential isolation. "God intends me to be lonely," he tells his sister Jemina. "I am not more lonely than I have been a long while; He has so framed my mind that I am in a great measure beyond the sympathies of other people and thrown upon myself." The letters of 1845 to this same sister and to Keble, his ever-patient friend, rehearse the end. It is here, as much as in the best of his verse, that the elegiac poet in Newman finds expression. Both correspondents possessed the gift of intimate emotional response, and Newman—in this religious parting of friends—elicited all their sympathy and pity.

The Littlemore period (from 1842—45) was an almost unbroken cycle of low-spirits. This chill upon his natural hopes

---

[1] Newman's ambition was directed towards the acceptance and success of his ideas rather than towards the elevation of his person. In the normal sense, he was not an ambitious man; but the importance he gave to his ideas strengthened his *amour-propre*.

and ambitions[1] may well have been conducive to Newman's powers of self-examination. At least, in spring and summer of 1844, he wrote a series of letters to Mrs. William Froude, wife of the distinguished scientist and later a member of the Roman Faith herself, in which he analysed the evolution of his dissatisfaction with the English Church. This is the fullest account of Newman's changing religious opinions to be found anywhere in his published letters, most of which has been included in the present collection.[1]

The note of play—that indication of personality intimately relaxed—does not feature greatly in his letters, save in certain early missives to his sisters. To Harriett he writes about the less tractable pupils that come to him to be tutored: "I have some trouble with my horses . . . for whenever they get a new coachman they make an effort to get the reins slack. But I shall be very obstinate, though their curvetting and shyings are very teasing." To his mother, residing at Brighton, he sends in the March of 1827 a postcript "pastoral" prose-poem: "Does the sea blossom? Are the green leaves budding on its waters, and is the scent of spring in the waves? Do birds begin to sing under its shadow, and to build their nests on its branches? Ah! mighty sea! Thou art a tree whose spring never yet came, for thou art an evergreen." To Harriett, again, in the same year, he writes that Pusey is convalescing at Brighton: "He is very unwell; his nerves very much tired . . . All of you be dull when he calls, for he can bear nothing but dullness, such as looking out upon the sea monotonously."

But instruction and self-improvement often supersede fantasy and teasing. Mary seeks information on how she is to read the early Fathers. Jemima is praised as "an ingenious girl" for having invented "a very correct illustration of the generation of asymptotic curves," while Harriett's work upon a passage from Gibbon "does her much credit." The family's collective thirst for knowledge was prodigious.

[1] Originally published in *Cardinal Newman and William Froude, F.R.S.: a correspondence* by Gordon Huntington Harper (Baltimore, 1933).

To sum up Newman's character, as shown in his letters, is not easy. He is such a chameleon, such a mineral of brilliant and flinty facets. Of all the great nineteenth-century figures, Newman is perhaps the most complex, not so much in his work (although that is rich and varied enough), but in the impulses and motives behind it, which were continually seeking resolution in the deliberated written word.

We see him in his letters: forceful, wayward, persuasive, self-willed, magisterial, subtle, ironical, occasionally witty, inward-looking yet often self-deceiving, many times righteous, sometimes contrite, sick with self-pity or haughty with assurance—a powerful masculine intellect yoked to a strangely feminine nature. And then we must remember that Newman was a poet (*genus irritabile,* and all which that entails).

A man sincerely loved and hated, Newman confessed himself blessed in his friends; and nothing which he wrote in his letters can outmatch the tender evidence of friendship with which Keble received and replied to the news of Newman's submission to Rome. "My dear Newman," he wrote at midnight on October 11, 1845, "you have been a kind and helpful friend to me in a way in which scarce anyone else could have been, and you are so mixed up in my mind with old and dear and sacred thoughts, that I cannot well bear to part with you, most unworthy as I know myself to be; and yet I cannot go along with you, I must cling to the belief that we are not really parted—you have taught me so, and I scarce think you can unteach me—and, having relieved my mind with this little word, I will only say God bless you and reward you a thousandfold all your help in every way to me unworthy, and to so many others. May you have peace where you are gone, and help us in some way to get peace; but somehow I scarce think it will be in the way of controversy. And so, with somewhat of a feeling as if the Spring had been taken out of my year, I am, always, your affectionate and grateful, J. KEBLE."

DEREK STANFORD.

1. TO HIS FATHER

11th June, 1817

The minute I had parted from you I went straight to the tailor's, who assured me that, if he made me twenty gowns, they would fit me no better. If he took it shorter—he would if I pleased—but I might grow, &c. &c. I then went *home* (!) and had hardly seated myself, when I heard a knock at the door, and opening it, one of the Commoners entered whom Mr. Short[1] had sent to me, having before come himself with this said Commoner, when I was out. He came to explain to me some of the customs of the College, and accompany me into the Hall at dinner. I have learned from him something I am much rejoiced at. 'Mr. Ingram,' said he, 'was very much liked; he was very good-natured; he was presented with a piece of plate the other day by the members of the College. Mr. Short on the contrary is not liked; he is strict; all wish Mr. Ingram were tutor still.' Thus I think I have gained by the exchange, and that is a lucky thing. Some time after, on my remarking that Mr. Short must be very clever, having been second master at Rugby, he replied, 'Do you think so?' Another proof that he is a strict tutor.

At dinner I was much entertained with the novelty of the thing. Fish, flesh and fowl, beautiful salmon, haunches of mutton, lamb, &c., fine strong beer; served up in old pewter plates and misshapen earthenware jugs. Tell mamma there were gooseberry, raspberry, and apricot pies. And in all this the joint did not go round, but there was such a profusion that scarcely two ate of the same. Neither do they sit according to their rank, but as they happen to come in.

I learned from the same source whence I learned concerning Mr. Short, that there are a great many juniors to me. I hear also that there are no more lectures this term, this being the

---

[1] The Rev. Thomas Short, for so many years the respected and popular tutor of the College.

week for examinations, and next week most of them go. I shall try to get all the information I am able respecting what books I ought to study, and hope, if my eyes are good-natured to me, to fag.[1]

Tell Harriett [his sister] I have seen the fat cook. The wine has come; 8⅓ per cent. is taken off for ready money. Two things I cannot get, milk and beer; so I am obliged to put up with cream for the one and ale for the other.

2. TO HIS FATHER

16th June, 1817

I was very uncomfortable the first day or two because my eyes were not well, so that I could not see to read, and whenever my eyes are bad I am low-spirited. Besides, I did not know anyone, and, after having been used to a number about me, I felt very solitary. But now my eyes are better, and I can read without hurting them, and I have begun to fag pretty well.

I am not noticed at all except by being silently stared at. I am glad, not because I wish to be apart from them and ill-natured, but because I really do not think I should gain the least advantage from their company. For H. the other day asked me to take a glass of wine with two or three others, and they drank and drank all the time I was there. I was very glad that prayers came half an hour after I came to them, for I am sure I was not entertained with either their drinking or their conversation.

3. TO THE REV. W. MAYER

Trinity Sunday, 1819

To-morrow is our Gaudy. If there be one time of the year in which the glory of our college is humbled, and all appearance of

[1] He suffered from weakness of the eyes at this time.

goodness fades away, it is on Trinity Monday. Oh, how the angels must lament over a whole society throwing off the allegiance and service of their Maker, which they have pledged the day before at His table, and showing themselves the sons of Belial!

It is sickening to see what I might call the apostasies of many. This year it was supposed there would have been no such merry-making. A quarrel existed among us: the college was divided into two sets, and no proposition for the usual subscription for wine was set on foot. Unhappily, a day or two before the time a reconciliation takes place; the wine party is agreed upon, and this wicked union, to be sealed with drunkenness, is profanely joked upon with allusions to one of the expressions in the Athanasian Creed.

To see the secret eagerness with which many wished there would be no Gaudy; to see how they took hope, as time advanced and no mention was made of it; but they are all gone, there has been weakness and fear of ridicule. Those who resisted last year are going this. I fear even for myself, so great a delusion seems suddenly to have come over all.

Oh that the purpose of some may be changed before the time! I know not how to make myself of use. I am intimate with very few. The Gaudy has done more harm to the college than the whole year can compensate. An habitual negligence of the awfulness of the Holy Communion is introduced. How can we prosper?

4. TO HIS FATHER

9th August, 1824

So far from this invasion of an Englishman's castle being galling to the feelings of the poor, I am convinced by facts that it is very acceptable. In all places I have been received with civility, in most with cheerfulness and a kind of glad surprise, and in many with quite a cordiality and warmth of feeling. One person says, 'Aye, I was sure that one time or other we should have a proper minister.' Another, that she had understood from such a one that a 'nice young gentleman had come to the parish'; a third 'begged I would do him the favour to call on him, whenever it was convenient to me.' (This general invitation has been by no means uncommon.) Another, speaking of the parish she came from, said, 'The old man preached very good doctrine, but he did not come to visit the people at their houses as the new one did.' Singularly enough, I had written down as a memorandum a day or two before I received your letter, 'I am more convinced than ever of the necessity of frequently visiting the poorer classes—they seem so gratified at it, and praise it.' Nor do I visit the poor only; I mean to go all through the parish; and have already visited the shopkeepers and principal people. These, it is obvious, have facilities for educating their children, which the poor have not; and on that ground it is that a clergyman is more concerned with the children of the latter, though our Church certainly intended that, not only schoolmasters of the poorer children, but all schoolmasters high and low, should be under her jurisdiction. The plan was not completed, and we must make the best of what we have got. I have not tried to bring over any regular dissenters. Indeed, I have told them all 'I shall make no difference between you and church-goers. I count you all my flock, and shall be most happy to do you a service out of church if I cannot within it.' A good dissenter is, of course, incomparably better than a bad churchman, but a good churchman I think better than a good dissenter. There is too much irreligion in the place for me to be so mad as to drive away so active an ally as Mr. Hinton seems to be. Thank you for your letter and pardon my freedom of reply.

5. TO HIS SISTER JEMIMA

Ulcombe.   *5th September, 1826*

I know you will not consider me unmindful of you because I am silent. Three letters I have received from you, and yet you have not heard from me; but now I will try to make amends. You must not suppose that the letters you send to Harriett are in any measure addressed to me or read by me; if that were the case, I should be still more in your debt than I am. But Harriett is very stingy, and dribbles out her morsels of information from your letters occasionally and graciously, and I have told her I mean to complain to you of it. I, on the contrary, am most liberal to her of my letters. And in her acts of grace she generally tells me what you and Mary &c. say in *her* words. Now it is not so much for the *matter* of letters that I like to read them as for their being written by those I love. It is nothing then to tell me that so and so 'tells no news,' 'says nothing,' &c.; for if he or she says *nothing*, still he or she *says*, and the *saying* is the thing. Am not I very sensible? You have received from H. such full information of our, I cannot say *movements*, but sittings, here, that it will be unnecessary for me to add anything.

I hope to finish Genesis the day after to-morrow (Thursday), having gained, as I hope, a considerable insight into the language. At first I found my analytical method hard work, but after a time it got much less laborious, and though as yet I have not any connected view of Hebrew grammar, yet the lines begin to converge and to show something of regularity and system. I think it a very interesting language, and would not (now I see what it is) have not learned it for any consideration. I shall make myself perfect in the Pentateuch before I proceed to any other part of Scripture, the style being, I conceive, somewhat different, and I wish to become sensible of the differences. I read it with the Septuagint.

6. TO THE REV. S. RICKARDS

Oriel College.   *26th November, 1826*

My dear Rickards,

In our last conversation I think you asked me whether any use had occurred to my mind to which your knowledge of our old divines might be applied. Now one has struck me—so I write. Yet very probably the idea is so obvious that it will not be new to you, and if so, you will not think it worth paying postage for. I begin by assuming that the old worthies of our Church are neither Orthodox nor Evangelical, but intractable persons, suspicious characters, neither one thing nor the other. Now it would be a most useful thing to give a kind of summary of their opinions. Passages we see constantly quoted from them for this side and for that; but I do not desiderate the work of an advocate, but the result of an investigation—not to bring them to us, but to go to them. If, then, in a calm, candid, impartial manner, their views were sought out and developed, would not the effect be good in a variety of ways? I would advise taking them *as a whole*—a corpus theolog. and ecclesiast.—*the* English Church—stating, indeed, *how far* they differ among themselves, yet distinctly marking out the grand, bold, scriptural features of that doctrine in which they all agree. They would then be a band of witnesses for the truth, not opposed to each other (as they now are), but *one*—each tending to the edification of the body of Christ, according to the effectual working of His Spirit in everyone, according to the diversity of their gifts, and the variety of circumstances under which each spake his testimony. For an undertaking like this few have the advantages you have; few the requisite knowledge, few the candour, few the powers of discrimination—very few all three requisites together. The leading doctrine to be discussed would be (I think) that of regeneration; for it is at the very root of the whole system, and branches out in different ways (according to the different views taken of it) into Church of Englandism, or into *Calvinism, Antipædo-baptism,* the *rejection of Church government and discipline,* and the *mere moral system.* It is connected with the doctrines of free-will, original sin, justification, holiness, good works, election, education, the visible Church, &c. Another leading doctrine would be that connected with the observance of the Lord's Day, connected with which the Sabbatarian controversy must be introduced. Again, on Church government, union, schism, order, &c.;

44

here about Bible Society, Church Missionary (*sodes!*) &c. Again upon the mutual uses, bearings, objects, &c., of the Jewish and Christian covenants, on which points I shall be rejoiced to find them (what *I* think) correct. This is, indeed, a large head of inquiry, for it includes the questions of the *lawfulness of persecution, national blessings, judgments, union of Church and State,* and again of the profitableness, often, of the uses and relative value of facts at the present day, of the gradual development of doctrines, of election, &c. Again the opinions of these doctors concerning the Trinity and Incarnation—how far they give in to Platonic doctrines, &c. &c. I have mixed subjects together unpardonably, and have made, as Whately would tell us, *cross divisions.* Never mind. The first subject, regeneration, is by far the most important and useful, I think . . .

It is six years yesterday since I passed my examination; and if you knew all about me which I know, at and since that time, you would know I have very much to be serious about and grateful for. I trust I am placed where I may be an instrument for good to the Church of God. May you (as you are, and more than you are) be a blessing to all around you for miles and miles. And may we both and all the members of Christ work together in their respective stations for the edification of the whole body. This is Sunday, and I cannot better conclude my letter than by such a prayer.

Ever yours very sincerely,
John H. Newman.

7. TO HIS SISTER HARRIETT

19th March, 1827

As to Mr. W.'s absurd question about my opinion on the Catholic question, tell him that I am old enough to see that I am not old enough to know anything about it. It seems to me a question of history. I am not skilled in the political and parliamentary history of Elizabeth, the Stuarts, and Hanoverians.

How *can* I decide it by means of mere argument—theoretical argument, declamations about liberty, the antecedent speculative probability of their doing no harm? In my mind he is no wise man who attempts, without a knowledge of history, to talk about it. If it were a religious question I might think it necessary to form a judgment; as it is not, it would be a waste of time. What would be thought of a man giving an opinion about the propriety of this or that agrarian law in Rome who was unacquainted with Roman history? At the same time I must express my belief that NOTHING will satisfy the Roman Catholics. If this be granted, unquestionably they will ask more.

News came this morning of the Dean of Durham's death, late head of Ch. Ch. Pusey has lost a brother.

8. TO HIS MOTHER

7th May, 1827

Tell Jemima Miss M. [Miss Mitford?] is clever, but her naturalness degenerates into affectation and her simplicity into prettiness. She is rather the ape of nature—a mimic—*ars est celare artem*. But some of her pieces are very good, *e.g.* the old bachelor. Tell her she has no business to say *we* are getting old. Let her speak for herself. Tell her I am quite vigorous; particularly the last week, when I have hunted from the college two men . . .

9. TO HIS SISTER HARRIETT

2nd December, 1827

Dear Pusey lodges at 5 Eastern Terrace. My Mother will send her card and he will call. He is very unwell; his nerves very much tried. He is not well in mind or body. All of you be very dull when he calls, for he can bear nothing but dullness, such as looking out upon the sea monotonously.

46

I do not see how my Mother can be civil to him. He does not go out to dinner, and as to breakfast, it would be so strange to ask him.

Well, Copleston is a bishop and a dean. Shall we have a new Head or not? Which will be best, Keble or Hawkins?[1]

10. TO THE REV. J. KEBLE

Marine Square, Brighton.   *19th December, 1827*

Though I have not written to you on the important college arrangement which is under our consideration at present, and in which you are so nearly concerned, you must not suppose my silence has arisen from any awkward feeling (which it has not) or any unwillingness to state to you personally what you must have some time heard indirectly. I have been silent because I did not conceive you knew or understood me well enough to be interested in hearing more than the fact, any how conveyed, which way my opinion lay in the question of the Provostship, between you and Hawkins. This may have been a refinement of modesty, but it was not intended as such, but was spontaneous.

I write now because Pusey has told me that you would like to receive a line from any of the Fellows, even though you have already heard their feelings on the subject before us all; and I am led to mention my reason for not having written before (which I otherwise should not have done), lest you should think my conduct less kind to you than in intention it has really been. I have been so conscious to myself of the love and affectionate regard which I feel towards you, that the circumstance of my not thinking you the fittest person among us in a particular case and for a particular purpose seemed to me an exception to my general sentiments too trivial to need explanation or remark— to myself; but I have forgotten that to *you* things may appear different—that this is the first time I have had an opportunity

---

[1] Copleston's consecration as Bishop left the Provostship of Oriel vacant. Of the two candidates, Keble and Hawkins, it was the latter who was elected. [D.S.]

of *expressing* any feeling towards you at all; and that, consequently, it would have been acting more kindly had I spoken to you rather than about you. Forgive me if I have in any way hurt you or appeared inconsiderate.

I have lived more with Hawkins than with any other Fellow, and have thus had opportunities for understanding him more than others. His general views so agree with my own, his practical notions, religious opinions and habits of thinking, that I feel vividly and powerfully the advantages the College would gain when governed by one who, pursuing ends which I cordially approve, would bring to the work powers of mind to which I have long looked up with great admiration. Whereas I have had but few opportunities of the pleasure and advantage of your society: and I rather suspect, though I may be mistaken, that, did I know you better, I should find you did not approve opinions, objects, and measures to which my own turn of mind has led me to assent. I allude, for instance, to the mode of governing a college, the desirableness of certain reforms in the University at large, their practicability, the measures to be adopted with reference to them, &c.

It is ungracious to go on, particularly in writing to you above others; for you could easily be made to believe anyone alive was more fit for the Provostship than yourself. I have said enough, perhaps, to relieve you of any uneasy feeling as regards myself: the deep feelings I bear towards you, these I shall keep to myself.

Yours ever affectionately.[1]

11.   TO HIS SISTER JEMIMA

Oriel College.   *10th May, 1828*

. . . Poor Pusey came here last Monday. He is much thrown back, and his spirits very low. He proposes being ordained on

[1] Anne Mozley—the Editor of the Anglican *Letters* adds the following note: The above letter from Mr. Newman to Mr. Keble will help to clear away the difficulties that have arisen as to Mr. Newman's part in the election which are noticed in Dean Burgon's *Twelve Good Men*.

Trinity Sunday. I suppose his marriage will take place shortly after. He, Pusey, is going to change his name to Bouverie, this, however, is quite a secret.

. . . In accordance with my steady wish to bring together members of different colleges, I have founded a dinner club of men about my own standing (my name does not appear, nor is known as the founder). We meet once a fortnight. One fundamental rule is to have very plain dinners.[1]

I am very regular in my riding [enjoined by his doctor], though the weather has not on the whole been favourable. On Thursday I rode over to Cuddesdon with W. and F. and dined with Saunders. It is so great a gain to throw off Oxford for a few hours, so completely as one does in dining out, that it is almost sure to do me good. The country, too, is beautiful; the fresh leaves, the scents, the varied landscape. Yet I never felt so intensely the transitory nature of this world as when most delighted with these country scenes. And in riding out to-day I have been impressed more powerfully than before I had an idea was possible with the two lines:

> Chanting with a *solemn* voice
> Minds us of our *better choice*.

I could hardly believe the lines were not my own, and Keble had not taken them from me. I wish it were possible for words to put down those indefinite, vague, and withal subtle feelings which quite pierce the soul and make it sick. Dear Mary seems embodied in every tree and hid behind every hill. What a veil and curtain this world of sense is! beautiful, but still a veil.

12. TO HIS MOTHER

13th March, 1829

What a scribbler I am become! But the fact is my mind is so full of ideas in consequence of this important event, and my

---

[1] The members were: 1, R. H. Froude; 2, R. I. Wilberforce; 3, J. H. Newman; 4, J. Bramston; 5, Rickards; 6, Round.

views have so much enlarged and expanded, that in justice to myself I ought to write a volume.

We live in a novel era—one in which there is an advance towards universal education. Men have hitherto depended on others, and especially on the clergy, for religious truth; now each man attempts to judge for himself. Now, without meaning of course that Christianity is in itself opposed to free inquiry, still I think it *in fact* at the present time opposed to the particular form which that liberty of thought has now assumed. Christianity is of faith, modesty, lowliness, subordination; but the spirit at work against it is one of latitudinarianism, indifferentism, and schism, a spirit which tends to overthrow doctrine, as if the fruit of bigotry and discipline—as if the instrument of priestcraft. All parties seem to acknowledge that the stream of opinion is setting against the Church. I do believe it will ultimately be separated from the State, and at this prospect I look with apprehension—(1) because all revolutions are awful things, and the effect of this revolution is unknown; (2) because the upper classes will be left almost religionless; (3) because there will not be that security for sound doctrine without change, which is given by Act of Parliament; (4) because the clergy will be thrown on their congregations for voluntary contributions.

It is no reply to say that the majesty of truth will triumph, for man's nature is corrupt; also, even should it triumph, still this will only be ultimately, and the meanwhile may last for centuries. Yet I do still think there is a promise of preservation to the Church; and in its Sacraments, preceding and attending religious education, there are such means of Heavenly grace, that I do not doubt it will live on in the most irreligious and atheistical times.

Its enemies at present are (1) the uneducated or partially educated mass in towns, whose organs are Wooler's, Carlisle's publications, &c. They are almost professedly deistical or worse. (2) The Utilitarians, political economists, useful knowledge people—their organs the 'Westminster Review,' the 'London University,' &c. (3) The Schismatics in and out of the Church, whose organs are the 'Eclectic Review,' the 'Christian Guardian,' &c. (4) The Baptists, whose system is consistent Calvinism—for, as far as I can see, Thomas Scott, &c., are inconsistent, and such inconsistent men would, in times of commotion, split, and go over to this side or that. (5) The high circles in London. (6) I might add the political indifferentists, but I do not know enough to speak, like men who join Roman Catholics on one hand and Socinians on the other. Now you must not understand me as speaking harshly of individuals; I am speaking of bodies and principles.

And now I come to another phenomenon: the talent of the day is against the Church. The Church party (visibly at least, for there may be latent talent, and great times give birth to great men) is poor in mental endowments. It has not activity, shrewdness, dexterity, eloquence, practical power. On what, then, does it depend? On prejudice and bigotry.

This is hardly an exaggeration; yet I have good meaning and one honourable to the Church. Listen to my theory. As each individual has certain instincts of right and wrong antecedently to reasoning, on which he acts—and rightly so—which perverse reasoning may supplant, which then can hardly be regained, but, if regained, will be regained from a different source—from reasoning, not from nature—so, I think, has the world of men collectively. God gave them truths in His miraculous revelations, and other truths in the unsophisticated infancy of nations, scarcely less necessary and divine. These are transmitted as 'the wisdom of our ancestors,' through men—many of whom cannot enter into them, or receive them themselves—still on, on, from age to age, not the less truths because many of the generations through which they are transmitted are unable to prove them, but hold them, either from pious and honest feeling (it may be), or from bigotry or from prejudice. That they are truths it is most difficult to prove, for great men alone can prove great ideas or grasp them. Such a mind was Hooker's, such Butler's; and, as moral evil triumphs over good on a small field of action, so in the argument of an hour or the compass of a volume would men like Brougham, or, again, Wesley, show to far greater advantage than Hooker or Butler. Moral truth is gained by patient study, by calm reflection, silently as the dew falls—unless miraculously given—and when gained it is transmitted by faith and by 'prejudice.' Keble's book is full of such truths, which any Cambridge man might refute with the greatest ease.

13. TO J. W. BOWDEN

13th March, 1831

I fully agree with you about the seriousness of the prospect we have before us, yet do not see what is to be done. The nation (*i.e.* numerically the $\pi\lambda\hat{\eta}\theta os$)[1] is for revolution . . . They certainly have the physical power, and it is the sophism of the day to put religious considerations out of sight, and, forgetting there is any power above man's, to think that what man can do he may do with impunity.

I fear that petitions against Reform would but show the weakness of the Conservative party by the small number which could be got together. At all events, I believe the University has never come forward on questions purely political, or at least before others. Besides, the Church has for a long time lost its influence as a body—*Exoriatur!* Nor do I think it is in a humour to exert it on this occasion, if it had any. It is partly cowed and partly offended. Two years back the State deserted it. I do not see when, in consequence of that treachery, the State has got itself into difficulties, that the Church is bound to expose itself in its service.

Not that the Church should be unforgiving; but, if others think with me, *what* great interest has it that things should remain as they are? I much fear society is rotten, to say a strong thing. Doubtless there are many specimens of excellence in the higher walks of life, but I am tempted to put it to you whether the persons you meet generally are—I do not say consistently

[1] The mob or multitude. [D.S.]

religious; we never can expect that in this world—but believers in Christianity in any true sense of the word. No, they are Liberals, and in saying this I conceive I am saying almost as bad of them as can be said of anyone. What will be the case if things remain as they are? Shall we not have men placed in the higher stations of the Church who are anything but real Churchmen? The Whigs have before now designed Parr for a Bishop; we shall have such as him. I would rather have the Church severed from its temporalities, and scattered to the four winds, than such a desecration of holy things. I dread above all things the pollution of such men as Lord Brougham, affecting to lay a friendly hand upon it . . .

You may not thank me for this long meditation; and to tell the truth I cannot, even in this long account of my thoughts express them fully.

Do you know that my brother Frank has gone out of the country as a missionary? He left Oxford last August, and was to arrive at Bagdad by the middle of January.

You ask me what I am doing. Why, I am going to be an author, but anonymously? I am thinking of writing two works on theological subjects, for a library which is coming out under the Bishop of London's sanction. And I am retiring from the tuition.

14. TO HIS MOTHER

24th October, 1831

I have to-day received a very valuable present of books from many of my new friends and pupils, consisting of thirty-six volumes of the Fathers; among these are the works of Austin, Athanasius, Cyril Alexandrinus, Epiphanius, Gregory Nyssen, Origen, Basil, Ambrose, and Irenæus. They are so fine in their outsides as to put my former ones to shame, and the editions are the best. Altogether, I am now set up in the patristical line, should I be blessed with health and ability to make use of them.

15. TO HIS MOTHER

Cambridge   *16th July, 1832*

Having come to this place with no anticipations, I am quite taken by surprise and overcome with delight. This, doubtless, you will think premature in me, inasmuch as I have seen yet scarcely anything, and have been writing letters of business to Mr. Rose, and Rivingtons. But really, when I saw at the distance of four miles, on an extended plain, wider than the Oxford, amid thicker and greener groves, the Alma Mater Cantabrigiensis lying before me, I thought I should not be able to contain myself, and, in spite of my regret at her present defects and past history, and all that is wrong about her, I seemed about to cry *'Floreat æternum.'* Surely there is a *genius loci* here, as in my own dear home; and the nearer I came to it the more I felt its power. I do really think the place finer than Oxford, though I suppose it isn't, for everyone says so. I like the narrow streets; they have a character, and they make the University buildings look larger by contrast. I cannot believe that King's College is not far grander than anything with us; the stone, too, is richer, and the foliage more thick and encompassing. I found my way from the town to Trinity College like old Œdipus, without guide, by instinct; how, I know not. I never studied the plan of Cambridge.

Mr. Rose[1] is away; he is very ill, which accounts for his silence. Should you see Froude, tell him he *is* married.

P.S.—Let me know about the cholera. I trust we shall have no cases, but it would distress me deeply should a case occur while I am away.

16. TO THE REV. R. H. FROUDE

13th September, 1832

As to your proposal for me to accompany you, it is very tempting.

[1] Editor of the *British Critic* at the inception of the Oxford Movement. It was in his vicarage at Hadleigh, Essex, that the first meeting of the Movement was held. [D.S.]

It quite unsettled me, and I have had a disturbed night with the thought of it. Indeed, it makes me quite sad to think what an evidence it has given me of the little real stability of mind I have yet attained. I cannot make out why I was so little, or rather not at all, excited by the coming of the cholera, and so much by this silly prospect which you have put before me. It is very inconsistent, except, perhaps, that the present novelty has come upon me suddenly. But enough of philosophising.

I am much tempted by your proposal, for several reasons, yet there is so much of impediment in the way of my accepting it. I cannot divest myself of the feeling that I may be intruding upon your father; but, supposing this away, I see much in favour of the scheme. Probably I never shall have such an opportunity again. I mean that of going with a man I know so well as yourself. And going with a person older than myself, as your father, is to me a great temptation. I am indolently distrustful of my own judgment in little matters, and like to be under yours. [N.B.—My leaving them, in the event, at Rome, and going through Sicily by myself is a curious comment upon this.]

Then what a name the Mediterranean is! And the time of the year, for I think summer would be too hot for me; and the opportunity of getting there without touching Gallic earth (for I suppose you go by water), which is an abomination. And if I ever am to travel, is not this the time when I am most at liberty for it? My engagements being slighter now than they have been these many years, and than they are likely to be hereafter. And I feel the need of it; I am suspicious of becoming narrow-minded, and at least I wish to experience the feeling and the trial of expansiveness of views, if it were but to be able to *say* I had, and to know how to meet it in the case of others. And then I think I may fairly say my health requires it. Not that I ever expect to be regularly well as long as I live. It is a thing I do not think of; but still I may be set up enough for years of work, for which, at present, I may be unequal.

But you must tell me (1) as to time. I could not allow myself to be absent from England beyond Easter (say the beginning of

April). Would it not be possible for me to part company with you? (2) As to expense, which, I apprehend, will be a serious subject . . . (3) As to my health. It is quite enough that *you* should be an invalid; but it would be an ungracious πάρεργον for me to fall sick also. Now I cannot answer for my health. If all of a sudden I fell ill?

My book [the 'Arians'] has long been out of hand. I suspect that Rose thinks it scarcely safe, and Rivington thinks it dull. However, I am quite satisfied with Rose; he is in ecstasies with parts of it, and, I sincerely believe, delays it under the wish to make it as good as possible. He seems to like the first chapter least, which is now in Lyell's hands. Rose is a very energetic, well-principled fellow. I have seen a good deal of him; whether he is firm remains to be seen. I will believe no one till he has committed himself.

Do send Mr. Rose one or two more architectural articles before you go.

17.   TO THE REV. S. RICKARDS

Naples.   *14th April, 1833*

I hope you received, in due course, a letter I addressed tardily to you from Falmouth. I had intended, before this, to make up for its tardiness by inflicting upon you a second letter; but again has my purpose been frustrated. So now you have tardy letter the second . . . We were five weeks at Rome, and spent a most delightful time—its memory will ever be soothing to me. Jerusalem alone could impart a more exalted comfort and calm than that of being among the tombs and churches of the first Christian saints. Rome is a very difficult place to speak of, from the mixture of good and evil in it. The heathen state was accursed as one of the infidel monsters of Daniel's visions; and the Christian system there is deplorably corrupt—yet the dust of the Apostles lies there, and the present clergy are their descendants.

[1] plagiarism. [D.S.]

A notion has struck me, on reading the Revelation again and again, that the Rome there mentioned is Rome considered as a city or *place* without any reference to the question whether it be Christian or Pagan. As a seat of government, it was the first cruel persecutor of the Church; and as such condemned to suffer God's judgments, which had not yet fully been poured out upon it, from the plain fact *that it still exists.* Babylon is gone. Rome is a city still, and judgments await her therefore. I have no intention of proving this here, but wish to state my view. When I had formed it I was surprised to find several confirmations of it in a book of Roman antiquities I happened to take up. Gregory the Great seems to have held the notion (three centuries after Rome became Christian) that still the spot was accursed. It was on this principle that he encouraged the demolition of the heathen edifices—such as the Coliseum—as monuments of sin; and I own he seems to me to have a sounder Christian judgment than the moderns, who have affected a classical tenderness for what were the high places of impiety and the scenes of primitive martyrdoms. It seems, too, he especially considered Rome reserved for future superhuman judgments; for he mentions with approbation the answer of some man, a servant of the Lord, to Alaric, that Rome was not to be destroyed by barbarians, but by earthquakes, tempests, &c.; and he adds, 'which we have partly seen accomplished in our own times'; and certainly, from the very magnitude of the masses which lie in ruins, one should suppose nothing but elemental convulsions could have effected their overthrow. An Irish Bishop of the eleventh century states the same doctrine in a so-called prophecy which remains, of the series of Popes to their termination. With the authenticity of this document I am not concerned, much less with its inspired character (though it is remarkable that the list he gives is now within about nine of the end)—it is sufficient it was produced, A.D. 1600 about, in order to secure the election of a particular Pope. Thus its doctrine evidently has been acknowledged by a considerable party in the Church; and, as a tradition, has a sort of authority of the opinion of the Church. It is contained in the concluding words, which are such as these—after filling up his list he says: 'Then shall she that sitteth upon the seven hills be destroyed when the Lord comes to judge the earth.' You will observe this document is written by an upholder of the Roman supremacy, who thus makes the *city and state* still accursed though God's Church be there. It may be said that it is impossible to distinguish between the State and the Church, since the Bishop of Rome has been the temporal sovereign. This is true, and accordingly (supposing this view to be correct) the question arises, *when* was he invested with the sovereignty, for that would be the period of apostasy. But, granting this, it does not follow that the Church is the woman of the Revelation any more than a man possessed with a devil is the devil. That the spirit of old Rome has possessed the Christian Church there is certain as a matter of fact; that the spirit *lives* is most true, quite independent of this theory; and, if it lives, must it not be led out to slaughter some day? The revivification of ancient Rome in modern has often been noticed; but it has been supposed that the Christian Church is that new form of the old evil, whereas it is really a sort of *genius loci*, which enthralls the Church which happens to be there. I am not so clear as I wish to be, but I think the distinction I make is important. Even were the old spirit dead, the city would be under the curse by which children suffer for their fathers' sins; but the spirit lives to show they are the children of those who killed the Prophets The Roman sway is still over its ancient territory even when the people disclaim its dominion (as in the territory of the Greek Church), it appoints its agents and representatives (bishops, patriarchs, &c.). Its language is still Latin, which is its bond of union as an empire. Its policy is still crafty, relentless and inflexible, and undeviating through a succession of rulers. It still sacrifices the good of its members to the splendour and strength of the Republic (what can be a greater instance of this than the custom of the forced celibacy of the clergy?) The religion it upholds is still polytheistic, degrading, idolatrous; and so strictly is all this connected with Rome as a local source, that its authorities lose their power if they quit Rome. We were surprised to hear that the reason Bonaparte did not (as he wished) make Paris the seat of the Popedom was that he found the Romish authorities could not act out of Rome. I am a great believer in the existence of *genii locorum*. Rome has had one character for 2,500 years; of late centures the Christian Church has been the instrument by which it has acted—it is its slave. The day will come when the captive will be set free; but how a distinction is to be drawn between two powers, spiritual and devilish, which are so strangely united, is as much beyond our imagination as it was beyond the power of the servants in the parable to pull up the tares from the wheat; but that it is incomprehensible is no objection to the notion of God's doing it. Indeed, the more I have seen of Rome the more wonderful I have thought that parable, as if it had a directly prophetic character which was fulfilled in the Papacy. To the above may be added, as affording thought to the Christian mind, the remarkable confidence of the Romans in their safety —their *securitas*. They think nothing can harm Rome. When the insurgents two years since were at their gates, they were not at all excited. They said nothing could harm Rome, and went on just as usual—it is a certain insensibility to fear. This is not unlike the temper which may have existed in Babylon, though in individuals very likely there is much piety in it. Indeed, I am very far from thinking there are not many good men among them. I like the look of a great many of their priests—there is such simplicity, gentleness and innocence among the monks: I quite love them; but I fear their system must cripple their $\mathring{\eta}\theta os$.[1]

Does it not seem strange that I who have been such a keeper at home should now be wandering among a people whose language I do not understand? And yet it seems to come natural to one, so soon is the mind habituated to circumstances. Though I should have liked a companion I am not unwilling to rove by myself. Bad times are coming, and no one can tell whether one may not have to travel as Wesley and Whitfield. Harriett says you have been inquiring after my book. It will make its appear-

[1] ethos, a word which was a favourite with Newman. [D.S.]

ance next October as an independent work. I shall re-write nearly a third of it. I think this will be a great improvement, though I rather dread the labour. I am very well, thank God, and though I never (doubtless) shall be in strong health, yet I trust this expedition will set me up. I think I wish nothing else than to spend my strength, whatever it is, in God's service, and I suppose I shall never again in my life have a cessation from work, of this duration, nor can I wish it. Do you know that Keble has begun writing verses in the 'British Magazine'? I hear you are soon to see him. In point of interest I have seen nothing like Ithaca, the Straits of Messina, and Egesta (I put aside Rome), and in point of scenery nothing like Corfu. As to Rome, I cannot help talking of it. You have the tombs of St. Paul and St. Peter and St. Clement; churches founded by St. Peter, and Dionysius (A.D. 260), and others in the Catacombs used in the times of persecution; the house and table of St. Gregory; the place of martyrdom of St. Peter and St. Paul; but the catalogue is endless. O Rome! that thou were not Rome!

18. TO HIS SISTER HARRIETT

Syracuse.   *27th April, 1833*

The two last miles we diverged from the road up a steep path, and soon came to the ancient stone ascent leading to Tauro-minium. I never saw anything more enchanting than this spot. It realised all one had read of in books about scenery—a deep valley, brawling streams, beautiful trees, the sea (heard) in the distance. But when, after breakfast, on a bright day, we mounted to the theatre, and saw the famous view, what shall I say? I never knew that Nature could be so beautiful; and to see that view was the nearest approach to seeing Eden. O happy I! It was worth coming all the way, to endure sadness, loneliness, weariness, to see it. I felt, for the first time in my life, that I should be a better and more religious man if I lived there. This superb view, the most wonderful I can ever see, is but one of at least half-a-dozen, all beautiful, close at hand. One view is at the back of the theatre, with a view of Calabria and the Messina side of Sicily. Another is going out of Taormini on the descent. The landlady of the fondaco asked me if I was going to Paris, and begged me to take a letter to her daughter, which I have done.

And so I went off to Giarre. There first I went through the river-beds. The hills receded—Etna was magnificent. The scene was sombre with clouds, when suddenly, as the sun descended upon the cone, its rays shot out between the clouds and the snow, turning the clouds into royal curtains, while on one side there was a sort of Jacob's ladder. I understood why the poets made the abode of the gods on Mount Olympus.

And now I have told you nearly everything pleasant up to this date—the 27th (except that the frogs between Giardini and Giarre, which are louder even than those at Albano, are the most musical animals I have hitherto met with—they have a trill like a nightingale). I am hitherto disappointed in birds and flowers. I never thought this expedition was to be one of pleasure only, for I wished to see what it was to be a solitary wanderer. On Monday night I had little sleep, and on Tuesday none, from the fleas. I counted quarter after quarter all through the night at Giarre, and there were noises in the next room which annoyed me. The fleas were innumerable, and they bite with a sting. In England we have no idea what a Sicilian flea is. On Wednesday I resolved to see the famous chestnut-trees, and so to go to Nicolosi under Etna. I went to see them as evidence of the wonderful fertility of the soil. From Nicolosi the ascent of Etna is made. The whole distance is not more than twenty-two miles, though very fatiguing. The distance from Giarre to the chestnuts is about six—a precipitous ascent over and along the beds of torrents. I was disappointed in them [they are nothing but roots, cut level with the ground]. We breakfasted in a house where was a sick man, who was attended by a village doctor. We were told it was three hours' march from thence to Nicolosi; it proved to be five; it is along fields of lava, very curious, certainly, but very hot with the sun on them—and curious conical hills, of the finest, richest light-brown earth, which seem dimpled by every breath of air, and lying in heaps as if turned out of a cart and left there.

At length we came to Nicolosi, where I had come in order to determine the possibility of going up Etna, as you never get right intelligence at a distance. I found every discouragement. The snow lay as it had lain two months before, and I was told I should have to walk for nine hours up and down, taking in the cone, half that time in the night, and all in the cold; and the leaves were not out, and there was nothing to see. And, on looking over the books of names of those who had ascended, everything was discouraging. One said, 'I have endured extreme fatigue, and advise no one to follow my example.' Another, 'Better be wise late than never. If you have been a fool in coming, do not be twice a fool in going up.' However, I think I should have attempted it, except that I had strained my leg in walking (but do not give this as the reason; the *season* is the straightforward reason), and my servant was tired.

The discomfort of the so-called inn was excessive; it was the most forlorn place I ever was in. It was a ground floor; one window and no glass; three doors with planks gaping to the external air; brick floor in pieces, and filthy walls. Mrs. Starke took me in by talking of 'reposing' before going up Etna. In addition, my spirits of wine failed, and I could not dress my dinner. I had lived on almost nothing for two days, and my servant had gone out to take care of himself. I lay down on my so-called bed, and thought of the sick-room at Ealing, and my mind felt very dry, and I thought, 'What if I should lose my reason?' and I was in dreadful irritation from the renewed attacks of the fleas. And I was altogether out of sorts. And the bed was on a board, and the bed things looked dirty, and I fancied it would all come to pieces in the night. But my servant came in and poached me some eggs, and threw down water under my bed against my enemies, and I lay down to sleep by eight or nine o'clock, and slept very soundly for eight hours, and got up on Thursday quite strong, with the happy prospect of walking in to breakfast to the comfortable town of Catania; and the morning was fine, and the road (twelve miles) a pleasant descent the whole way; and I lodged myself very happily there, and, though weak, I was recruited.

And now here I am at Syracuse, miserable again; and I seem to think I shall never get home—that is, though quite well, I cannot realise it. I still think of the 121st Psalm.

19. TO F. ROGERS

Palermo.   *5th June, 1833*

With what joy did I see in 'Galignani' yesterday that you were one of us. It was quite a chance I saw it. I had some days before looked over the papers of the last six weeks, having seen none during that time; and yesterday the person who lent them me said: 'There may be one or two yet which you have not taken —hunt over the heap again.' I took home four to read, and, as I was poring over some article on politics (I believe), the wind blew over the page, and I was arrested by the title of 'University Intelligence.' The first words were 'F. Rogers,' &c.

And now I suppose you are wondering what I do now at Palermo; and perhaps my friends at Oxford have been wondering, unless they have sat down in the comfortable conclusion that I am imprisoned here for want of a vessel. I only hope the Rose Hill people are not uneasy. I have *not* been weather-bound or shipless, taken by the Barbary pirates, or seized as a propagandist of Liberalism. No; but, you will be sorry to hear, confined with a very dangerous fever in the centre of Sicily for three weeks. I will give you an account of it, if my hand and my head let me. Only do not mention it till you hear I am at home, which I trust will be in about a fortnight or three weeks. I sail, please God, in a Marseilles vessel on Saturday next, the 8th, whence I shall despatch this to you.

This season has been remarkable for rain in this part of the world, as Froude, if he is returned, has perhaps told you. At Catania, Dr. Gemellaro told me that there sometimes fell only seven inches of rain in the wet months, but that this year there had fallen thirty-four. In consequence, a bad fever, of the nature of the scarlet, was epidemic; which I did not know, nor should have thought of perhaps, if I had. The immediate cause of my illness seems to have been my expedition from Catania to Syracuse; but doubtless I was predisposed to take injury from any bad state of the atmosphere, by the sleepless nights and famished days (though few) which I had had immediately before. Sicilian couches abound in the most inveterate enemies of slumber, and my provisions—for you get none at the inns—though they ought not, were affected by the weather, or were in themselves bad. (I bought them at Naples). And about Etna the transitions from heat to cold are very rapid and severe—in the same day I was almost cut in two, and exhausted with the scorching and dust of lava, though I believe I never got chilled. And in many places they have no glass in the windows, and the shutters do not fit tight, which is bad of a night. Now you will say, how was it *I* alone suffered all this of all Sicilian travellers? Why, to tell the truth, *the* way to avoid it would have been to have taken a Sicilian regular lioniser and purveyor, who would have avoided all difficulties; but this for *one* person is very expensive, and it falls light on several. I had a Neapolitan servant, a good cook (I had bought my provisions before I took him, and they *seemed* good), but knowing nothing of Sicily. I knew a great deal of Sicily from others—everyone was giving me advice to do things *they had not tried themselves*. It was from one of these plans I suffered. Now all this, that I have put down in the last half-page, sounds so *gauche*, that I beg you would keep it to yourself; for it is a gratuitous exposure on my part, and only takes up room in my letter, as you will see from what follows.

Everyone recommended me to go from Catania to Syracuse in a speronaro (by water). The distance by land and sea is forty miles—by land the road is indescribably bad, especially after rain —and the distance too long for mules in one day, and there is no inn on the road. The time by sea was unanimously declared by different persons to be seven hours—the boatmen said five. Dr. Gemellaro so fully acquiesced in these statements as to allow of my making an engagement with him for the middle of the day on which I was to set out from Syracuse on my return. I set out for Syracuse by 7 or 8 A.M. Well, when we were about half-way, a sirocco sprang up, and by degrees it became evident we could not reach Syracuse that night. We made for *Thapsus*, and slept in the boat off the peninsula. On my return, which I made by sea from the probability of the scirocco continuing, and the probable state of the road, the same ill luck attended me. The wind changed, and I slept in the boat. Next morning we made for Agosta (all we could do), the ancient Hybla. (Megara Hyblæa —whence the honey).—We arrived by 8 *a.m.* at Agosta. Delays of obtaining pratique, passport, &c. &c., kept us till 3 P.M., when we set forward on mules for Catania with the belief that the distance was twenty-two miles. By the time it grew dusk we had gone fourteen miles, and descended to the water's side; when to our dismay we learned we had eighteen miles before us, three rivers to ford or ferry, a deep sand to traverse for half the way, and the danger of being plundered. To complete the whole, when we got to the most suspicious part of our journey our guide lost his way. However, he found it again, and alarms are nothing when they are over, but half an hour was a substantial loss. We got to Catania between eleven and twelve at night. The sun had been broiling during the day—the night was damp. I must add, that the first day I was in the speronaro I had had no food for twenty-four hours—having of course taken no provision with me—that at Syracuse I had eaten very little, and only a breakfast on the day of this fatiguing journey; and, out of the three nights, I had slept only one, and that but a little. I am ashamed of the minuteness with which I am telling all this—but my head is not yet entirely my own.

From my return to Catania I sickened. When the idea of illness first came upon me I do not know, but I was obliged on May 1 to lie down for some time when I had got half through my day's journey; and the next morning I could not proceed. This was at Leonforte, above one hundred miles from Palermo. Three days I remained at the inn there with the fever increasing, and no medical aid. On the night of the third day I had a strange (but providential) notion that I was quite well. So on the next morning I ordered the mules, and set off towards Girgenti, my destination. I had not gone far when a distressing choking feeling (constriction?) of the throat and chest came on; and at the end of seven miles I lay down exhausted in a cabin near the road. Here, as I lay on the ground, after a time, I felt a hand at my pulse; it was a medical man who by chance was at hand, and he prescribed for me, and enabled me by the evening to get to Castro Giovanni (the ancient Enna). At first I had difficulty in getting a lodging—had it been known I had the fever I suppose it would have been impossible, for numbers were dying of it there, at Girgenti, and, I believe, everywhere. However, at last I got most comfortably housed. I did not then know what was the matter with me, I believe, but at Leonforte I had thought myself so bad that I gave my servant directions how to convey news of my death (should it be so) to England, at the same time expressing to him a clear and confident conviction that I should *not* die. The reason I gave was that 'I thought God had work for me.' I do not think there was anything wrong in this, on consideration.

At Castro Giovanni I was immediately bled—an essential service—but with this exception it seems as if nature recovered herself; but not till the eleventh day, during which time the fever was increasing, and my attendants thought I could not get over it. Since, I have gained strength in the most wonderful manner. My strength was so prostrated, I could not raise myself in bed or feed myself. The eight after the crisis I began to walk about (with help). On the twelfth I began a journey of three days to Palermo, going one day sixty-two miles; and here, where I have been these ten days, I have surprised everyone by my improvement (though I cannot run yet; the weather is very relaxing). When I came here I could not read nor write, nor talk nor think. I had no memory, and very little of the reasoning faculty. My head had been quite clear (at least at intervals) during the early part of my illness, and I had all through the fever corresponded with the doctor in (really very good) Latin; but a letter from home was brought me, containing letters from five persons, and I pored through it to find news of your election, you unworthy fellow, which it did not contain. This threw the blood into my head, which I have not yet quite recovered.

And now you will say my expedition to Sicily has been a failure. By no means. Do I repent of coming? Why, certainly I should not have come had I known that it was at the danger of my life. I had two objects in coming—to see the antiquities and to see the country. In the former I have failed. I have lost Girgenti and Selinunti, and I have lost the series of perfumed gardens through which the mule track near Selinunti is carried. But I have seen Taormini, and the country from Adernò to Palermo, and can only say that I did not know before nature could be so beautiful. It *is* a country. It passes belief. It is like the Garden of Eden, and though it ran in the *line* of my anticipations (as I say), it far exceeded them.

I continually say *En unquam*,[1] being *very* homesick.

June 17th—At last our vessel is nearing Marseilles. I hope to send you a newspaper from London or Oxford to announce my arrival.

20. TO F. ROGERS

Oriel College.   *31st August, 1833*

. . . Thanks for the two letters, and the song, which will be the more acceptable because the present time is evil. A strange notion yours! as if we were not disposed more to cling to what was, on the ground of its being 'fuit.' Do you understand? Charles I. and his line are the more dear on account of the

[1] Vigr. *Ecl.* i. 68.

apostasy of others. Yet, I confess, Tory as I still am, theoretically and historically, I begin to be a Radical practically. Do not let me misrepresent myself. I, of course, think that the most natural and becoming state of things is for the aristocratical power to be the upholder of the Church; yet I cannot deny the plain fact that in most ages the latter has been based on a popular power. It was so in its rise, in the days of Ambrose and in the days of Becket, and it will be so again. I am preparing myself for such a state of things, and for this simple reason, *because* the State has deserted us and we cannot help ourselves. You must not think, however, that I myself meant to hasten the downfall of the Monarchy by word or deed. I trust the Whigs and Radicals will reap their proper glory, and we but enjoy their fruit without committing ourselves. On this ground, I am against all measures on our part tending to the separation of Church and State, such as putting the bishops out of Parliament, &c., though I confess, if the destructives go much further in their persecution of us— *e.g.* if they made Arnold a bishop—I might consider it wrong to maintain that position longer, much as I should wish to do so. *Entre nous,* we have set up Societies over the kingdom in defence of the Church. Certainly this is, you will say, a singular confidential communication, being shared by so many; but the *entre nous* relates to *we*. We do not like our names known. You may say as much as you will to any one about the fact of the Societies and their object. They are already started (in germ) in Oxfordshire, Devonshire, Gloucestershire, Berks, Suffolk and Kent—the object being 'to make the clergy alive to their situation, to enforce the Apostolical Succession, and to defend the Liturgy.' We mean to publish and circulate tracts. I have started with four. We think of a quarterly magazine. I wish I had more money (a respectable wish), but I have squandered mine in Sicily. All this plan of publication will not interfere with Rose's Magazine. Everything as yet promises well—but we are merely talking about it as yet, and have got no rules even. My work is passing through the press. Do you recollect how I was fussed about it this time two years, when I had not written a word?

It has now been done the better part of a year and a half! I am somewhat in a stew with all sorts of indefinite fears—yet I hope I have committed no blunders.

We are bringing out a stinging 'Lyra' this September—moderate, well-judging men will be shocked at it. I am pleased to find we are called enthusiasts—pleased, for when did a cause which could be so designated fail of success? I have been writing a series of papers for Rose, called the 'Church of the Fathers,' which commences in October; I began another work besides, which is not known yet. You will be amused at this account about myself, but at present I have nothing else to talk or think about. Everyone is from Oxford, and nothing going on; and your letter certainly did not contain materials for much comment or development. One would think that a man who uses his eyes and pen but seldom would abound in deep sayings when he put pen to paper. Every sentence ought to be a view.

I am surprisingly well, except that my hair has all deserted me, as is usual after fevers. It seems so astonishing to be in England after so many sad forebodings: *i.e.* I could not reconcile my imagination, only my reason, to the notion I should ever get back. The way seemed so very long. Yet now I am beginning to get very dissatisfied with not having done more in Sicily. It was most unlucky to be detained three weeks in Palermo, when I might have been roving over the island. How glad I shall be to see you as a Fellow. Everything went so against me in Sicily that I made up my mind you were unsuccessful. I am particularly obliged to you for your kind attentions to my Mother, according to my request. You have no notion how useful your Tillemont already is. The 'Church of the Fathers' is in great measure drawn up from it.

21. TO THE REV. WM. PALMER

24th October, 1833

I put down my thoughts hastily for you, intending them rather as notes to remind you of what I mean than anything else.

I do not like the notion of forming a Society, or Association even, for many reasons.

First, there is an awkwardness in doing so without the sanction of the Bishops; and, though it is enough for satisfying our conscience to know that really they are privately with us, yet the world cannot know this, and it goes out to the world as a bad precedent, and an inconsistency in the case of those who have (rightly) made the absence of episcopal sanction an objection to certain Societies hitherto.

2. Again, a Society is a formidable undertaking to start with. Many of us are inexperienced and have to learn how to conduct an important and difficult scheme. It is a dangerous thing to set up a large system at once. The London University started with an apparatus of professors, which first ensured ridicule, and then disappointment. Besides, a profession of something great excites jealousy and suspicion. There would be the notion abroad that we were taking too much upon ourselves, whereas no one can complain of *individual* exertion.

3. And further, if we profess to be an Association, we are under the necessity of bringing into the government of it men who do not agree with us. We feel our opinions are true; we are sure that, few though we be, we shall be able to propagate them by the force of the truth; we have no need, rather we cannot afford, to dilute them, which must be the consequence of joining those who do not go as far as we do. I am not denying (far from it) the inexpediency of obtruding at once all we really hold; but I consider it a loss of time and trouble to *unite* with those who differ with us—that is, with any who are not disposed to aim at obtaining the liberty of the Church and the restoration of discipline. And if any men think these objects chimerical, then I see no reason for stirring myself at all.

4. Moreover, there is a growing feeling that Societies are bad things, which is in my mind an objection to any such project, both as being a true feeling and as being held as true. The dissensions in the Bible Society and the present state of the

Christian Knowledge Society make people feel that they are instruments of evil much more than of good; or at least of a diluted meagre sort of good.

True it is, the Church is a Society, but it is a Society with a *head;* in all other societies the real movers are secret and irresponsible; and thus second-rate men with low views get the upper hand. Individuals who are seen and heard, who act and suffer, are the instruments of Providence in all great successes.

Again, there is an awkwardness in tracts coming from a Society. It is an assumption of teaching. And, further, they must in consequence be weighed and carefully corrected: and thus they become cold and formal, and (so to say) *im*personal. An address with much in it which others question, yet coming from an individual mind, has a life about it which is sure to make an impression.

Lastly, to form an Association, one ought to have a very definite object. Practical men shrink from engaging without knowing *what* is to be done; but 'to defend the doctrine and discipline of the Church' is very vague; vague for this reason— that we are on the defensive, and not knowing *when* and *how* we shall be attacked, we cannot say *how* we are to act.

For such reasons as these I would advocate a less formal scheme: not that I am not eventually for an Association, but not till the Bishop puts himself at our head in this or that diocese. I would merely exert myself in my own place, and with my own immediate friends, in declaring and teaching the half-forgotten truths of Church union and order to all within my influence. I address friends in other dioceses in turn, and urge them to do the same—in Keble's words, wishing them and ourselves to say to each other, 'We pledge ourselves to each other, reserving our canonical obedience.' We merely encourage and instruct each other: and, being able to say that others are doing elsewhere the same as we are, we have an excuse for being more bold: the circumstance that we have pledged ourselves allows us to introduce ourselves to strangers, &c. &c. We print and circulate tracts;

our friends in other dioceses read them, approve, and partly disapprove. We say, 'Make what use you will of them, and alter them in your own way: reprint them and circulate them in turn, and send us yours to do the same with.' We try to get a footing in our county newspapers; and recommend our friends elsewhere to do the same. Thus gradually certain centres, in correspondence with each other and of a proselytising nature in their respective neighbourhoods, are formed.

But you will say that we are moving too slow, while external events are pressing upon us. 'Parliament will meet and settle matters while we are but forming.' Well then, here is a measure which will at once meet the danger and hasten the formation of the Association. Let us, for example, draw up a declaration or address to the Archbishop, an expression of our attachment to the doctrine and discipline of the Church. Rose recommends it, and it is evidently natural and seasonable. Let each of our centres, *i.e.* corresponding members, exert himself to get signatures in his own neighbourhood. This very attempt will lay the rudiments of a number of associations; channels of communication will be opened with a most definite object; and whether the attempt succeeds or not, the groundwork of a second future attempt will be laid, and this without any display of our real object, *i.e.* the organisation of the clergy. As this process is repeated again and again, being called for naturally by external events, an Association will gradually develop itself; and when, in the course of events, the Bishop in this or that place puts himself at its head, then at length it may be avowed. Thus it will be formed as a habit by energising.

Another advantage of this plan is, that we need not formally adjust our opinions with each other. We have the same general views and aims, but one diocese may be more High Church than another, may modify the tracts of another, &c.

Do not suppose I am blind to the appearance of fancifulness and theorising in the above sketch; but such must all anticipation of the future be. Doubtless many things would modify the plan in detail, when we came to put it in practice; but its great advantage is, that it *may* be modified; whereas, if we set up any Association at once, we commit ourselves.

You will see I am for no committee, secretaries, &c., but merely for certain individuals in every part of the country in correspondence with each other, instructing and encouraging each other, and acting with all their might in their respective circles.

Ever yours, J. H. N.

22. TO THE REV. S. RICKARDS

Oriel College. *30th July, 1834*

Thank you for a sight of Lady W.'s letter. Since you have let me see her opinion of me, I suppose the best return I can make is to let you know my opinion of her. And I am led first of all to express my thanks at her benevolent intention of having me shown up in some Review or other, which is not the less benevolent because it is impracticable in *the way* she wishes. I mean it would be easy to get some party or professedly eclectic Review to lash me, but that would not answer her purpose. On the other hand, a Church Review, such as the 'British Critic,' though it might not agree with me, would know enough of Church theology to find it was a very difficult thing to convict me of running counter to the great stream of our divines. *Sit anima mea cum Hammondo* and such like. This is, indeed, a very curious feature of her remarks. She knows (apparently) nothing of the Church of England *as such.* She jumbles *us* with what she calls 'Protestants,' and thinks it sufficient to prove that so-and-so is not the 'Protestant' doctrine. Now I should frighten good people if I were to say I disown the word 'Protestant,' yet in the sense she uses it I do disown it. I protest as much against Calvin as against the Council of Trent, whereas Protestant in her sense is a crooked stick, bent on one side. The word Protestant does not, as far as I know, occur in our formularies. It is an uncomfortable, perplexing word, intended to connect us—and actually connecting us—with the Protestants abroad. We are a

73

'Reformed' Church, not a 'Protestant.' I care not a whit for the Diet of Augsburg. Calvin is no guide to me, not even as an authority, and as for Bucer I wish he had never crossed the sea. That the Puritanic spirit spread in Elizabeth's and James's time, and did sad havoc, tainting even good and wise men, is certain. Blessed is he who is not corrupted by his age, who keeps his garments white and clean! Who can do it except, so to say, by miracle? Even Hooker, I should think (I speak under correction), but gradually worked his way out of his Puritanic education, but he *did* do so. The spirit of Puritanism has been succeeded by the Methodistic. (Of course, I do not use the word reproachfully, but historically). We, the while, children of the Holy Church, whencesoever brought into it, whether by early training or afterthought, have had one voice, that one voice which the Church has had from the beginning. As far as I can make out, the good and holy men of every age have not much differed from each other—Hooker and Taylor from St. Bernard, St. Bernard from St. Chrysostom. Meanwhile, the Church of Rome apostatised at Trent. It is too much to say that we, the children of Ridley and Laud, are innovators, introducing opinions, and open to warnings such as Lady W. gives us. Show me I am an innovator, and without question I will be silent. Then she need not speak of *consequences* of my doctrine, and I will be silent in that. But if I but speak as the Church has ever spoken, let her, if she will, still 'protest,' but let her quite understand her position, as external to the Church, as herself being one of, on the whole, an innovating party. Whether right or wrong, she, not I, must show cause why she says what she says. But doubtless the torrent of the day is so much with *her,* that I must consent to be in an apparent minority, and to rest on the scenes of past years, from 'the upper room' in Acts i. to the Court of Carisbrooke or Uxbridge. Doubtless I have made up my mind, as every one must who tries to stand against the torrent, to be misunderstood and called names. She may be quite sure that not a word has she said by way of accounting for my holding what I hold, but I could have said more plausibly before her; I could have made out a more specious story against myself, have spoken of reaction, &c. But, after all, what is the fact? That, however I came to hold what I hold, I hold it with such men as Hammond and Wilson, and therefore I am consoled, as well as prepared for the names Pelagian, Papist, or anything else— μὴ γένοιτο.[1]

I would wish to ask Lady W. whether she uses such words as Pelagian historically or not. If she does, let her tell me what Pelagius's doctrine was, and show I agree with it; if not, it is indirectly *assuming* that I have so committed myself as to fall under the expressed censure of the Church, which is unfair. Next, I observe that it is inconsistent in her calling me a Pelagian and yet spiritually-minded. Let her be quite sure that when I think a person a heretic, I shall never call him religious. A spiritually-minded heretic may exist in the 'Protestant' world, but not in the Church.

I conceive a clergyman is likely to have seen as much of persons in distress of mind as Lady W.

To conclude, I doubt not you have before now given my Lady a hint on the confident way in which she, a lay person, speaks of Christ's ministers. At first I was amused at the way in which she laid down the law, but on second thoughts it seemed a more serious thing. It is part of the evil of our present system, which puts great people about the Church, and, if they are religious, makes them little Queen Besses. She may be quite sure that, if she comes into collision with me, I shall take some *quiet* opportunity of hinting this to her. I write *currente calamo,* having no time for a very finished letter.

23. TO DR. HAMPDEN, PRINCIPAL OF ST. MARY HALL

28th November, 1834

The kindness which has led to your presenting me with your

[1] May it not be so.

pamphlet[1] encourages me to hope that you will forgive me, if I take the opportunity it affords to express to you my very sincere and deep regret that it has been published.

Such an opportunity I could not let slip without being unfaithful to my own serious thoughts on the subject.

While I respect the tone of piety in which the pamphlet is written, I feel an aversion to the principles it professes, as (in my opinion) legitimately tending to formal Socinianism.

And also I lament that, by its appearance, the first step has been taken towards an interruption of that peace and mutual good understanding which has prevailed so long in this place; and which, if ever seriously disturbed, will be succeeded by dissensions the more intractable, because justified in the minds of those who resist innovations, by a feeling of imperative duty.[2]

24. TO HIS SISTER HARRIETT

10th October, 1835

. . . Rationalism is the attempt to know *how* things are about which you can know nothing. When we give reasons for alleged facts and reduce them into dependence on each other, we feel a satisfaction which is wanting when we receive them as isolated and unaccountable, *i.e.* a satisfaction of the *reason*. On the other hand, when they stand unaccounted for, they impart a satisfaction of their own kind—namely, of the *imagination*. When we ask for reasons when we should not, we *rationalise*. When we detach and isolate things which we should connect, we are superstitious.

25. TO J. W. BOWDEN

Oriel College.   *2nd March, 1836*

Yesterday morning brought me the news of Froude's death; and

---

[1] The pamphlet was Hampden's application of his Bampton Lectures to the question of Subscription in Oxford.

[2] This letter, notes Newman, was the beginning of hostilities in the University.[D.S.]

if I could collect my thoughts at this moment, I would say something to you about him, but I scarcely can. He has been so very dear to me, that it is an effort to me to reflect on my own thoughts about him. I can never have a greater loss, looking on for the whole of my life; for he was to me, and he was likely to be ever, in the same degree of continual familiarity which I enjoyed with yourself in our Undergraduate days; so much so that I was from time to time confusing him with you, and only calling him by his right name and recollecting what belonged to him, what to you, by an act of memory.

It would have been a great satisfaction to me had you known him. You once saw him indeed, but it was when his health was gone, and when you could have no idea of him. It is very mysterious that any one so remarkably and variously gifted, and with talents so fitted for these times, should be removed. I never, on the whole, fell in with so gifted a person. In variety and perfection of gifts I think he far exceeded even Keble. For myself, I cannot describe what I owe to him as regards the intellectual principles [*i.e.* philosophy] of religion and morals. It is useless to go on to speak of him, yet it has pleased God to take him, in mercy to him, but by a very heavy visitation to all who were intimate with him. Yet everything was so bright and beautiful about him, that to think of him must always be a comfort. The sad feeling I have is, that one cannot retain in one's memory all one wishes to keep there, and that, as year passes after year, the image of him will be fainter and fainter.

26. TO MRS. JOHN MOZLEY[1]

Oriel.   *19th January, 1837*

. . . Tell Miss M. that I fear I must decline the place in her poetical collection. I never can write except in a season of idleness. When I have been doing nothing awhile, poems spring up as weeds in fallow fields.

[1] his sister Jemina, who had married the Rev. John Mozley. [D.S.]

I have been reading 'Emma.' Everything Miss Austen writes is clever, but I desiderate something. There is a want of *body* to the story. The action is frittered away in over-little things. There are some beautiful things in it. Emma herself is the most interesting to me of all her heroines. I feel kind to her whenever I think of her. But Miss Austen has no romance—none at all. What vile creatures her parsons are! she has not a dream of the high Catholic $\eta\theta\sigma s$.[1] That other woman, Fairfax, is a dolt—but I like Emma.

I have nearly finished Southey's 'Wesley,' which is a very superficial concern indeed: interesting of course. He does not treat it historically in its connexion with the age, and he cannot treat it theologically, if he would . . . I do not like Wesley—putting aside his exceeding self-confidence, he seems to me to have a black self-will, a bitterness of religious passion, which is very unamiable. Whitfield seems far better.

27. TO MRS. JOHN MOZLEY

St. Mark's. 25th April, 1837

What you say about my book ['Prophetical Office'] is very gratifying. I hear the same in various other quarters, and it is selling very well. It only shows how deep the absurd notion was in men's minds that I was a Papist; and now they are agreeably surprised. Thus I gain, as commonly happens in the long run, by being misrepresented, thanks to 'Record' & Co. &c. . . . I call the notion of my being a Papist absurd, for it argues an utter ignorance of theology. We have all fallen back from the time of the Restoration in a wonderful way. Any one who knew anything of theology would not have confounded me with the Papists; and if he gave me any credit for knowledge of theology,

[1] ethos. Anne Mozley, in whose collection of letters this appears, adds the following note: The ethos, as Mr. Newman calls it, of a book came always foremost in his critical estimation. He condoned a good deal when this satisfied him. Miss Austen described parsons as she saw them, and did not recognise it as in her province to preach to them, except indirectly by portraying the Mr. Collinses and Mr. Eltons of the day.

or for clearheadedness, he would not have thought me in danger of becoming one. True it is, every one who by his *own wit* had gone as far as I *from* popular Protestantism, or who had been taught from *without*, not being up to the differences of things, and trained to discrimination, might have been in danger of going further; but no one who either had learned his doctrine *historically* or had tolerable clearness of head could be in more danger than in confusing the sun and moon.

However, I frankly own that if, in some important points, our Anglican ἦθος [1] differs from Popery, in others it is like it, and on the whole far more like it than like Protestantism. So one must expect a revival of the slander or misapprehension in some shape or other. And we shall never be free from it, of course.

28. TO MRS. JOHN MOZLEY

29th January, 1838

The glass in my inner room has stood at 10°—that is, 22° below freezing-point. I have never had it so cold for a continuance, or at all, since I have been in the rooms.

I am quite sick at the thoughts of having the 'British Critic,' but there was no one else, and I did not like so important a work to get into hands I could not trust. I do not begin with it till the July number.

My book on Justification has taken incredible time. I am quite worn out with correcting. I do really think that every correction I make is for the better, and that I am not wasting time in an over-fastidious way, or even making it worse than it was; but I can only say this—openings for correction are inexhaustible.

I write, I write again: I write a third time in the course of six months. Then I take the third: I literally fill the paper with corrections, so that another person could not read it. I then write it out fair for the printer. I put it by; I take it up; I begin to correct again: it will not do. Alterations multiply, pages are

[1] ethos. [D.S.]

re-written, little lines sneak in and crawl about. The whole page is disfigured; I write again; I cannot count how many times this process is repeated.

29. TO F. ROGERS

Oriel. *15th September, 1839*

Your account of your priest is amusing. *Can* the R.C.'s have any tender feeling towards Anglicanism? Who among us ever showed them any kindness? Are we not the pets of a State which has made it felony to celebrate Mass even (I believe) in private, a law which (Ward declares) remained in existence till 1780 . . .

You see, if things were to come to the worst, I should turn Brother of Charity in London—an object which, *quite* independently of any such perplexities, is growing on me, and, peradventure, will some day be accomplished, if other things do not impede me. That Capuchin in the 'Promessi Sposi' has struck in my heart like a dart. I have never got over him. Only I think it would be, in sober seriousness, far too great an honour for such as me to have such a post, being little worthy or fit for it.

30. TO F. ROGERS

Oriel College. *22nd September, 1839*

Since I wrote to you, I have had the first real hit from Romanism which has happened to me. R. W., who has been passing through, directed my attention to Dr. Wiseman's article in the new 'Dublin.'[1] I must confess it has given me a stomach-ache. You see the whole history of the Monophysites has been a sort of alterative. And now comes this dose at the end of it. It does certainly come upon one that we are not at the bottom of things. At this moment we have sprung a leak; and the worst of it is that those sharp fellows, Ward, Stanley, and Co. will not let one go to sleep upon it. *Curavimus Babylonem et non est curata* was

[1] *Dublin Review*, April 1869.

an awkward omen. I have not said so much to any one.

I seriously think this a most uncomfortable article on every account, though of course it is *ex parte* . . . I think I shall get Keble to answer it. As to Pusey, I am curious to see how it works with him.

And now, *carissime,* good-bye. It is no laughing matter. I will not blink the question, so be it; but you don't suppose I am a madcap to take up notions suddenly—only there is an uncomfortable vista opened which was closed before. I am writing upon my first feelings.

31.   TO MRS. JOHN MOZLEY

25th February, 1840

I have got very sluggish about writing, for various reasons: first, I am so busy; next, my hand is so tired; and, thirdly, I am somehow desponding about the state of things, and this disinclines me to exert myself.

Everything is miserable. I expect a great attack upon the Bible—indeed, I have long expected it. At the present moment indications of what is coming gather. Those wretched Socialists on the one hand, then Carlyle on the other—a man of first-rate ability, I suppose, and quite fascinating as a writer. His book on the 'French Revolution' is most taking (to me). I had hoped he might have come round right, for it was easy to see he was not a believer; but they say he has settled the wrong way. His view is that Christianity has good in it, or is good *as far as it goes,* which, when applied to Scripture, is, of course, a picking and choosing of its contents. Then, again, you have Arnold's school, such as it is (I do hope he will be frightened back), giving up the inspiration of the Old Testament, or of all Scripture (I do not say Arnold himself does). Then you have Milman, clenching his 'History of the Jews' by a 'History of Christianity' which they say is worse; and just in the same line. Then you have all your political economists, who *cannot* accept (it is impossible) the

Scripture rules about almsgiving, renunciation of wealth, self-denial, &c., and then your geologists, giving up parts of the Old Testament. All these and many more spirits seem uniting and forming into something shocking.

But this is not all. I begin to have serious apprehensions lest any religious body is strong enough to withstand the league of evil but the Roman Church. At the end of the first millenary it withstood the fury of Satan, and now the end of the second is drawing on.

Certainly the way that good principles have shot up is wonderful; but I am not clear that they are not tending to Rome—not from any necessity in the principles themselves, but from the much greater proximity between Rome and us than between infidelity and us, and that in a time of trouble we naturally look about for allies. I cannot say enough of the wonderful way in which the waters are rising here, and one should be very thankful. All this is a miserable prose, and regular talk worth nothing, and soon to be falsified by the event.

I am going up to Littlemore till Easter. While there I may have more time to write to Harriett and you. Tell her so.

32. TO MRS. JOHN MOZLEY

Littlemore.   *1st April, 1840*

I am getting on here; the children are improving in their singing. I have had the audacity to lead them and teach them some new tunes. Also I have rummaged out a violin and strung it, and on Mondays and Thursdays have begun to *lead* them with it, a party of between twenty and thirty great and little in the schoolroom. I am catechising them in church, too, and have got them so far that they take an interest in it. I have only one girl as much as ten, and not two more than eight or nine, except some Sunday scholars. I have effected a great reform (for the time) in the girls' hands and faces. Lectured with unblushing effrontery on the necessity of their keeping their work clean, and set them to knit stockings.

Also I have drawn up a sort of Liturgy for School Prayers, varying with the seasons, on a hint I gained from some printed prayers, &c., done by some ladies in Sussex.

I think I shall be a good deal here in future.

33.   TO THE REV. THOMAS MOZLEY

Oriel College.   *20th May, 1840*

. . . We have bought nine acres, and want to build a μονή.[1] Give me some hint about building. My notion is to build *a bit,* and then stop, but to build it on a plan, which will admit of being added to. Were I a draughtsman I would hit off something good; as it is, take the following (with a plan):

The library admits of increase along one side, and is to be lighted with upper windows only, the room being (say) 16 to 18 feet high.

The cells to be added as required, being (say) 9 or 10 feet high.

The oratory or chapel a matter altogether for future consideration.

I want a cell to contain three rooms: 1, a sitting-room 12 by 9 (say); 2, a bed-room 6 by 6?; and 3, a cold-bath room 6 by 3?

34.   TO THE REV. A. PERCEVAL

Oriel.   *12th March, 1841*

My dear Perceval,

Many thanks for your kind note just received. I certainly am at this instant in a pretty considerable scrape, but am only surprised at the long run of luck we have had.

The Tract was necessary to keep people either from Rome or schism or an uncomfortable conscience. It was necessary for my own peace so much as this, that I felt people *did not know me,*

[1] a resting place. [D.S.]

and were trusting me when otherwise they would not. I really cannot repent having done it. As to the newspapers, it is a curious coincidence—but all these things will turn to good. The Tract was in print, not to say published, before the papers opened the subject.

I did not think it would have made a noise. I expected it to come in quietly—and it would, but for two things—first Golightly, who is the Fire-the-Faggot of the affair, and who would be pleased to know I felt him to be so—and secondly, Lord Morpeth's speech in the House the other night.

Repeating my thanks, I am,

My dear Perceval,

Yrs. affectionately,

J. H. NEWMAN.

P.S.—Mr. Pauli is a Christian and has been Pusey's assistant in Hebrew and takes Pupils here. He is well thought of, I believe.

Palmer, I am glad to say, quite sanctions the Tract.

35.   TO THE REV. C. RUSSELL[1]

Oriel College.   *13th April, 1841*

Dear Sir,

Nothing can be kinder or more considerate than the tone of your letter, for which I sincerely thank you. It will relieve you to know that I do *not* accuse your communion of holding Transubstantiation in the shocking sense which we both repudiate, but I impute that idea of it to our Articles which, I conceive condemn a certain extreme view of it which some persons or party [?] in your Church have put forward against the sense of the sounder portion of it. I am quite aware of Bellarmine's explanations; I am aware that well-informed R.C.'s hold the spiritual presence in the Eucharist; but should be very loth to think that our Article was regarding such a belief when it spoke of Transubstantiation. If I have not said so in the Tract, it was

[1] A Roman priest who had begun a correspondence with Newman. [D.S.]

because my object in it was not to defend you, but to exonerate our Articles from what is traditionally imputed to them. And in doing so I was taking the line of your own writer Davenport, or a Santa Clara, who, if I mistake not, commenting on this particular Article, says, 'Capharnaitarum haeresim procul dubio spectat.'

I heartily wish that I could extend to all your received doctrines the admission I make concerning this—which is that you have adopted a word 'Transubstantiation' conveying a wrong idea, which practically you explain away. O that you would reform your worship, that you would disown the extreme honours paid to St. Mary and the Saints, your traditionary view of Indulgences, and the veneration paid in foreign countries to Images. And as to our own country, O that, abandoning your connection with a political party, you would, as a body, 'lead quiet and peaceable lives in all godliness and honesty.' It would do your religious interests as much good in our eyes, as it would tend to rid your religious system of those peculiarities which distinguish it from primitive Christianity.

I will thankfully accept Veron's book at your hands, if there is any easy mode of conveyance for it.

I am etc.

36.　TO J. R. HOPE

October, 1841

Your account of the Jerusalem matter is fearful—the more I think of it the more I am dismayed. On me it falls very hard—here I am labouring with all my might to keep men from Rome, and as if I had not enough trouble, a new element of separation is introduced. I feel so strongly about it that when I once begin to publish my 'Protest,'[1] I think I shall introduce it as a preface or appendix to every book and every edition of a book I print. If people are driving me quite against all my feelings out of the

[1] The "Protest" can be read in Anne Mozley's *Letters and Corr.* ii. 324, or the *Apologia*. It was sent to the Archbishop of Canterbury and the Bishop of Oxford on November 11.

Church of England, they shall know that they are doing so. Is there no means of impeaching or indicting someone or other? Lawyers can throw anything into form. Should Bishop Alexander commit any irregularity out in Palestine might not one bring him into Court in England? I really can fancy our people giving an indirect sanction or connivance in the course of a few years to that dreadful scheme, which writers in the *Record* and elsewhere have put forth, of building the Jewish Temple for Jewish service.

My *reasons* for thinking of an action (prospectively) against the *Standard* or the like was this—that till I was cross-examined on my oath people would not believe I had not some understanding with the Pope.

Ever yours,

JOHN H. NEWMAN.

37. TO THE REV. S. RICKARDS

Oriel College.   *1st December, 1841*

My dear Rickards,

My silence must seem to you quite unkind, though it does not at all arise from not thinking of you and Mrs. Rickards; but, besides my very great engagements, these lie so much in writing that my hand is in a state of continued weariness, and it is a great effort to me to sit down to a letter. However, now that I am about it, I will try to tell you one or two things of myself, which, by-the-bye, I doubt whether I have told, or at least set about telling, or told in any connected way, to any one else.

For two years and more I have been in a state of great uneasiness as to my position here, owing to the consciousness I felt, that my opinions went far beyond what had been customary in the English Church. Not that I felt it any personal trouble, for I thought and think that such opinions were allowed in our Church fully; but that, looking on my position here, I seemed to be a sort of schismatic or demagogue, supporting a party against the religious authorities of the place. In what I have done in my parish, whether in the ordinary routine of duty, or any improvements or additions which I have attempted, I have uniformly kept my parishioners before my mind, and wished to act for *them*. But almost in every case my endeavours have fallen dead upon them as a whole, but have been eagerly apprehended and welcomed by University men, and of these a great many Undergraduates. In proportion, then, as I had reason to believe that the Heads of Houses were dissatisfied with me, did I seem to myself in the position of one who, to the neglect, at least virtual, of his own duties, was interfering with those committed to the charge of others against their will, and that for the propagation of feelings and opinions which I felt were not so truly those of the English Church as their own. And all this in spite of my preaching very little on directly doctrinal subjects, but on practical; for somehow what came out from me in an ethical form took the shape of doctrine by the time it reached other minds. In consequence, for two years past my view of my duty and my prospective plans here have been very unsettled. I have had many schemes floating on my mind how to get out of a position which of all others is to me most odious—that of a teacher setting up for himself against authority, though, I suppose, (if it may be said reverently), our Saviour bore this Cross as others. The most persistent feeling on my mind has been to give up St. Mary's.

The reason I say all this to you now is that, whether it will turn ultimately for the better or worse, certainly at present the greater gloom in which the prospects of the Church lie, has had for the time the effect of clearing away clouds before my own path. I mean that the most serious things which are happening, in word and deed, around us have in great measure taken away that delicacy towards authorities which has hitherto been so painfully harassing to me . . . As to this Jerusalem Bishopric, I seriously think that, if the measure is fairly carried out, it will do more to unchurch us than any event for the last three hundred years. With these feelings it is not wonderful that I should see my present position here in a very different light. O my dear Rickards, pray excuse all this sad talk about myself, which disgust me as I make it, and I fear I am writing you a most pompous sort of letter, but I think you will like to hear about me, and it is a comfort to me to write it out, and I have no time to pick and choose my words. But to return. It really seems to me that the Heads of Houses are now not defending the English Church, but virtually and practically, though they may not mean it, joining with this heretical spirit and supporting *it*; so that the contest is no longer one of what would be represented as a quasi-Romanism against Anglicanism, but of Catholicism against heresy. And thus, to my mind, at present a much broader question swallows up the particular one.

38. TO MRS. JOHN MOZLEY

6th February, 1842

I am going up to Littlemore [*i.e.* for good] and my books are all in motion—part gone; the rest in a day or two. It makes me very downcast; it is such a nuisance taking steps. But for years three lines of Horace have been in my ears:

> Lusisti satis, edisti satis atque bibisti:
> Tempus abire tibi est; ne potum largius æquo
> Rideat et pulset lasciva decentius ætas.[1]

Of Tract No. 90, 12,500 copies have been sold, and a third edition is printed. An American clergyman, who was here lately, told me he saw it in every house.

39. TO THE BISHOP OF OXFORD[2]

14th April, 1842

I am very much obliged by your Lordship's kindness in allowing

[1] Hor. *Ep*. ii. 2. 214.
[2] The Rt. Rev. Charles Lloyd. [D.S.]

me to write to you on the subject of my house at Littlemore; at the same time I feel it hard both on your Lordship and myself that the restlessness of the public mind should oblige you to require an explanation of me.

It is now a whole year since I have been the subject of incessant misrepresentation. A year since I submitted entirely to your Lordship's authority; and with the intention of following out the particular act enjoined upon me, I not only stopped the series of tracts on which I was engaged, but withdrew from all public discussion of Church matters of the day, or what may be called ecclesiastical politics. I turned myself at once to the preparation for the press of the translations of St. Athanasius to which I had long wished to devote myself, and I intended and intend to employ myself in the like theological studies, and in the concerns of my own parish and in practical works.

With the same view of personal improvement I was led more seriously to a design which had been long on my mind. For many years, at least thirteen, I have wished to give myself to a life of greater religious regularity than I have hitherto led; but it is very unpleasant to confess such a wish even to my Bishop, because it seems arrogant, and because it is committing me to a profession which may come to nothing. What have I done that I am to be called to account by the world for my private actions in a way in which no one else is called? Why may I not have that liberty which all others are allowed? I am often accused of being underhand and uncandid in respect to the intentions to which I have been alluding: but no one likes his own good resolutions noised about, both from mere common delicacy, and from fear lest he should not be able to fulfil them. I feel it very cruel, though the parties in fault do not know what they are doing, that very sacred matters between me and my conscience are made a matter of public talk. May I take a case parallel, though different? Suppose a person in prospect of marriage: would he like the subject discussed in newspapers, and parties, circumstances, &c. &c., publicly demanded of him at the penalty of being accused of craft and duplicity?

The resolution I speak of has been taken with reference to myself alone, and has been contemplated quite independent of the co-operation of any other human being, and without reference to success or failure other than personal, and without regard to the blame or approbation of man. And being a resolution of years, and one to which I feel God has called me, and in which I am violating no rule of the Church any more than if I married, I should have to answer for it, if I did not pursue it, as a good Providence made openings for it. In pursuing it, then, I am thinking of myself alone, not aiming at any ecclesiastical or external effects. At the same time, of course, it would be a great comfort for me to know that God had put it into the hearts of others to pursue their personal edification in the same way, and unnatural not to wish to have the benefit of their presence and encouragement, or not to think it a great infringement on the rights of conscience if such personal and private resolutions were interfered with. Your Lordship will allow me to add my firm conviction that such religious resolutions are most necessary for keeping a certain class of minds firm in their allegiance to our Church; but still I can as truly say that my own reason for anything I have done has been a personal one, without which I should not have entered upon it, and which I hope to pursue whether with or without the sympathies of others pursuing a similar course . . .

As to my intentions, I purpose to live there myself a good deal, as I have a resident curate in Oxford. In doing this I believe I am consulting for the good of my parish, as my population in Littlemore is at least equal to that of St. Mary's in Oxford, and the *whole* of Littlemore is double of it. It has been very much neglected; and in providing a parsonage-house at Littlemore, as this will be and will be called, I conceive I am doing a very great benefit to my people. At the same time it has appeared to me that a partial or temporary retirement from St. Mary's Church might be expedient under the prevailing excitement.

As to the quotation from the [newspaper] which I have not seen, your Lordship will perceive from what I have said that no 'monastery is in process of erection,' there is no 'chapel,' no 'refectory,' hardly a dining-room or parlour. The 'cloisters' are my shed connecting the cottages. I do not understand what 'cells[1] of dormitories' means. Of course I can repeat your Lordship's words, that 'I am not attempting a revival of the Monastic Orders in anything approaching to the Romanist sense of the term,' or 'taking on myself to originate any measure of importance without authority from the Heads of the Church.' I am attempting nothing ecclesiastical, but something personal and private, and which can only be made public, not private, by newspapers and letter-writers, in which sense the most sacred and conscientious resolves and acts may certainly be made the objects of an unmannerly and unfeeling curiosity.

40. TO THE REV. J. KEBLE

Basingstoke.   *5th September, 1843*

My dear Keble,

I am indeed to you a Job's messenger. Here am I, having been summoned from Oxford yesterday on a very painful errand. *Another* person,[2] still more important, as I should say, than the last mentioned has surprised me by telling me he must go over to Rome, and I really cannot tell whether I have succeeded in stopping him. At least I cannot get him to give me any promise.

Really I cannot keep St. Mary's on—and what is so very uncomfortable, these efforts to stop others do *me* harm—for I feel that the collision which drives them from Rome drives me, as is natural, in the other direction. I know I cannot speak in a sufficient *real* way about it and did I feel ever so duly, my words would be cold upon paper, but I much fear to-day's conversation has done me a good deal of harm, that is, has increased my conviction of the false position we are in, if that is harm.

[1] but note his own choice of this word in Letter 33. [D.S.]
[2] William Lockhart of the Littlemore community. [D.S.]

I wish I felt more deeply than I do how I am paining you. But surely I must tell you how things are.

Ever yours affectionately,

J. H. N.

41. TO THE BISHOP OF OXFORD

7th September, 1843

My dear Lord,

I shall give your Lordship much pain I fear by the request which it is necessary for me to make of your Lordship before I proceed to act upon a resolution, on which I have made up my mind, for a considerable time to act. It is to ask your Lordship's permission to resign St. Mary's. If I intended such a step three years since, as I have said to your Lordship in print, it is not surprising that I should have determined on it now, when so many Bishops have said such things of me, and no one [has] undertaken my part in respect to that interpretation of the Articles under which alone I can subscribe them. I will not ask your Lordship to put yourself to the pain of replying to this request, but shall interpret your silence as an assent.

Were I writing to any one but your Lordship it might be presumption to suppose I should be asked to reconsider the request which I have been making, but kindness like yours may lead you to suspend your permission. If so, I may be allowed to say in a matter on which I am able to speak, that I should much deplore such an impediment, as probably leading to results, which would more than disappoint your Lordship's intentions in interposing it. My resolution is already no secret to my friends and others. Let me heartily thank your Lordship for all your past acts of friendship and favour to one who has been quite unworthy of them, and believe me my Lord to be keenly alive to your anxieties about the state of the Church, and to feel great sorrow as far as I am the occasion of them. On the other hand I will say on my own behalf that I have ever felt great love and devotion towards your Lordship, that I have ever wished to please you, that I have honestly tried to bear in mind that I was in a place of high trust in the Church, and have laboured hard to uphold and strengthen her, and to retain her members. I am not relaxing my zeal till it has been disowned by her rulers. I have not retired from her service till I have lost or forfeited her confidence.

That your Lordship's many good words and works for her welfare may be a blessing in this life, and a full reward in the next is the prayer of your Lordship's

Affectionate servant,

J. H. NEWMAN.

42.   TO THE REV. W. DODSWORTH

Littlemore.   *18th March, 1844*

It is not easy to return an answer to your question. In matter of fact we are full here, but I suppose we might make more room—but under the circumstances great caution is necessary for the sake of all parties in forming such relations as you speak of with anyone. I say under the circumstances, for I suppose, had we any right to be considered what we are aiming at, we should be wrong to consult personal feelings and likings, or to be guided by knowledge of individuals, &c. I suppose a religious house ought frankly to receive anyone who shows himself in earnest, without respect of persons. But this presupposes a state of things very different from that under which we find ourselves. The principle of obedience does not exist in our Church—i.e. (as regards a religious House) the principle of assimilation, or a digestive power. We have no head to whom obedience is due. We have no ecclesiastical authority, no episcopal blessing. We have no vows, obliging persons to be resigned, when the spirit or flesh rebels. We have no sacramental services, compensating for hardships, relieving the dreariness or monotony (as some would find it) of a retreat. For all these reasons it seems allowable or necessary to pick and choose our associates, and to make personal attachment the principle of admission. Else the whole attempt would be overset. Nor am I speaking merely theoretically. You see then I can return no answer to your question.

One thing, I think, we seem to be agreed upon—though I should not like it mentioned—to make sacramental confession a *sine qua non* among those who belong to us—and as there is more than one priest here, this does not involve any general subjection to one person.

Perceval called on me here. He had sent me a letter in the beginning of February, from which I inferred too truly how it was with him. He since has asked for it back—so I suppose means to publish it. It will not strike others however.

43.   TO MRS. WILLIAM FROUDE

Littlemore.   *3rd April, 1844*

My dear Mrs. Froude,

Pray take my writing as a proof of my anxiety to act rightly towards persons I love so much as William and you—and please continue to do what I am sure you do already, remember at sacred times and places me and my difficulties.

What I was going to remark upon yesterday was what seemed W's chief distress, viz. that my changing opinion seemed to unsettle one's confidence in truth and falsehood as external things, and led one to be as suspicious of the new opinion as one became distrustful of the old. Now in what I shall say, I am not going to speak in favour of my second thoughts in comparison of my first, but against such scepticism and unsettlement about truth and falsehood generally—the idea of which is very painful —at least this will be my main subject.

The case with me then was this, and not surely an unnatural one:—as a matter of feeling and of duty I threw myself into the system which I found myself in. I saw that the English

94

Church had a theological idea or theory as such, as I took it up. I read Laud on Tradition, and thought it (as I still think it) very masterly. The Anglican theory was very distinctive. I admired it, and took it on faith. It did not (I think) occur to me to doubt it, and I saw that it was *able,* and supported by learning, and I felt it was a *duty* to maintain it. Further on looking into antiquity and reading the Fathers, I saw such portions of it as I examined fully confirmed (e.g. the Supremacy of Scripture). There was only one question about which I had a doubt, viz. whether it would *work,* for it had never been more than a paper system.

Of course it is a difficulty to speak from memory of feelings and thoughts which belong to eight and nine years ago, and moreover to an exciting and busy time—yet I trust I have represented my former self correctly, though such a representation needs as much caution as I can give it.

One thing of course I saw clearly—that there was a great risk of Anglican principles running into Roman. They i.e., primitive, had done so once—as I notice in the Advertisements to my third volume of Sermons—they might do so again. And I felt both admiration and love of Rome, as far as I dare. This is plain from one of the notes in smaller type on the Translation of Vincentino in Records of the Church (in the Tracts) No. xxiv, in which I say, "Considering the high gifts and the strong claims of the Church of Rome, etc, on our admiration, reverence, love, and gratitude, how could we withstand it, as we do; how could we refrain from being melted into tenderness and rushing into communion with it, but for the words of Truth itself etc. 'He that loveth father or mother more than Me etc.?' " Other of the early Tracts show the same thing—and some of the Lyras "O Mother Church of Rome" and "O that thy creed were sound."

Nothing then but a strong positive difficulty or repulsion has kept me from surrendering my heart to the authority of the Church of Rome; a repulsive principle, not growing out of Catholic, Anglican or Primitive doctrine, in the way in which I viewed that doctrine, but something antagonistic, arising from *particular doctrines* of the Church of Rome, particular historical views, etc., etc.

And this very circumstance led me to be violent against the church of Rome—because it was the only way of resisting it. A bulwark and breakwater was necessary to the position of the English Church and theory. And in being violent, I was not acting on private judgment against so great a Communion, but I had the authority, or rather the command of all our Divines, who, doubtless from the same constraining necessity, have ever been violent against her also. To be violent against Rome was to be dutiful to England, as well as a measure of necessity for the English theory.

Now on all these respects I was contrasted, as you may easily see, with Hurrell Froude. He went by no theory, he was bent on defending no system, he was no Advocate, laughed at economies, merely investigated—and in consequence, and just in the same proportion, did not attack the Church of Rome, and disliked attacks upon it.

But to be brief—such were my feelings and views from 1833 to 1839. It was my great aim to build up the English system into something like consistency, to develop its idea, to get rid of anomalies, and to harmonize precedents and documents. I thought, and still think, its theory a great one. What then was my dismay or excitement, call you which you will, when in 1839 it flashed upon me in the course of reading the Fathers, which I had hitherto read with the eyes of our own Divines, that (not only was it a theory never realized) but a theory unproved or rather disproved by Antiquity? but I must stop.

Your affecte friend,

JOHN H. NEWMAN.

44.   TO MRS. WILLIAM FROUDE

Littlemore. *4th April, 1844*

In bonâ Domini—(all good gifts to you at this season). My dear Mrs. Froude,

Without waiting for any answer from you, here I go on, making up pretty considerably for my delay and silence; and all about myself.

So far from my change of opinion having any fair tendency to unsettle persons as to truth and falsehood as objective realities, it should be considered whether such change is not necessary should truth be a real objective thing, and made to confront a person who has been brought up in a system *short of* truth. Surely the *continuance* of a person who wishes to go right in a wrong system, and not his giving it up, would be that which militated against the objectiveness of Truth—leading to the suspicion that one thing and another were equally pleasing to our Maker where men were sincere.

Nor surely is it a thing that I need be sorry for that I defended the system in which I found myself, and have had to unsay my words. For is it not one's duty, instead of beginning with criticism, to throw oneself generously into that form of religion which is providentially put before one? Is it right, is it not wrong, to begin with private judgment? May we not on the other hand look for a blessing *through* obedience even to an erroneous system, and a guidance by means of it out of it? Were those who were strict and conscientious in their Judaism, or those who were lukewarm and sceptical, more likely to be led into Christianity when Christ came? Yet in proportion to their previous zeal, would be their appearance of inconsistency. Certainly I have always contended that obedience even to an erring conscience was the way to gain light—and that it mattered not when a man began, so that he began on what came to hand and in faith—that anything might become a divine method of Truth, that to the pure all things are pure, and have a self-correcting virtue and a power of germinating. And though I have no right at all to assume that this mercy is granted to me, yet the fact that a person in my situation *may* have it granted seems to me to remove the perplexity which my change of opinion may occasion.

I am writing in a most miserably prosy way, which I cannot

just now get out of. Perhaps it will go of itself presently. Well, but it may be said, I have said it to myself—"Why however did you *publish?* had you waited quietly, you would have changed your opinion without any of the misery, which now is involved in the change, of disappointing and distressing people." I answer that things are so bound up together as to form a whole, and one cannot tell what is not a condition of what. I do not see how possibly I could have published the Tracts or other works professing to defend our Church without accompanying them with a strong protest or argument against Rome. The one obvious objection against the whole Anglican line is, that it is Roman, and I really think there is no alternative between silence altogether and forming a theory and attacking the Roman system. In my lectures on the Prophetical Office I apologise for doing the latter from "the circumstances of the moment," both because "till they (persons who attack the 'Holy Cath. Church') do more *than they have hitherto done,*" "they hazard a deviation into Romanism etc." and next because in teaching that doctrine "the plan of attacking Romanism" is "the most convenient way of showing what our own views are." As far as I recollect I give the same *defensive* reason in the first of the "Tracts against Romanism," No. 71 I think. Either then I was obliged to commit myself to a theory of the Church and against Rome publicly and argumentatively, or not a Tract could be written. And where I myself should now be in opinion as well as many others, if no Tracts had appeared, is a speculation quite beyond me.

Nothing indeed all through this course of things strikes me as more strange than the intertwining of things good and bad. E.g. one is tempted to say, knowing what misery has resulted and does result from Dr. Hawkins being Provost of Oriel, "O that Hurrell's wish had been accomplished of placing Keble in his place!" But if Keble had been Provost, I for one should probably be Tutor of Oriel to this day. What great things K. might have done then, of course, is quite hid from us—they would have been great—but we should have never been dismissed from the Tuition, we (K., R. H. F., and I.) should never have turned our minds so keenly to other subjects, not a Tract would have been written. I should have gone on with Mathematics (which I was bent on doing and did, till Jenkyns *on the ground* of my leaving the Tutorship introduced me to *Rose* and so to the History of Arianism) I should have gone on with Niebuhr and Aristotle.

You must not suppose I am arguing against my having committed all sorts of faults in my *mode* of doing things, so much so, that all the comfort I might have had is taken away, of feeling an *assurance* that I have been brought on by a divine guidance to my present point. Alas! though I do not think there is anything in the mere fact of my change to show that I am wrong or to unsettle people, yet I have so bad a conscience in details as to have *very little* claim to feel confidence that I am right. This of course is what keeps me back. And now this unsufferable prose has exhausted my paper. O, my dear Mrs. Froude, I am very much disgusted at it.

Ever yrs affectionately,

John H. Newman.

45. TO MRS. WILLIAM FROUDE

Littlemore. *Good Friday Evening, 5th April, 1844*

My dear Mrs. Froude,

I write with some apprehension lest I should be making a great fuss about nothing and to no good—and yet I think too that what I have said and shall say may tend to make you less uncomfortable.

My confidence against the Church of Rome lay in two things, first my feeling that we had the Apostolical Succession—next my conviction that her peculiar doctrines were not held by the Fathers.

As to the first of these, I acknowledged great irregularity in the transmission, and vast and various disorders and faults in our Church. But I got over all by the parallel of the Jewish Church, which was a Church when Christ came, in spite of anomalies as great as ours. My view is drawn out in my last Lecture on the Prophetical Office.

As to the second it was to me as clear as day (as it is now) that the honours paid in the Church of Rome to St. Mary were not primitive. On this I rested our case mainly for those honors are at once the furthest removed from primitive usage and especially characteristic of the Roman Church. I have drawn out the general argument in Lecture ii on "Romanism as neglectful of Antiquity."

My defence of the English Church against Rome was conducted under the shelter of these two convictions, with the expression of which my lectures begin and end. They were written in 1834—1837; and during 1836 and 7 the Tracts against Rome.

In the Summer of 1839 I was led in the course of my *regular reading* (which is a point on which some stress might be laid) to the Monophysite controversy, and to the Council of Chalcedon and St. Leo's works inclusively. I found what surprised me very much. It struck me at once, but when it began to assume an unsettling character I do not recollect—but I found more matter for serious thought in that history than in anything I had read. The Council of Ch. is the fourth A.D. 452 Ecumenical Council, which it is generally considered the English Church receives. Our Divines consider its opponents heretics, as denying that "Jesus Christ has come in the flesh." Eutyches was condemned then, he said there was but one nature in our Lord. Now I cannot bring together all the strange things I found in its history. I found the Eastern Church under the superintendence (as I may call it) of Pope Leo. I found that *he* had made the Fathers of the Council unsay their decree and pass another, so that (humanly speaking) we owe it to Pope Leo at this day that the Catholic Church holds the true doctrine. I found that Pope Leo based his authority upon St. Peter. I found the Fathers of the Council crying out "Peter hath spoken by the mouth of Leo," when they altered their decree. I found a portentously large body of

Christians thrown into schism by this Council, at this day the Churches of Egypt, Syria (in part) and Armenia; and the schismatics not like the Arians, of a rationalist, but with a theology of a warm and elevating character. I found that they appealed, and with much plausibility, to certain of the Fathers, as St. Athanasius and St. Cyril of Alex.—that they professed to be maintainers of the antiquity—that they called their opponents (the Catholics) *Chalcedonians,* as we call the R.C.'s Tridentines, that their cause was taken up by the civil power, and created a contention between Emperors and the Church. Further I found there was a large middle party as well as an extreme. There was a distinct Via Media, which indeed the Emperor took up, and there was a large body who went on for some centuries without Bishops. I am writing from memory, but I am sure I am right in all points of consequence—and in a word I found a complete and wonderful parallel, as if a prophecy, of the state of the Reformation controversy, and that we were on the Anti-Catholic side.

I will go on with this part of the subject at the expense of the order of time. I add then that from that time to this, the view thus brought before me has grown upon me. I had hitherto read ecclesiastical history with the eyes of our Divines, and taken what they said on faith, but now I had got *a key,* which interpreted large passages of history which had been locked up from me. I found everywhere one and the same picture, prophetic of our present state, the Church in communion with Rome decreeing, and heretics resisting. Especially as regards the Arian controversy, how could I be so blind before! except that I looked at things bit by bit, instead of putting them together. There was Pope Julius resisting the whole East in defence of St. Athanasius, the Eusebians at the great Council of Antioch resisting him, and he appealing to his own authority (in which the historians support him) and declaring that he filled the See of St. Peter. The lapse of Pope Liberius, carefully as it needs considering, does not interfere with the general view. There were two parties, a Via Media, and an extreme, both heretical, but the Via Media containing pious men, whom St. Athanasius and others sympathise in—there were the kings of the earth taking up the heresy against the Church—there was precisely the same appeal to Scripture, which now attains, and that grounded on a literal interpretation of its text, to which St. Athanasius always opposes the "ecclesiastical sense"—there was the same complaint of introducing novel and unscriptural terms into the Creed of the Church, "Consubstantial," and "Transubstantiation" being both of philosophical origin, and if Trent has opposed some previous Councils (which I do not recollect) at least the Nicene Council adopted the very term "Consubstantial" which a celebrated Council of Antioch 60 or 70 years before condemned or discountenanced.

When shall I come to an end?

Ever yrs affectionately,

John H. Newman.

46. TO MRS. WILLIAM FROUDE

Littlemore.   *Easter Tuesday, 9th April, 1844*

My dear Mrs. Froude,

I have received your kind letter this morning and at present cannot make up my mind whether I ought to send you any more of these harassing letters. Not that I meant them either to be many or harassing, I set about overcoming what seemed to be a difficulty pressing on William—and I suspect I both exaggerated it, and have been led into a great error in my way of meeting it. However I write on, whether you see it or not, writing (since I have begun to do, what I had no notice of doing in my first letter to you) to complete what otherwise probably I may never get myself to do.

What I described in my last was the view that burst upon me, that separation from the body of Christendom, and again, or especially, from the see of Rome, is (to those who would go by primitive views of Christianity) a *presumption* of error. I cannot recollect by what degrees or at what time it became an unsettling principle in my mind, though I perfectly recollect the lively feelings produced in me by the Monophysite history. These I mentioned to H. Wilberforce among others at the end of July when we met at the consecration of the New Church at Otterbourne. But I cannot make out that I realised them practically till the end of the Long Vacation, then something else occurred to give them very serious force.

I know how very coolly, that is, historically, I must seem to you to be writing on these most serious matters. But it does no good to be roundabout. If I am to write, I must write plainly, yet I can hardly get myself to say what now comes, though it is difficult to say why. At the end of the Long Vac. (1839) a number of the Dublin Review appeared containing an Article by Dr. Wiseman which made some talk in Oxford. I looked at it, and treated it very lightly. Persons who (I suppose) half took up our views, said we were bound to answer it, meaning it was a great difficulty in the way of the Anglican theory. I recollect saying it was "all the old story" and would not think about it. I do not know what made me take up the Number again, but I found it on careful attention to contain so powerful an argument that I became (I may say) excited about it. I was leaving Oxford for a few weeks, in the course of which I paid visits to Rogers and to H. Wilberforce, and to both I mentioned that I was shaken in my confidence in the Anglican theory, but to no one else.

The argument in the Article in question was drawn from the History of the Donatists, and was directed to show that the English Church was in schism. The fact to which the Monophysite controversy had opened my eyes, that antagonists of Rome, and churches in isolation, were always wrong in primitive times, and which I had felt as a presumption against ourselves, this article went on to maintain as a recognized principle and rule in those same ages. It professed that the *fact* of isolation and opposition was *always taken* as a *sufficient* condemnation of bodies so circumstanced, and to that extent, that the question was not asked how *that the quarrel arose*? which was right, and which wrong? who made the separation? but that the *fact* of separation was reckoned anciently as decisive against the body separated. This was argued chiefly from the language of St. Augustine as elicited in the Donatist controversy, and the same sort of *minute* parallel was drawn between the state of the Donatists and our own, which I had felt on reading the history of the Monophysites.

On my return to Oxford, my immediate business was to set about answering this argument. It is my sincere belief and principle that it is right to resist doubts and to put aside objections to the form of doctrine and the religious system in which we find ourselves. I think such resistance pleasing to God. If it is His will to lead us from them, if the doubt comes from Him, He will repeat the suggestion, He will call us again as He called Samuel, He will make our way clear to us. Fancies, excitement, feelings go and never return—truth comes again and is importunate. The system in which we have been placed is God's voice to us till He supersede it, and those means by which He supersedes it must be more distinct than the impression produced on us by that system itself. Accordingly I then set about, as I have since, to keep myself in my own place. What I wrote appeared as an article in the British Critic in January (I think) 1840, under the title of "Catholicity of the English Church," and, though important practical effects followed from the shock I had received, the view of the subject which it contains kept me quiet for nearly two years, that is, till the autumn of 1841.

The practical effects which I speak of, were such as these:— 1. to attempt to give up St. Mary's. I brought this before the College in 1840, wishing to retain Littlemore, but the Provost would not hear of the separation of the Living. In 1841 I took the Cottages I now inhabit, and from the beginning of 1841 I had a curate at St. Mary's and gradually took less and less share in the duty there. Last year, as you know, I resigned it. 2. I gave up society etc., in Oxford as far as might be. The affair of No. 90 was an excuse for this. In consequence, i.e. in 1841, our theological meetings at Pusey's came to an end, and my weekly evening parties also. 3. I gave up the British Critic in the spring of 1841, this was settled, before the affair of No. 90. 4. As far as possible, I left off writing on any subjects of the Day (except in Sermons, then I felt it my duty while I held St. Mary's). My contributions to the Tracts, as a course, came to an end in 1838. In 1840 I added the Devotions of Bp. Andrews—and nothing else, except indeed No. 90, which shall be mentioned presently. As to my University Sermons I went on with them as finishing a course; the last, which has made some talk, I wrote quite lately, but I will speak of this elsewhere, if I ever write so much. Except No. 90, I have not as far as I remember written anything on subjects of the Day since 1838, six years. I have already excepted Sermons. (I suppose you will say certain letters in the Times in the beginning of 1841 are exceptions. I was *pressed* to write them). 5. Of course I became very careful of saying things against Rome. In new Editions of my volumes I corrected many passages, and at the end of 1842, I took measures for the publication of a retractation of certain passages which called for it. I published an article on anti-Christ in the B. C. in 1840 I think. (By the bye several B. C. articles form another important exception since 1838). 6. I was very desirous of an adjustment, or at least of the contemplation of an adjustment between ourselves and the Church of Rome, and without feeling I knew enough about the matter to dare to pronounce that it might be upon the basis of the Council of Trent, I hoped it might be so. And feeling very strongly the corruptions in the Church, I felt more and more inclined to regard them, as had very frequently been done, by our writers, as *in* the Church, not *of* the Church. 7. No. 90 originated in various causes. The desire just mentioned of drawing towards Rome; a feeling of the need which various persons had to know *how* Catholicly to interpret certain articles; a feeling as if our opponents had a right to ask and ought to be told, and as if it were disingenuous, and would clearly seem so, not to state plainly how we reconciled our subscriptions without opinions; and moreover a hope that to *state* the Catholic interpretation was to *make* it; for what was allowed, became de facto an interpretation. I did not foresee the great opposition made to it and such condemnation from authority. I had taken up my notes here for writing it in Lent 1840, but I did not write it till the beginning of 1841.

At the time of publication of No. 90, I was 1. desirous of union with Rome, i.e. Church with Church. 2. I was strongly opposed to the idea of *individual* moves. 3. I thought the *practical* system of Rome very corrupt and thought those corruptions *balanced* our quasi-schism (I have drawn out my view in the B.C. of July 1841, Article on Private Judgment). 4. I thought my own occupation quite gone in the Anglican Church. My feeling is shown in a Preface I wrote to Nelson's Life of Bull (I think) in 1840.

You will clearly see, if you see this letter at all, that it is written with a minuteness consistent with what I have stated in the first lines of it, rather than in a way which will interest you.

Yours affectionate Friend,

John H. Newman.

47. TO MRS. WILLIAM FROUDE

Littlemore.   *19th May, 1844*

My dear Mrs. Froude,

I said in my last that difficulties presented themselves to me in the Anglican theory of the Church from which the Roman is free. On both theories the Church is considered, as the Creed declares it, *one*—now the meaning of "one" is simple, if "one Church" means one *kingdom*, one body politic, but in what sense do Anglicans consider it one? They consider it a *succession*, propagated through different countries, independent in each country and claiming adherence of Christians in this or that country to itself as it exists in this or that country. Each Bishop is isolated from every other and supreme in his own diocese, and if he unites with others, it is only as the civil power or his own choice happens to unite him. He claims obedience yet without claiming to be a depository and transmitter of true *doctrine*, the succession being a point of order, not a condition and witness of Christian faith. And all other bishops or religious bodies acting in his diocese without his leave are schismatical. Now if this be so, the question occurs in what sense do Anglicans consider the Church *one*? in what sense are Rome and England one?

If Rome and England *are* one, what is meant by the common phrase of "the church of our baptism"? Baptism is "one," and admits into the "one body"; not into any local society. A child baptized by a clergyman of Oxford is not admitted into that diocese or Church, but into the Catholic Body, which is diffused throughout the world, and which is the real Church "of his baptism." It puzzled me to make out, in what sense, on the hypothesis that Rome and England formed one Church, a man changed his Church who went from the English to the Roman branch, any more than he changed it, if he communicated here with the Church of Oxford, there with the Church of London. He changed his *faith* indeed; that is another matter; but how was he guilty of schism, how could he *change* his Church, when there was no *other* Church to change to?

To meet this difficulty Anglicans are forced into the following argument—that is, I believe so; and certainly I was, and have expressed it, among other places, in the Article on the Catholicity of the English Church and in a note at p. 150 of the Oxford Translation of St. Cyprian's Treatises. (No—I have explained the *general theory* in these places). They say, that since there is but one Bishop and Church in each place, and our succession, not the Roman, has possession in England, therefore the Roman succession and Church are intruders here. But surely this is very technical and unreal; for who can deny that the true difference between us and Rome is one of *doctrine and practice*? Yet such an explanation sinks that difference altogether, and reduces our quarrel with Rome to one of ecclesiastical arrangement. Its irrelevance is shown as soon as you put the question of members of our Church going abroad; are they to communicate with the Roman Church in places where that Church has possession? If we are one Church with Rome, only locally distinct, they ought, yet few would feel it right to do so; and if they do not, we are *not* one Church with Rome. The Anglican theory then cannot be acted upon, it is a mere set of words—facts confute it.

It was, I think, in the beginning of 1840, that a lawyer, with whom I was slightly acquainted wrote me several letters on this subject, in opposition to Palmer, which had the effect of convincing me that it was absurd to call the Roman Catholics schismatics in England. As I recollect, his plain argument was, how preposterous that a man who across the Channel believes in purgatory, the Mass, the Pope's Supremacy etc. must all of a sudden, if he comes to England, change his creed and worship, and become member of a local community which denies all he has hitherto received? This led me to investigate the Anglican theory of local Episcopacy itself, from which these absurdities follow, and I found it as untenable as its consequences; as a few words will show.

May 29th. I think it is Hooker who tells us the distinction between "Bishops by restraint" and "Bishops at large." Bishops by restraint are Bishops with a certain definite jurisdiction. Bishops at large are Bishops over the *whole* Church. Now I believe it is generally granted that this "restraint" is the consequence of a byelaw of the Church, and that local jurisdiction, which it implies, is not of the essence of the Episcopate. In the theory of Episcopacy there is never more than *one* Bishop in the whole Church—for every Bishop is but the shadow and repetition of every other. Every Bishop has the full Episcopate in his own person, as in a firm every partner has all the responsibilities of the whole house. They are, to use a law phrase, "joint tenants" in power, or (as St. Cyprian expresses it) they have the Episcopate "in solidum." There is then one and one only Bishop in the Church, with a universal jurisdiction, the Vicar of Christ, and the Pastor of Souls. *Each* Bishop is *all this* in *his essential* character; such is the theory which I think you find in Bingham,

and among ancient writers in St. Cyprian's Treatise De Unitate
. . . But now it is obvious how inconvenient, or rather how
impossible such a theory is in practice, while men are men. If a
thousand absolute and independent monarchs rule over the
whole heritage of Christ, what is to secure their agreement? who
is to decide their differences? This being so, by a series of bye
laws and usages (similar to that by which three Bishops at least
are necessary for a consecration, though in the theory and really,
one is enough) the intrinsic power of individual Bishops is
curtailed, and one is put under another. The great majority of
Bishops deprive themselves of their intrinsic universal jurisdiction and take a subordinate place under others, and all limit
their *immediate* jurisdiction to some particular spot, or what is
called a Diocese. They are then called what they all are in fact,
"Bishops by restraint," and thence results the great Patriarchal
system. They divide between them, for the sake of order, their
own power—one is a suffragan, another a metropolitan, another
a private. And again, since such an arrangement depends on
byelaws or canons, when matters arise of greater consequence
than canons, e.g. matters of faith, then all parties return to first
principles and rights. Thus, as you will read in Bingham, during
the Arian troubles each Catholic Bishop considered himself quite
free to consecrate and order things anywhere, when Arianism
prevailed. They then became Bishops at large again, or had a
universal jurisdiction.

But if this be so, how absurd is it, I was going to say hypocritical, when we have actually broken from Rome in matters
of faith and order, when we have asserted an independence
which can only be defended by an abolition of all usages in
canons, then again to effect a delicacy and profess an etiquette
on the point of local jurisdiction. This is straining at a gnat
and swallowing a camel. We have a greater right to place a
Bishop at Malta, than we had to disobey the Pope, local episcopacy and the Popedom—stand on the same basis, viz. that
of canons. And the R. C.'s have as great a right to create a
Church in England, or we to create a Church out of the Roman

communion—if their congregations are disobedient to the Bishop of London or Winchester, yet so are the Dioceses of London and Winchester to the Pope. At the Reformation the Patriarchal system was broken up as in Arian times, Bishops at large succeeded to Bishops by restraint, and though we may have rules among ourselves, as Roman Catholics have, yet England and Rome, viewed as Churches, each claims its inherent original jurisdiction over the whole Church. If at the Reformation there was division indeed, but not a schism, much less are the particular acts growing out of that division deserving that serious name. The presence of Rome in England and of England in Rome is the legitimate and necessary consequence of that great event.

Moreover, this being the case, we see how preposterous it is to talk of the Pope's "usurped power." As to his exercising power over the *whole Church,* he only does what all Bishops have a right to do, except they are restrained by definite provisions. As to his claiming power over the Bishops, he only does it by usage, by prescription, by the canons as the Archbishop of Canterbury. If he goes beyond these warrants he acts unjustifiably. While he can appeal to them, he is blameless. What he possesses, is either what he retains or what he has received. And in saying this, I am not going to the question whether his power is by divine right or not, even though it has been brought about by natural and human means, it may be a fulfilment of the prophetic promise to St. Peter as recorded in xvi of St. Matthew.

A further conclusion seemed to follow from what has been said. If the ecumenical authority of the Pope has been created, not by his exaltation but by the canonical depression of other Bishops, and is no assumption, but the result of a voluntary arrangement, it follows that while it is lawful as being in their own power, it must necessarily be gradual as being the consequence of their positive acts. Canons are not framed, nor do usages obtain, in a day—nor do the dispositions and ordinances which are the subject of them. The Papacy then could not but be of slow growth, and if it were the subject of prophecy in Matt. xvi, there is still greater reason for saying so. All then that we look for in antiquity, is tendencies and beginnings of its greatness, and these are found abundantly. This is the further conclusion which I meant, and with reference to it I will bring this long letter to an end.

I write from memory, and therefore may make some mistakes in detail, though I am correct on the whole. St. Clement, Bishop of Rome, (vid. Library of Fathers, vol. 8, p. 44, note f) who is mentioned by St. Paul, wrote a pastoral letter which is extant to the Church of Corinth. St. Ignatius addresses the Church of Rome as the Church "which presides" or "is the first see in the country of the Romans." Dionysius of Corinth in the second century speaks of its alms and benevolences as extending all over the Church. St. Irenaeus in the same century calls it the Church with which all others must concur. Pope Victor at the same time threatened the Churches of Asia Minor with excommunication. Tertullian, Origen and St. Cyprian use language in the third like Irenaeus's. Pope Stephen repeats towards St. Cyprian the threat of Pope Victor. Pope Dionysius is appealed to against Dionysius Bp of Alexandria in a matter of doctrine by Alexandrians, entertains the appeal, requires an explanation of him, and receives it and the Roman civil government submits the deprivation of Pauı, Bp of Antioch, to the decision of the see of Rome. In the fourth century St. Athanasius and his friends appeal to the Roman see, and St. Jerome professes in a matter of doctrine and in the choice of a patriarch of Antioch, to rule himself by its decision. Moreover in every case the view whether of doctrine or discipline taken by the see of Rome, ultimately prevailed, and, if success is the token of truth, is the true one. It is the Pope who has determined the rule for observing Easter, and for treating the baptisms of heretics, who has confirmed or pronounced the condemnation of Arianism, Apollinarianism, Pelagianism, and the other numerous heresies which distracted the early Church. He appears to exercise an infallibility which in after ages he has more distinctly claimed.

All these things being considered, I was forced to admit that the doctrine of the Papacy was a primitive one—for

1st. If we do not allow of developments, especially in a matter which from the nature of the case *requires* time for its due exhibition, hardly any doctrine can be proved by antiquity.

2. Nor is it anything to the purpose that the Pope's power was withstood in early times, e.g. by St. Cyprian—for when a doctrine or ordinance has to be developed, collision or disturbances seem previous conditions of its final adjustment.

3. Nor is it to the purpose that certain passages such as those which I have referred to above from writers of the first centuries may otherwise be explained—for the question is which of the two interpretations is the more likely—and the event seems to suggest the true interpretation, as in the case of a prophecy.

But I am getting hard and dry, if I have not been so all along.

Ever yr affectionate friend,

John H. Newman.

P.S. Your letter of this morning has led to my finishing this. Since my object in writing has ceased to be that with which I began (viz. that of removing a painful feeling which William seemed to have) I have become both somewhat indolent about writing, and also very anxious about the *effect* of my letters to you. Both these feelings will account for my long silence. The same change of purpose makes me indifferent as to hearing what you think about my letters, so that I am made certain they do not unsettle you, for I am not writing with a purpose so much as finishing a subject I may not otherwise get myself to work out.

48.   TO THE REV. J. KEBLE

Littlemore.   *8th June, 1844*

My dear Keble,

Pattison wishes me to tell you that friends of his, a lady and daughter, are going into your Parish. So far you must know—at least you know *them*, and have been civil to them already—but what you do not know, and he wishes you to know, is, that they have come to Hursley to be 'under your superintendence.' I do not know what the phrase means, but when he and I had repeated it several times, and no light seemed thrown upon it, I dropped the subject. Perhaps he does not know either. If you wish, I can inquire.

I ought to take this opportunity of writing to you a long letter, to which I have a great repugnance because it is about myself—not to say that writing intelligibly makes my hand ache. But you should know my state of mind—and though the disgust of writing, and the thought of the worry and worse that my letters give you, almost deter me, and I don't know how I shall get on, I will attempt to do it.

I have thought much lately of the words in Bishop Andrewes' Morning Prayer—'Despise not the work of Thine own hands'—he repeats it in various forms, as addressed to Each of the Persons of the Most Holy Trinity. May I not take comfort in this plea which they contain? 'Thine Hands have made me and fashioned me.' I look back to past years, or rather to all my years since I was a boy, and I say, 'Is it come to this? has God forgotten to be gracious? would He have led me on so far to cast me off? what have I done to be given over, if it be such, to a spirit of delusion? where is my fault?which has been the false step, if such there be?'

I know He taketh up and setteth down—and of course I know that I have done enough to provoke Him to give me over and to deserve all that is evil. But still such is not His way, and I cannot get myself to believe that He means evil towards me, yet month by month my convictions grow in one direction.

When I was a boy of fifteen, and living a life of sin, with a very dark conscience and a very profane spirit, He mercifully touched my heart; and, with innumerable sins, yet I have not forsaken Him from that time, nor He me. He has upheld me to this hour, and I have called myself His servant. When I came up to reside at Trinity, this verse of the Psalms, which was most in my heart and on my lips, and it has brought tears into my eyes to think of it, was 'Thou shalt guide me with Thy counsel,' etc. He then brought me through numberless trials safely and happily on the whole—and why should He now leave me to a blinded mind? I know I have done enough to provoke Him; but will He?

He led me forward by a series of Providences from the age of nineteen till twenty-seven. I *was* 'the work of His hands,' for He repeatedly and variously chastised me and at last to win me from the world, He took from me a dear sister—and just at the same time He gave me kind friends to teach me His way more perfectly.

Time went on, and various things happened by which He went on training me—but what most impresses itself upon me, is the strange feelings and convictions about His will towards me which came on me, when I was abroad. When I went down to Sicily by myself, I had a strong idea that He was going to effect some purpose by me. And from Rome I wrote to some one, I think Christie, saying I thought I was to be made something of in His Hands, 'though, if not, the happier for me.' And when I was in Sicily by myself, it seemed as if some one were battling against me, and the idea has long been in my mind, though I cannot say when it came on, that my enemy was then attempting to destroy me. A number of sins were committed[1] in the very act of my going down by *myself*—to say nothing else, I was wilful, and neglected warnings—from that time everything went wrong. As I lay ill at Leonforte, before I got to Castro Giovanni, while I was laid up, I felt this strongly. My servant thought I was dying—but I expected to recover, and kept saying, as giving the reason, 'I have not sinned against light.' I had the fullest persuasion I should recover, and think I then gave as the reason, that some work was in store for me. But any how when I was getting up again, after it was over, this feeling was strong upon me, I recollect, when travelling down the country from Castro G. to Palermo, (the ecclesiastical year was on the same days as this year, and as the year of my getting in to Oriel, so that Rogers and I were both elected on the 12th of April) it must have been Whitsunday or Monday morning, sitting on my bed as I was dressing, and crying profusely. My servant, who was

[1] ' Involved ' is written over ' committed.'

obliged to help me from my great weakness (for I could not walk by myself) of course could not think the meaning of it—and I could but say to him, what was quite as unintelligible as my tears, that I thought God had some work for me. And then when I got to England, the very first Sunday after my arrival (July 14) you preached your sermon on National Apostasy, which was the beginning of the movement.

And now at the end of eleven years from that time, [what] is my own state? why, that for the last five years (almost) of it, I have had a strong feeling, often rising to an habitual conviction, though in the early portion of it after a while dormant, but very active now for two years and a half, and growing more urgent and imperative continually, that the Roman Communion is the only true Church. And this conviction came upon me while I was reading the Fathers and from the Fathers—and when I was reading them theologically, not ecclesiastically, in that particular line of study, that of the ancient heresies, to which circumstances, external to myself, had led me fourteen years ago, before the movement began.

And when this trial came upon me, I told only two persons with whom I happened to be at the time—and set myself to resist the impression. As you know, I wrote against it, and I am not aware in what respect I have indulged it. And I have attempted to live a stricter life. Every Lent since it first came on me I have spent up here, except such necessary returns to Oxford in the course of the week as Oxford duties made necessary—and for the last two years I have been here almost entirely. And I have made great efforts to keep others from moving in the direction of Rome also.

Of course there is no fear of your supposing me not to be conscious of innumerable weaknesses and errors in my heart and conduct—but I cannot help trusting they need not come into account here. Or, even though there has been at times sin more than ordinary, I trust it is not being laid to my charge.

Moreover I certainly think I may say, that in many respects my heart and conduct have improved in the course of this five years, and that in respects in which I have prayed for improvement. Then the question comes upon me, why should Providence have granted my prayers in these respects, and not when I have prayed for light and guidance?

And then, as far as I see, all inducements and temptations are for remaining quiet, and against moving. The loss of friends what a great evil is this! the loss of position, of name, of esteem —such a stultification of myself—such a triumph to others. It is no proud thing to unsay what I have said, to pull down what I have attempted to build up. And again, what quite pierces me, the disturbance of mind which a change on my part would cause to so many—the casting adrift, to the loss both of religious stability and comfort—the temptation to which many would be exposed of scepticism, indifference, and even infidelity.

These last considerations are so serious, in the standard of reason as well as in the way of inducement, that, if it were not for antagonist difficulties, I don't see how I could ever overcome them. But it does strike me on the other side, 'What if you are the cause of souls dying out of the Communion of Rome, who have had a *call* to join it, which you have repressed? what, if this has happened already?' Surely time enough has been allowed me for wavering and preparation—I have fought against these feelings in myself and others long enough. And then another terrible thought strikes me. We hear of physicians thinking they have cured a complaint, when they have but thrown their patient into a contrary one—and enough has happened to make me fear greatly lest a sort of latitudinarianism and liberalism *may* be the end of them (though forbid it!) whom I am keeping from Rome. I am quite sure there is this *danger*. I dread it in particular persons. The time may even come, when I shall beg them to join the Church of Rome and they will refuse. Indeed I sometimes feel uncomfortable about myself—a sceptical, unrealizing temper is far from unnatural to me—and I may be suffered to relapse into it as a judgment.

What then is the will of Providence about me? The time for argument is passed. I have been in one settled conviction for so

long a time, which every new thought seems to strengthen.
When I fall in with friends who think differently, the temptation
to remain quiet becomes stronger, very strong—but I really do
not think my conviction is a bit shaken. So then I end as I began
—Am I in a delusion, given over to believe a lie? Am I deceiving
myself and thinking myself convinced when I am not? Does any
subtle feeling or temptation, which I cannot detect, govern me,
and bias my judgment? But is it possible that Divine Mercy
should not wish me, if so, to discover and escape it? Has He led
me thus far to destroy me in the wilderness?

Really I dread what would be the consequence if any intimate
friend of mine joined the Church of Rome. Might I not feel it
impossible to disobey what seemed a warning to me, whatever
trial and pain of mind it involved?

How this letter will distress you! I am ever thinking of you,
My dear Keble,

Yours affectionately,

J. H. N.

49. TO MRS. WILLIAM FROUDE

Littlemore.   *14th July, 1844*

My dear Mrs. Froude,

I find the subject I have now got into is endless, and I must
cut it short. I meant to have drawn out the mode in which I
have got reconciled to the (apparently) modern portions of the
Roman system. It has been by applying to them that *principle*
which, as my last letter showed, had long been in my mind, the
principle of developments. From the time I wrote the Arians, or
at least from 1836, I have had in my thoughts, though I could
not bring it out, that argument or theory, which at last appeared
as my closing University Sermon.[1] It was delayed as long as I
could in the series of Sermons from inability, or fear of not

[1] Sermon XV, " The Theory of Developments in Religious Doctrine."

doing justice to it, as it ought, in the due order, to have preceded the one before it.

Yet I must confess that the Sermon does not, as Palmer has observed in his Pamphlet, go the whole length of theory which is necessary for the Roman system, and that something is still necessary to the discussion of the *theory*, though I have no difficulties about receiving the system in matter of fact. The kind of considerations which do weigh with me, are such as the following: —

1. I am far more certain (according to the Fathers) that we *are* in a state of culpable separation *than* that developments do *not* exist under the gospel, and that the Roman developments are *not* true ones.

2. I am far more certain that *our* (modern) doctrines are wrong, *than* that the Roman (modern) doctrines are wrong.

3. Granting that the Roman (special) doctrines are not found drawn out in the early Church, yet I think there is sufficient trace of them in it, to recommend and prove them, *on the hypothesis* of the Church having a divine guidance, though not sufficient to prove them by itself. So that the question simply turns on the nature of the promise of the Spirit made to the Church.

4. The proof of the *Roman* (special) doctrines is as strong (or stronger) in Antiquity, as that of certain doctrines which *both we and the Romans* hold. E.g. there is more evidence in Antiquity for the necessity of Unity than for that of the Apostolical succession—for the supremacy of the see of Rome than for the Presence in the Eucharist—for the practice of Invocation than for certain books in the present Canon of Scripture, etc., etc.

5. The analogy of the Old Testament and the New leads to the acknowledgement of doctrinal developments. E.g. the prophetical notices concerning our Lord before His coming. Again the gradual revelation of the calling of the Gentiles through St. Peter and St. Paul. Again, the distinct theological announcements of St. John's gospel compared with those which preceded it. Again it is undeniable that the doctrine of the Holy Trinity, as we now hold it, is historically the result of a great deal of

discipline and controversy, of much heresy and much antagonist development. Again the rule for baptizing heretics, or of infant baptism etc., etc. was unsettled and contested in early times, but at last universally obtained as it is at present.

And now I have said enough on the whole subject—and I cannot get over the feeling that I have intruded it upon you.

Your affectionate friend,

John H. Newman.

50. TO THE REV. J. KEBLE

Littlemore.   *14th September, 1844*

My dear Keble,

I have been going to write to you for some days, to tell you what there was to be told about dear Bowden, and your letter has just come.

I was at Clifton on Wednesday and Thursday last, not having seen him for a month. He was sadly altered. Fever has come on and perspirations. He certainly would not get from Clifton, except that he has in a way set his heart on waiting God's time at St. Leonard's, where he was all last winter and has a house now ready for him. It so happens he has no home, though he has just come into property by his father's death, Roehampton having gone out of his hands last month. Perhaps I may stay with him when he gets to St. Leonard's, for he seemed to wish it, I thought—but I shall hear more in a day or two.

He gave me an account how he got through the day.

September 15th. He does not like not to come down stairs while he can, though it is a great effort to him, particularly dressing. He lies on his sofa with Bible, Prayer Book, Breviary, and 'Paradisus Animæ' on a little desk before him; but his thoughts are so unsteady now, that he has wished much, but sought in vain in Bristol, some sacred emblem or picture which may meet his eyes without effort. I took him the 'Paradisus' by accident for another purpose two months ago, and he has seized upon it with great delight, and says it is a great comfort to him. He made me read Compline, Terce and Sext with him. Besides that he manages to get through the Morning and Evening prayer, I believe—and sometimes the Penitential Psalms in the Breviary. Morning is his best time for eating, and he takes his principal meal then. His worst time is between six and eight in the evening. He gets out, or did, but a day makes a change now, in a Bath Chair—but he cannot bear the beautiful scenery at Clifton—it tries him. At length the hours have passed away, and no more expedients are needed. Evening comes, and he seems to have some quiet sleep of a night which recruits him, and he lies very tranquilly in bed. So he is lifted upstairs by his two servants, making a sort of low interjection, not of pain but of relief, 'lo, lo, lo,' or the like, and says, as he told me, 'Well, another crest has been topped, another billow is over,' calling the days his billows, with an allusion to 'Who would count the billows past?' He made me come and see what he called his 'procession' —his wife first with the candle, then he in the arms of the two men. While going up, he turned about his head, to be sure I was looking.

One forgets past feelings, else I would say that I had never had pain before like the present. I thought so yesterday, and said so; but I suppose it is not so. Yet I am in very great distress, and do trust I shall be kept from gloom and ill temper. I have given him up since October last, yet have not realized his loss till now, if now. He is my oldest friend. I have been most intimate with him for above twenty-seven years. He was sent to call on me the day after I came into residence—he introduced me to College and University—he is the link between me and Oxford. I have ever known Oxford in him. In losing him I seem to lose Oxford. We used to live in each other's rooms as Undergraduates, and men used to mistake our names and call us by each other's. When he married, he used to make a similar mistake himself, and call me Elizabeth and her Newman. And now for several years past, though loving him with all my heart, I have shrunk from him, feeling that I had opinions that I dared not tell him, and that I must be constrained or almost hypocritical if I was with him.

Lewis has come up to tell me the news that dear Bowden is gone—I suppose this morning. I am going off at once to Clifton. I have heard no particulars. But it distresses me to have parted so suddenly with him on Thursday when he wished me to stay and did not know I was going.

Ever yours affectionately,
J. H. N.

51.   TO MRS. JOHN MOZLEY

31st October, 1844

I begin this letter for a not very complimentary reason, but from having a headache, a very unusual visitor, which hinders me from working.

You ask me about my meeting Arnold, and though there is nothing but what is commonplace to tell, I cannot tell it without introducing myself more than is pleasant. Indeed, the less I have to say, the more I must bring in myself, if I am to say anything; but even then I have little enough.

The second of February, as you know, is our great Gaudy of the year. The Provost dines in Hall at the top of the table; and in the Common-Room, to which the party adjourn, sits at the right hand of the Dean, as being the guest of the Fellows. Eden was Dean, and was taken ill, I think, when the news came that Arnold was coming with the Provost, and I, being Senior Fellow, must take the Dean's place. My first feeling was to shirk. 'It is not my place,' I said, 'to take the office upon me. It is nothing to me. I am not bound to entertain Arnold,' &c., &c. However, I thought it would be cowardly, so after all I went, knowing that both in Hall and Common-Room the trio at the top of the table would be Provost, Arnold, and I, and that in the Common-Room I should sit at the top between them as the entertainer.

The Provost came into Hall with Arnold and Baden-Powell (who made a fourth), I being already in my place at table, waiting for them. The Provost came up in a brisk, smart way, as if to cut through an awkward beginning, and said quickly, 'Arnold, I don't think you know Newman'; on which Arnold and I bowed, and I spoke. I was most absolutely cool, or rather calm and unconcerned, all through the meeting from beginning to end; but I don't know whether you have seen me enough in such situations to know (what I really believe is not any affectation at all on my part; I am not at all conscious of any such thing, though people would think it) that I seem, if you will let me say it, to *put on* a very simple, innocent, and modest manner. I sometimes laugh at myself, and at the absurdities which result from it; but really I cannot help it, and I really do believe it to be genuine. On one occasion in the course of our conversation I actually blushed high at some mistake I made, and yet on the whole I am quite collected. Now, are you not amused at all this? or ought not I to blush now? I never said a word of all this about myself to anyone in my life before; though, perhaps, that does not mend the matter that I should say it now. However, to proceed.

So when the Provost said, 'I don't think, Arnold, you know Newman,' I was sly enough to say, very gently and clearly, that I had before then had the pleasure of meeting Dr. Arnold, for I had disputed with him in the Divinity School before his B.D. degree, when he was appointed to Rugby. At which Baden-Powell laughed, and Arnold seemed a little awkward and said, 'Oh, I thought it had been Pusey.' You must know that in the said disputation I was doing him a favour, for he could get no one to go in with him, when I volunteered; though in the event it turned to my advantage, for I had not to dispute before Hampden when I actually took my degree [in 1836].

We then sat down to table, and I thought of all the matters possible which it was safe to talk on. I recollected he had travelled with William Churton, and that made one topic. Others equally felicitous I forget. But I recollect the productions of North Africa was a fruitful subject; and I have some dream of having talked of a great tree, the name of which I now forget, as big as a hill, and which they bring as an argument for the indefinite duration of the present earth *a parte ante*.

In the Common-Room I had to take a still more prominent part, and the contrast was very marked between Arnold and the Provost—the Provost so dry and unbending, and seeming to shrink from whatever I said, and Arnold who was natural and easy, at least to all appearance. I was told afterwards that on one occasion Baden-Powell made some irreverent remark, and people were amused to see how both Arnold and myself in different ways, as far as manner was concerned, retired from it. At last the Provost and Arnold rose up to go, and I held out my hand, which he took, and we parted.

I never saw him again; he died the June [2nd June, 1842] after. He is a man whom I have always separated from the people he was with, always respected, often defended, though from an accident he got a notion, I believe, that I was a fire-brand, and particularly hostile to *him*. There is no doubt he was surprised and thrown out on finding I did not seem to be what he had fancied. He told Stanley that it would not do to meet me often. When Stanley tried to clench the remark, he drew back, and said he meant that it was not desirable to meet often persons one disagreed with, or something of the sort. This is what I heard, to the best of my recollection, after his death. For myself, I don't think I was desirous of pleasing him or not; but was secretly amused from the idea that he certainly would be taken aback by coming across me *in propria persona;* at least so I think.

52.   TO THE REV. F. W. FABER

Littlemore.   *Advent Sunday [1st December], 1844*

My dear Faber,

I find it very difficult to answer you, both on your own account, and from diffidence which you will easily understand, in my own judgment. Perhaps it will be best for me to put some of my reasons before you, as far as I can.

I can understand certainly that Oret may be intolerably cold. It does not strike me that you infringed your rule by using the Confiteor;—but now as to direct and habitual invocations.

Really I have a great repugnance at mixing religions or worships together, it is like sowing the field with mingled seed. A system is a whole; one cannot tell the effect of one part disjoined from the rest. All this you know better than I can state it. Observances which may be very right in Saints, or in a Church which creates saints, in a communion in which the aids of grace are such and such, may be dangerous in a communion which has them not. I do not like decanting Rome into England; the bottles may break. Indeed I look with much anxiety to what is doing now in many quarters—not the least to the inculcation of extraordinary degrees of asceticism; extreme strictness about indifferent matters, heights of devotion and meditation, self-forgetfulness and self-abandonment, and the like. What is natural in Saints and in a saintly system, becomes a mere form in others. Of course the Invocations you write about would be no form in you, but others evils might come of them.

Again, I am not sure there is not danger of presumption in taking what belongs to another system at will. Private judgment comes in, and eclecticism. There is an absence of submission to religion as a rule. And I am not satisfied that our Church has not a claim in such observances on the obedience of her members to her directions. And when a man is holding office in the Church, so to speak, as you are, I think there is a still greater difficulty in the adoption of such observances.

You will understand without a word of mine, that I am saying all this by way of showing you the grounds of my opinion, and not as forcing it upon you. I am far too much perplexed myself in various ways, to feel it pleasant to give advice at all—much more to suffer what I say to be taken as a decision on the point. I hope you will but use what I have said as suggestions for your guidance.

I cannot think that Oakeley's arguments in the E. Ch. will stand, more than you, and I shall be surprised if the Bishop of L. likes to be told that O. considers that the Pope has a prior claim on his obedience.

Ward has been had up—and Romanizing propositions submitted to him to deny. He has got till Tuesday to answer.

I hear people speak with great commendation of Sir Launcelot and hope soon to have time to read it. I hope you have recovered the fatigue of St. Wilfred.

Yours most sincerely,
John H. Newman.

53. TO MRS. JOHN MOZLEY

Littlemore.   *15th March, 1845*

I have just received your very painful letter, and wish I saw any way of making things easier to you or to myself.

If I went by what I wished, I should complete my seven years of waiting. Surely more than this, or as much, cannot be expected of me—cannot be right in me to give at my age. How life is going! I see men dying who were boys, almost children, when I was born. Pass a very few years, and I am an old man. What means of judging can I have more than I have? What maturity of mind am I to expect? If I am right to move at all, surely it is high time not to delay about it longer. Let me give my strength to the work, not my weakness—years in which I can profit the cause which calls me, not the dregs of life. Is it not like a deathbed repentance to put off what one feels one ought to do?

As to my convictions, I can but say what I have told you already, that I cannot at all make out *why* I should determine on moving, except as thinking I should offend God by not doing so. I cannot make out what I am *at* except on this supposition. At my time of life men love ease. I love ease myself. I am giving up a maintenance involving no duties, and adequate to all my wants. What in the world am I doing this for (I ask *myself* this), except I think I am called to do so? I am making a large income by my sermons. I am, to say the very least, risking this; the chance is that my sermons will have no further sale at all. I have a good name with many; I am deliberately sacrificing it. I have a bad name with more; I am fulfilling all their worst wishes, and giving them their most coveted triumph. I am distressing all I love, unsettling all I have instructed or aided. I am going to those whom I do not know, and of whom I expect very little. I am making myself an outcast, and that at my age. Oh, what can it be but a stern necessity which causes this?

Pity me, my dear Jemima. What have I done thus to be deserted, thus to be left to take a wrong course, if it is wrong? I began by defending my own Church with all my might when others would not defend her. I went through obloquy in defending her. I in a fair measure succeed. At the very time of my reading it breaks upon me that I am in a schismatical Church. I oppose myself to the notion; I write against it—year after year I write against it, and I do my utmost to keep others in the Church. From the time my doubts come upon me I begin to live more strictly; and really from that time to this I have done more towards my inward improvement, as far as I can judge, than in any time of my life. Of course I have all through had many imperfections, and might have done every single thing I have done much better than I have done it. Make all deductions on this score, still, after all, may I not humbly trust that I have not so acted as to forfeit God's gracious guidance? And how is it that I have improved in other points if in respect of this momentous matter I am so fearfully blinded? . . .

Why should I distress your kind heart with all my miseries? Yet you must know them, to avoid the greater misery of looking at me externally, and wondering and grieving over what seems incomprehensible. Shall I add that, distressing as is my state, it has not once come upon me to say, O that I had never begun to read theology! O that I had never meddled in ecclesiastical matters! O that I had never written the Tracts, &c.! I lay no stress on this, but state it . . . Of course the human heart is mysterious. I may have some deep evil in me which I cannot fathom; I may have done some irreparable thing which demands punishment; but may not one humbly trust that the earnest prayers of many good people will be heard for me? May not one resign oneself to the event, whatever it turns out to be? May one not hope and believe, though one does not see it, that God's hand is in the deed, if a deed there is to be; that He has a purpose, and will bring it to good, and will show us that it is good, in His own time? Let us not doubt, may we never have cause to doubt, that He is with us. Continually do I pray that He would discover to me if I am under a delusion; what can I do more? What hope have I but in Him? To whom should I go? Who can do me any good? Who can speak a word of comfort but He? Who is there but looks on me with a sorrowful face?—but He can lift up the light of His countenance upon me. All is against me—may He not add Himself as an adversary! May He tell me, may I listen to Him, if His will is other than I think it to be!

Palm Sunday— . . . So, my dear Jemima, if you can suggest any warnings to me which I am not considering, well, and thank you; else do take comfort, and think that perhaps you have a right to have faith in me, perhaps you have a right to believe that He who has led me hitherto will not suffer me to go wrong. I am somehow in better spirits this morning, and I say what it occurs to me to say at the time. Have I not a right to ask you not to say, as you have said in your letter, that I shall do wrong? What right have you to judge me? Who of my equals, who of the many who will talk flippantly about me, has a right? Who has a right to judge me but my Judge? Who has taken such pains to know *my* duty (poor as they have been) as myself? Who is more likely than I to know what I ought to do? I may be wrong, but He that judgeth me is the Lord, and 'Judge nothing before the time.'

His ways are not our ways, nor His thoughts as our thoughts. He may have purposes as merciful as they are beyond us. Let us do our best, and leave the event to Him; He will give us strength to bear. Surely I have to bear most; and if I do not shrink from bearing it others must not shrink. May I do my best; am I not trying to do my best?—may we not trust it will turn to the best?

54. TO W. H. GLADSTONE

18th April, 1845

My dear Mr. Gladstone,

I should not venture to encroach upon your time with this note of mine, but for your letters to me last autumn, which make me read with great interest, of course, everything which is in the papers about you, and encourage me to think that you will not think me intrusive.

As various persons ask me what I understand is your present position, I will put down what I conceive it to be; and I will beg you to correct my account of it just as much or just as little as you please, and to determine, as you think best, whether I shall say I have your authority for any statements you may kindly make in your answer or not.

Useless words always look cold and formal on paper. I should not think of saying (what I really hope it will not even come into your passing thoughts to doubt) how great interest I feel in the line of thought which is at present engaging your mind, and how sure I am you will be conducted to right conclusions. Nor is there anything to startle or distress me in what you are reported to have said in the House.

I say then: 'Mr. Gladstone has said the State *ought* to have a conscience—but it has not a conscience. Can *he* give it a conscience? Is he to impose his own conscience on the State? He would be very glad to do so, if it thereby would become the State's conscience. But that is absurd. He must deal with facts. It has a thousand consciences, as being in its legislative and executive capacities, the aggregate of a hundred minds—that is, it has no conscience.

'You will say, "Well, the obvious thing would be, if the State has not a conscience, that he should cease to be answerable for it." So he has—he has retired from the Ministry. While he thought he could believe it had a conscience—till he was forced to give up, what it was his duty to cherish as long as ever he could, the notion that the British Empire was a subject and servant of the Kingdom of Christ—he served the State. Now that he finds this to be a mere dream, much as it ought to be otherwise, much as it once was otherwise, he has said, "I cannot serve such a mistress."

'But really,' I continue, 'do you in your heart mean to say that he *should* absolutely and for ever give up the State and the country? I hope not—I do not think he has so committed himself. That the conclusion he has come to is a very grave one, and not consistent with his going on blindly in the din and hurry of business, without having principles to guide him, I admit; and this I conceive is his reason for at once retiring from the Ministry, that he may contemplate the state of things calmly and from without. But I really cannot pronounce, nor can you, nor can he perhaps at once, what is a Christian's duty under these new circumstances—whether to remain in retirement from public affairs or not. Retirement, however, could not be done by halves. If he is absolutely to give up all management of public affairs, he must retire not only from the Ministry, but from Parliament.

'I see another reason for his retiring from the Ministry. The public thought they had in his book a pledge that the Government would not take such a step with respect to Maynooth as is now before the country. Had he continued in the Ministry, he would, to a certain extent, have been misleading the country.

'You say, "He made some show of seeing his way in future, for he gave advice. He said it would be well for all parties to yield something. To see his way and to give advice is as if he had found a principle, but he gave that advice which facts, or what he called circumstances, made necessary, and which, if followed out, will, it is to be hoped, lead to some basis of principle which we do not see at present.'

This letter[1] has run to a greater length than I had expected, but I thought I would do my best to bring out the impression which your speech has given me of your meaning.

I am, My dear Mr. Gladstone,
Very truly yours,
John H. Newman

55. TO THE REV. E. B. PUSEY

3rd October, 1845

My dear Pusey,

I have written to the Provost to-day to resign my fellowship. Anything may happen to me now any day. Anyhow, believe me,
My dear Pusey,
Yours most affectionately ever,
J. H. N.

56. TO MRS. JOHN MOZLEY

Littlemore.   *8th October, 1845*

My dear Jemima,

I must tell you what will pain you greatly, but I will make it as short as you would wish me to do.

This night Father Dominic, the Passionist, sleeps here. He does not know of my intention, but I shall ask him to receive me into what I believe to be the One Fold of the Redeemer.

This will not go till all is over.
Ever yours affectionately,
John H. Newman.

---

[1] Mr. Gladstone, in his reply, assented to Newman's representation. "I do not know," he said, " that I should have the least difficulty in subscribing to your letter as it stands; and I could much rather say ditto to you than do your work over again in my own language."

PART II

NEWMAN AS CATHOLIC
BY
MURIEL SPARK

INTRODUCTION

I

The letters which appear in this section cover a period of over forty years. It may assist readers who are unfamiliar with Newman biography if we recall some of the events of his life as a Catholic which these letters touch upon, before considering the fascinating points of his personality which emerge from the letters.

In the eyes of many his life seemed to be finished when he entered the Catholic Church. It was, indeed, many years before he regained his lost status among his countrymen, and then it was as if he emerged a different man; no longer the audacious Tractarian and prophet of Development, but the benign charmer of the *Apologia*. However, he was the same man. The development of Newman, his adjustment to new circumstances, was less abrupt than the change in his environment. He found himself in a new world, at first alien and yet attractive, later irritating and yet wonderful, always 'awful,' as he would say, and always, for him inevitable.

After his reception into the Church Newman remained for a few months at Littlemore, leaving it with his band of convert followers in the spring of 1846 to reside at Old Oscott in a house which they named Maryvale. In the autumn of that year Newman with his friend Ambrose St. John went to Rome to further their studies and to consider their future course. Newman's reception among Catholic society at Rome was a mixture of enthusiasm and suspicion. It was a time of political crisis in Rome, and attention was necessarily diverted from the illustrious convert by the forces which threatened the Pope. One of Newman's difficulties was that he never mastered Italian, which was then almost exclusively used among Church officials and dignitaries.

At Rome, he wrote his first novel, *Loss and Gain*, the story of an Oxford conversion, very much coloured by his own experience.

Newman and his companion were ordained the following year, and finding the flexible Oratorian tradition attractive and agreeable to their English temperament, decided to be Oratorians. Newman returned to England at the end of 1847 to found an Oratory which, in the next year, was established at Birmingham, his home to the end of his days.

The founder-community of Oratorians was formed of prominent Anglican converts, friends of Newman who rallied to his Superiority. The setting up of the Oratory took time. The convert community was under the somewhat predatory eyes of the hereditary Catholics who regarded their academicism on the one hand, and their Italianate zeal on the other, with a tiresome readiness to find fault. These 'old' Catholics were apt to look for quick and spectacular results—an attitude quite foreign to Newman, who went on his own way. A London Oratory was founded by Newman under the Rectorship of Father Frederick William Faber, and at London was ultimately gathered a band of Oratorians somewhat different in temperament from those who remained with Newman at Birmingham.

In 1850 Newman was persuaded to give a series of lectures to a London audience, which he later published as *The Difficulties of Anglicans*. He is described by one of his audience in terms reminiscent of the effect he produced in his great pulpit days at St. Mary's, Oxford:

Never did a voice seem better adapted to persuade without irritating. Singularly sweet, perfectly free from any dictatorial note, and yet rich in all the cadences proper to the expression of pathos, of wonder, and of ridicule, there was still nothing in it that any one could properly describe as insinuating, for its simplicity, and frankness, and freedom from the half-smothered notes which express indirect purpose, was as remarkable as its sweetness, its freshness, and its gentle distinctness. As he described the growth of his disillusionment with the Church of England, and compared it to the transformation which takes place in fairy tales when the magic castle vanishes, the spell is broken, "and nothing is seen but the wild heath, the barren rock, and the forlorn sheep-walk," no one could have doubted that he was describing with perfect truth the change that had taken place in his own mind.[1]

Newman gave these lectures with some reluctance; he was conscious, with his delicate insight, of the great diversity of Anglican opinion. Not all experienced the same 'difficulties,' and some might be repelled by his words. The lectures were, however, received with delight and respect; they attracted converts to the Church. Following the lectures, Newman received an honorary degree of Doctor of Divinity from Rome.

Another series of lectures, which he delivered at the Corn Exchange at Birmingham in 1851, brought Newman into prolonged misfortune. The establishment of the Catholic Hierarchy had just then provoked a great deal of anti-Catholic feeling in England, further stimulated by Cardinal Wiseman's tactless public enthusiasm. Newman's task was to answer the current popular objections to the Catholic Faith. His lively set of lectures, in which he employed fully his great gifts of irony, were later published as *The Present Position of Catholics in England.* One of these lectures he devoted to a certain Dr. Achilli, a renegade Dominican friar, who was then making a good thing for himself by publicly denouncing the authorities at Rome in a series of highly-coloured 'disclosures.' Achilli himself had already been quietly exposed by Dr. Wiseman in the *Dublin Review.* In his lecture, Newman repeated the charges against this Achilli who was making the scandalous stir. Newman gave facts and dates. He was assured by his informants of their truth; but it was difficult for him to substantiate them when called upon to do so by a Court action.

Newman's friend, Maria Giberne came to his aid. She set off purposefully to Italy, returning with a band of women, Achilli's former victims, ready to testify against him. Wiseman, upon

[1] *Cardinal Newman* by R. H. Hutton; quoted in Wilfrid Ward's *Life of Cardinal Newman*, i, 233.

whose article Newman had relied, was not very helpful. He could not produce his documentary evidence—Newman suggested that the Cardinal did not even look for some of the papers until it was too late! A large sum was raised from the laity throughout the world to finance Newman. He needed it. The prosecution, aware of his formidable witnesses, contrived to prolong the case. The witnesses, anxious to get it over and be repatriated, had to be maintained close at hand for some months, supervised by the indefatigable Miss Giberne. The trial was held in June 1852. It lasted five days. Newman's witnesses supported his main indictments. The Crown claimed that all were perjurers, Achilli alone was truthful. Judgment was given against Newman, which did his reputation some indirect good. *The Times* was highly indignant at such a flagrant distortion of justice, and so was the body of intelligent opinion throughout the country. Newman was prepared for imprisonment, but it did not come to this. He was fined £100 with costs, which amounted to about £10,000. With the balance of the Achilli fund Newman later built a church in Dublin.

About this time Newman undertook to found a Catholic university in Ireland. This was a project initiated by the Irish bishops. It was a semi-political move; the government, answering the pressure of Irish demands, had established the non-religious Queen's Colleges in Dublin. The Catholic bishops had no intention of permitting their laity to attend a completely secular institution. A Catholic university was the answer; unassailable status could be given to it by the presence of Dr. Newman as Rector. In reality, there was little desire among Irish Catholics for a university education, and the English laity were diffident about sending their sons to Ireland to be educated. The bishops seem to have been fairly cynical about the scheme, or at least short-sighted. Newman, although he knew his name was being used to frustrate Sir Robert Peel, none the less took the project seriously. He gave seven years to his efforts in Dublin, and returned with a sense of having wasted his best time of life. "When I am gone," he wrote, "something may come of what I have done in Dublin." And indeed, that humiliating interval did yield its fine fruits. We have to thank the Dublin scheme for Newman's *Idea of a University*, that compilation of lectures in which he considered the nature of education as it then was and of a Catholic education as it might be, defining "the great principle of the University" as "the indissoluble union of philosophy with religion."

In practice, the University not only fell short of his great ideal, it barely came into being. Having been kept waiting for two years Newman arrived in Dublin to find much verbal enthusiasm, much practical indifference. He had received a message from Rome that he was to be made a bishop, Cardinal Wiseman begging the honour of consecrating him. He was presented by prominent Catholics with an episcopal cross, ring, and other regalia. He received congratulations from all quarters as the news spread round. But due to the intervention of the Irish bishops, fearful of giving Newman too much power, he heard no more from Rome on the subject. "Dr. Cullen [the Irish Archbishop] put a spoke in the wheel," Newman wrote in later years, "for which he is my great benefactor." Newman kept his episcopal cross, ring and chain, as curios to show to his intimate friends.

He was not used to these peculiar dealings. He is said to have declared of the Irish bishops, "They regard any intellectual man as being on the road to perdition." In Dublin he was never allowed a free hand; his duties as Rector were superseded by the bishops; if he brought over a scholar from Oxford they were jealous; he frequently described himself in letters as "harnessed as a horse to a cart"; if he desired explanations from Dr. Cullen he received no reply to his letters. The Irish, of course, treated him with much personal warmth, but where the university was concerned they were, Newman said, "like Frankenstein, scared at their own monster." "I doubt not the question recurred to me," he wrote in retrospect, "'Are they doing me a favour in sending for me from England, or am I doing them a favour by coming?'"

While in Ireland he wrote his second novel, *Callista,* a tale of the third-century African Church.

About this time another ill-fated proposition was put to Newman: he should edit a new translation of the Scriptures. The scheme received public attention and acclaim. But once again, his serious start on the work was apparently wasted. On hearing that a similar project had been started in America the bishops simply lost interest in Newman's efforts. He had already engaged translators, and before the Bible scheme was finally dropped he had lost money, time, and confidence in his superiors.

In 1856 Newman had to contend with a trying domestic problem. There had been disagreement between the London and Birmingham Oratories following which a point in the Oratorian rule had been investigated by a Roman delegate without Newman's knowledge. The Birmingham Fathers sent him to Rome where he found he had been misrepresented, and did his best to straighten out the matter. The Oratories were finally separated, to the satisfaction of both, but Newman did not trust the London Oratory under Fr. Faber, and refers in his journal to: "the thousand whisperings against me at the London Oratory, which have succeeded in prejudicing the Catholic body to a great extent against me."

Affairs at Birmingham Oratory occupied much of Newman's time. In 1859 the Oratory school was founded, and although Newman did not take a direct part in its conduct, he adapted plays of Terence and Plautus for school use. He encouraged the performance and appreciation of music, being himself an accomplished violinist.

He had been in close contact and sympathy with a number of intelligent Catholics of a 'liberal' turn, prominent among whom was Lord Acton, a pupil of Dr. Döllinger whom Newman had met. Acton, with Richard Simpson, an Oriel convert, and F. M. Capes who had preceded Newman into the Church, were actively campaigning for an approach to Catholic theology more in keeping with the scientific mind of the age than the traditional apologetics afforded. Their platform was *The Rambler,* edited by Simpson. This group was opposed by W. G. Ward, a convert with somewhat fanatical views, who now became editor of the *Dublin Review,* and by H. E. Manning who later succeeded Wiseman at Westminster.

Newman had a hard time with his friends of the *Rambler* faction; he desired to encourage their adventurous spirit, at the same time as he discerned where they distorted Catholic doctrine. He was especially critical of their provocative tone, and tried hard to teach tact to Richard Simpson. At last, to save the paper from ecclesiastical censure, Newman agreed to edit it. However, he did not make sufficiently drastic changes to satisfy the bishops, far less Ward and Manning; the *Rambler* continued to be violently attacked in other Catholic papers. Newman was too delicate to risk impugning his friends by a complete reversal of their policy. "I thought it unfair, ungenerous, impertinent, and cowardly to make in their behalf acts of confession and contrition, and to make a display of change of editorship and (as if) so virtuous a change . . ." he explained.

Newman's own Bishop, Ullathorne of Birmingham, a simple, shrewd and well-disposed man, advised Newman to resign the *Rambler,* which he promptly did. In the last number which appeared before he abandoned the editorship was a fateful article by himself entitled 'On consulting the Faithful in matters of Doctrine'; this was no more, apparently, than a piece of ecclesiastical history set forth with Newman's typical precision and point. It was misunderstood by hasty hawk-eyed readers, and on the strength of it Newman was delated at Rome. This damaged his reputation there for some years.

In dissociating himself from the *Rambler* group, who felt that Newman had failed them, he took equal care not to commit himself to their opponent extremists who at that time were much vexed on the question of the Pope's temporal power. Newman was up against people who would have this temporal question elevated to *de fide* doctrine. He therefore lost popularity on both sides.

In 1861 he was visited with one of his periodic undefined

semi-nervous illnesses. "The truth is," he wrote to Sir John Acton, "I have been in constant hot water of one sort or degree or another for full thirty years—and it has, at length, boiled me. I wish it may serve in part for a purgatory." His doctors ordered him to take a holiday, and from Brighton he writes to his old friend Miss Holmes: "I have been going about seeing once again, and taking leave for good, of the places I knew as a child. I have been looking at the windows of our house at Ham near Richmond, where I lay aged 5 looking at the candles stuck in them in celebration of the Victory of Trafalgar . . . Also I tried to find the solitary cottage in which I passed my summer and autumn holydays at Norwood, when I was a schoolboy . . ."

Within a few years, this tendency of mind to look back over the past and to turn from his present frustrations bore happy fruit in his *Apologia Pro Vita Sua,* the work by which Newman is best known. The occasion and prompting of that work seems in retrospect comparatively insignificant. Charles Kingsley who was then Professor of Modern History at Cambridge, a vigorous, outward-looking, philanthropic, more-than-typical English clergyman, an opponent of the Tractarians, chose to oppose Newman. He was in many ways Newman's natural opposite; his talent was bold and simple where Newman's was tenuous and complex. Kingsley simply wrote in *Macmillan's Magazine* to the effect that the Church of Rome was not interested in the truth; to prove this, and by a process of popular demonology, he fixed on Father Newman who, according to Kingsley, had displayed his equivocal tendencies even while preaching from his Littlemore pulpit. Newman answered him, and was answered, in a series of published letters. Sympathy was gained by Newman. Kingsley wrote a pamphlet, Newman an article. It was, besides a religious argument, a combat between men of letters, and as such the tones of the case are familiar to English literary dialectics. Kingsley, for example:

> If I, like a hundred more, have mistaken his meaning and intent, he must blame not me, but himself. If he will indulge in subtle paradoxes, in rhetorical exaggerations; if, whenever

he touches on the question of truth and honesty he will take a perverse pleasure in saying something shocking to plain English notions, he must take the consequences of his own eccentricities.

and Newman:

He has no mercy for the man who will define his thought and choose his language so subtly that the mass of his hearers may fail to perceive his distinctions, and be led into dangerous errors—because he cannot endure making a fine art of speech.

But the predominant issue was the honour of Newman and his Church. Constant misrepresentations from all quarters seem now to have goaded Newman into the realization that nothing but a spiritual autobiography could begin to open before the world the complexity and sincerity of his motives. "I recognised what I had to do," he announced in the *Apologia* itself, "though I shrank from both the task and the exposure which it would entail. I must, I said, give the true key to my whole life . . . I wish to be known as a living man, and not as a scarecrow which is dressed up in my clothes."

He wrote the *Apologia* in about eight weeks, publishing it in serial form. He turned to his trusted Oxford friends for the letters and documents he needed to revive his memory of the time when he was leader of the Movement. It has been said that as a history of his religious opinions the *Apologia* is at times not accurate. How could it be, in the hurried circumstances? It is a document of memory at white-heat; as an autobiography it is artistic in nature; as a work of art it is autobiographical in kind. It represents Newman's position not only in the years that had passed, but in a special manner, in the years to come. It is the consummation of the Newman idea. In 1864 it not only silenced Kingsley, it established Newman; it won him the confidence of his fellow-Catholics and high repute among English Protestants.

Even Newman's detractors at Rome were impressed by his

success. A certain Monsignor Talbot, an English official at the Vatican, who has immortalized his name by his repulsive treatment of Newman, made a few patronising overtures, which Newman rejected with apparent relish.

A scheme was in force at this time among the Catholic laity, who were anxious to send their sons to Oxford. Newman's friends urged him to set up an Oratory there; Bishop Ullathorne was in favour of the scheme. The Roman authorities, on the representations of Talbot and Manning, were against it, fearful, they claimed, for the Catholic youth amid the temptations of the University, and the plan lay dormant for a time. It is difficult to see from Newman's various statements, the position of his mind—one recalls the exasperation of Kingsley with Newman's inability to speak plainly on one literal level of meaning. Newman later declared he did not want to go to Oxford, and never wanted to go. Yet he clearly put much effort towards promoting the project.

In 1865, while the Oxford scheme was in suspense, Newman's position amongst English Catholics became further entrenched by his *Letter to Pusey*. Pusey had been in controversy with Manning, and in his *Eirenicon* had attacked the Catholic devotion to the Blessed Virgin along with other Roman practices. Intervening with his *Letter,* Newman contrived both to refute Pusey and to dissociate himself from the excessive enthusiasms and practices of some fellow-converts such as Faber and Ward, which Pusey had cited as if they enjoyed universal acceptance in the Church. Privately, Newman taxed Pusey, "How is it fair to throw together Suarez, St. Bernardine, Eadmer, and Faber? As to Faber, I never read his books." The *Letter to Pusey* was generally well received. Newman had become a national figure, his influence exceeding that of Manning and Ward, this was a trying situation for them, for they genuinely feared his views and possibly, his power. But it was not a simple case of Manning and Ward uniting to form a personal faction against Newman. They represented a large body of Catholic opinion. Ward preferred Newman to Manning as a person. Manning seems to have desired friendship with Newman on an agree-to-differ basis, which Newman, whose personality was involved in all his undertakings, could not accept.

When the Oxford scheme was revived in 1866, and plans for the building of a Church there were already in progress, Newman's high hopes of success were well known to his friends. Now in his mid-sixties, it was not easy for Newman to contemplate a new life, and to uproot himself from his Birmingham home. But he and his supporters became aware of something like an ecclesiastical intrigue on the part of Talbot at Rome and Manning, now Archbishop of Westminster, with the support of vociferous laymen like Ward to cheat Catholics out of a higher education. Newman was, moreover, always drawn towards youth; the prospect of once more moving in his former environment amongst converts, undoubtedly fascinated him. One of his fellow Oratorians reported him to say, "Earlier failures do not matter now; I see that I have been reserved by God for this . . . It may prove to be the inauguration of a second Oxford Movement."

Permission had been given for the Oratory to set up an Oxford mission for the benefit of Catholics already there. It was taken for granted that Newman should head the mission. The means by which the plan was frustrated bears, at this distance of time, a slightly comic Italianate appearance, at the same time as it seriously reflects the sort of opposition Newman had to contend with. While permission was granted for the mission to proceed, the Bishop of Birmingham was given a secret instruction by Cardinal Barnabo, the Prefect of Propaganda, that in the event of Newman himself going to reside at Oxford, he should be "blandly and suavely" recalled. Newman had by this time circularised Catholics about the proposed Church, and had raised funds. The objection to Newman's going to Oxford was that his presence there would inevitably persuade Catholics to send their sons to the University. In fact, Newman himself had previously told his bishop in passing that he had no intention of *residing* at Oxford. And yet it seems that Newman's main objection was not so much to the prohibition as to the humiliating phraseology used by Barnabo—that "blande et sauviter" stuck and rankled in Newman's mind. He reverts to it again and again. Newman's friends were likewise stung by this discourtesy to an eminent revered personage, and were angry that he should be treated like a callow seminarist. The "secret instruction" leaked out just in time to prevent the founding of the Oxford mission; for without Newman the scheme was pointless. The Newmanite laity now got up a somewhat extravagantly-worded public address to Newman: "We, the undersigned, have been deeply pained at some anonymous attacks which have been made upon you. They may be of little importance in themselves, but we feel that every blow that touches you inflicts a wound upon the Catholic Church in this country . . ."

Whereupon Talbot addressed himself to Manning in melo-dramatic terms more in keeping with Elizabethan times than the temper of a mere ninety years ago. "Dr. Newman," he declared, "is the most dangerous man in England, and you will see that he will make use of the laity against your Grace. You must not be afraid of him. It will require much prudence, but you must be firm, as the Holy Father still places his confidence in you; but if you yield and do not fight the battle of the Holy See against the detestable spirit growing up in England, he will begin to regret Cardinal Wiseman, who knew how to keep the laity in order. I tell you all this in confidence, because I already begin to hear some whisperings . . ."

Talbot had already done his best to damage Newman's name by putting it about that he had preached in favour of Garibaldi at the time of the Papal troubles in Italy. But a more material accusation was now brought against Newman. "It is perfectly *true*" Talbot informed Manning, "that a cloud has been hanging over Dr. Newman in Rome ever since the Bishop of Newport delated him to Rome for heresy in his article in the *Rambler* on consulting the laity on matters of faith."[1] Newman was aware

[1] The correct title of the article was " On Consulting the Faithful in Matters of Doctrine ".

that the *Rambler* article had been the subject of discussion at Rome. He had sent an explanation of it to Cardinal Wiseman, and had eventually been informed by Manning that the matter was settled.

With the support of the Oratorians and his loyal lay friends, Newman now decided to send a deputation to Rome to plead his cause. He had not yet given up hopes of Oxford. Fathers St. John and Bittleston reached Rome in the spring of 1867, from where they sent a series of colourful reports to Birmingham of their many conversations and efforts to clear Newman's name in the Oxford matter. "Father Newman, I can assure you," said the admirable Ambrose St. John to the first dignitary he encountered, "has always acted in the spirit of obedience to the Holy See in this matter. He himself does not, and has not wished to go to Oxford." "Then we are all agreed," replied the bewildered Monsignor.

In the end Newman had to resign the Oxford mission, but the delegation to Rome succeeded in bringing to light the complaint about his *Rambler* article, which he had been led to consider a closed matter. Newman now sent a copy of his original explanation, which Wiseman had apparently failed to produce. Cardinal Barnabo expressed the grestest esteem for Newman. He burst into tears. He said, "Tell Newman I will do anything I can for him."

"I am *not a bit* softened about Barnabo," Newman wrote to his two friends. "He has not at all explained the 'blanda et suavis revocatio' which was to be *concealed* from me *till* I attempted to go to Oxford—*not at all.*"

That Newman's reputation was not seriously beclouded is evident from the fact that in the following year the Pope invited him to assist in preparations for the forthcoming Vatican Council which defined the Dogma of Papal Infallibility. Newman did not attend the Council.

His attitude to Papal Infallibility seems to have puzzled many, both in and out of the Church. In retrospect his position seems not at all equivocal. He himself, in his life as a Catholic, always held the doctrine; before the definition of the Dogma he did not feel it should be made a binding object of Catholic faith. However, believing whatever the Church believed, he assented to the Dogma as such when it was defined, while he welcomed the limits which the terms of definition imposed upon it. But because, while it was still an open question, he opposed the definition, he was assumed by some to commit intellectual dishonesty by accepting Infallibility. He makes his position clear in many letters, some preceding the time when the question became prominent.

In the year of the famous Definition, Newman published the work of a life-long desire, his *Essay in Aid of a Grammar of Assent*. He claimed that it was the only work he had done without a direct 'call' or outward stimulus, for it was not written in answer to any current controversy or prominent heresy; it fulfilled what he had long conceived as a need for a more psychological and immediate approach to theology in general and revealed religion in particular, than those traditional methods which were currently but ineffectively employed. In the *Grammar of Assent* he proposed, "that in any inquiry about things in the concrete, men differ from each other, not so much in the soundness of their reasoning as in the principles which govern its exercise, that those principles are of a personal character, that where there is no common measure of minds, there is no common measure of arguments, and that the validity of proof is determined, not by any scientific test, but by the illative sense."

Newman regarded this as his last work. It was well received, for Newman was now highly regarded, even amongst his former opponents. It was well-timed, for the 'illative sense,' generally regarded as Newman's discovery, was a question-raising commodity, a sort of spontaneous "right judgment in ratiocination" which opened exciting new possibilities of thought that are not yet exhausted. In its proper context, like Newman himself, it was not easy to understand, and therefore difficult to grapple with and oppose. Congratulations reached him from many different quarters, Newman responding to all with equal courteous gravity, and with signs of the stimulation his mind had received from the task. To one correspondent he gave the interesting information:

> I have not insisted on the argument from *design*, because I am writing for the 19th Century, by which, as represented by its philosophers, design is not admitted as proved. And to tell the truth, though I should not wish to preach on the subject, for 40 years I have been unable to see the logical force of the argument myself. I believe in design because I believe in God; not in a God because I see design.

And to a lady who had expressed her pleasure in the book he writes, "It will please me much if you say of the last 100 pages what you say for the chapter on certitude—for they were written especially . . . for such ladies as are bullied by infidels and do not know how to answer them . . ."

"The book itself" he noted in his journal, "I have aimed at writing these twenty years;—and now that it is written I do not quite recognise it for what it was meant to be, though I suppose it is such."

Newman's work was not finished, as he supposed, with the *Grammar of Assent*. In 1874 Gladstone initiated a series of attacks on the Vatican decrees of 1870. As in his reply to Pusey, Newman took advantage of his reply to Gladstone (his *Letter to the Duke of Norfolk*) to distinguish between true Catholic obligations of belief and the extreme claims of zealots. Newman undertook this task from a sense of responsibility towards converts who had followed him into the Church, and who might have lost courage as a result of the recent troublesome controversy surrounding the Dogma. Conscious of his own liberty of expression, and the latitude of reception accorded even to his *Grammar of Assent*, Newman was indignant against Gladstone's "charging people quite as free in mind as he is, of being moral and mental slaves." Newman really enjoyed controversy, however much he affected anxiety when it arose. "I thought I should be in peace for the remainder of my life—and now I am in controversy again!" he writes with evident satisfaction.

He had been for some years republishing editions of his Anglican works. More and more he was becoming in the eyes of his countrymen one of those Victorian prophet-figures. A fellow-Oratorian describes how, in Newman's latter years,

> . . . all sorts of persons with religious difficulties have had recourse to him. Members, often ministers, of various religious bodies, Methodists, Presbyterians, &c. with no sort of leaning towards the Church, have sought his guidance and advice and sympathy; and his correspondence of this sort, until writing became an impossibility for him, was enormous. Indeed, now and again one came across something which almost looked like a *cultus* of Cardinal Newman outside the Church.

In 1877 Newman received a mark of esteem which caused him special high elation. Trinity College, Oxford, where he had been an undergraduate, made him an Honorary Fellow.

Under the new Pope, Leo XIII, Newman's position at Rome had undergone a favourable change. In his seventy-ninth year he was offered a Cardinalate. The tension between himself and Manning now reappeared. Newman, through his extreme of reticence, all but muffed the matter of the Cardinalate, aided by Manning who acted with extreme obtuseness if not, as some hold, malice. Hardly anything happened to Newman in a simple manner, without a fuss.

Replying to his bishop's intimation of the proposed offer, Newman intended to express his acceptance on condition of being allowed to remain at Birmingham in his declining years, instead of residing at Rome. But he was too delicate bluntly to dictate conditions to Rome; Newman's letter, therefore, could be read as if declining the offer. Privately, however, he made his true feelings clear to Bishop Ullathorne, who in turn intimated them to Manning when forwarding Newman's letter. To everyone's surprise, not the least Newman's, an announcement swiftly followed in *The Times,* that Dr. Newman had been offered and had declined, the Cardinal's Hat. The offer had so far been tendered unofficially; Newman wrote to *The Times* denying the report, on the grounds that as he had not been offered the honour, he could not refuse it. At the same time he bethought himself how a private communication, intended for Rome, could have reached the newspapers before it reached Rome.

Despite further correspondence, the clarity and meaning of which seems unquestionable, Manning persisted in having it that Newman had refused. It appears that a small campaign began on the part of Newman's few remaining enemies. But the feelings of the English Catholics were strongly for Newman. Manning, having intimated a refusal to the Holy See, was faced with his mistake. He gave his word that he had misread the whole correspondence, and possibly by some psychological lapse, this was so. He himself was now at Rome, and he made the necessary explanations. The Pope agreed to Newman's residence at Birmingham. For the ceremony, Newman travelled to Rome, arriving frail and exhausted in April 1879, and was formally created Cardinal in May. He took as his motto "Cor ad cor loquitur"—in so many ways the symbolic expression of his nature.

With the Cardinalate, Newman felt that the cloud of suspicion under which he had laboured during his life as a Catholic was lifted. It gave prestige and authority rather to his work in retrospect than to his future activities. He was now more or less retired, though he continued to contribute controversial articles to such papers as *The Contemporary Review* and *The Nine-teenth Century*. He conducted a large correspondence which became progressively smaller as his eyes and hand weakened. "Infirm but not ill" was his description of himself. He showed a curiously clear objectivity about his infirmity, as when he wrote in 1882,

I am over eighty, and it is with difficulty that I walk, eat, read, write or talk. My breath is short and my brain works slow, and, like other old men, I am so much the creature of hours, rooms, and of routine generally, that to go from home is almost like tearing off my skin, and I suffer from it afterwards. On the other hand, except in failure of memory, and continual little mistakes in the use of words, and confusion in the use of names, I am not conscious that my mind is weaker than it was.

In 1883 he gave his beloved violin to the daughter of Dean Church from whom, in 1865, he had received it as a gift. "I had constant use and pleasure in the use till lately" he writes, "—but I find now I have no command of it; nay, strange to say I cannot count or keep time. This is a trouble to me; one gets an affection for a fiddle, and I should not like to go without getting it a good master or mistress."

A memoir by his contemporary Oratorian, Father Neville, tells us, "When he could no longer read the daily Office in the Breviary, he substituted the Rosary, and said it was 'the most beautiful of all devotions and that it contained all in itself.' "

Newman received the last Sacraments on August 10, 1890, and died the following day. He was buried, as he wished, in the grave of Ambrose St. John who had preceded him by fifteen years.

II

That Newman's life should be represented by his letters is in accordance with his own mind. On the subject of biography, he informed a correspondent in 1866, "My own notion of writing a life is the notion of Hurrell Froude—viz. to do it by letters, and to bring in as little letterpress of one's own as possible . . . It is far more real, and therefore interesting than any other way." And a few years earlier he had pointed out in a letter to his sister, "Contemporary letters are facts, and as such they reveal the true life of a man."

It is doubtful if Newman's letters *can* be said to reveal his true life; certainly they do not reflect the whole of his mind or personality—because they do not represent the full range of his style. One misses the balance and grace of the historical essays, the surge and point of the sermons, the irony, the leisured point-by-point polemic (not that these features are entirely absent from his letters). So far as the style is the man, his letters stand for one special aspect of Newman, that of his personal relation-ships. This, in a man who approached everything with a personal involvement, is an important aspect.

He regarded his letters as part of his literary output. Looking back over his work for the fifteen years preceding 1874, he asked himself, "What was I doing all that time? . . . First, must be recollected all through the fifteen years the great number of letters I wrote, whatever be their worth . . ." His correspon-dence was voluminous; in his letters he expressed his diversity of moods, unburdened his mind to his friends, exerted an influence on those who sought his guidance. He grumbled frequently, especially to his intimate friends. "To let out one's sorrow" he wrote to Ambrose St. John who had teased him about his complaining, "is a great relief, and I don't think an unlawful one . . . Job too had three friends and to them he let out. Yet he was the most patient of men. I think you don't discriminate between complaining and realizing. What is so common in the Psalms and in Jeremias, as the sentiment 'Just art Thou, O Lord, yet will I plead with Thee?'" He kept copies of his letters, hoarded them for reference, and generally treated them with importance. In a sense, they were written for posterity.

As with everything he wrote, the prose of the letters is graceful and pure. He writes, unless occasion demands otherwise, con-versationally. He did not, like so many of his contemporaries, preserve a special altiloquent epistolary style. And the fact that we can observe, admire and criticize his personality in his letters, particularly in his Catholic years, shows how frank he was, how regardless of criticism. In his old age, commenting on his writings in general he wrote, " . . . I have used words which, when I used them I saw could be used against me, but did not care whether they were so used or not, from a clear conscience that it would be a mistaken use of them, if they were." A state-ment which applies as much to Newman's letters as to anything else he wrote.

III

1

Newman was one of those large intricate personalities whom it is only possible partially to understand in any one age, and he himself knew this, " . . . even those who think highly of me have the vaguest, most shadowy, fantastic notions attached to their idea of me; and feel a respect, not for me, but for some imagination of their own which bears my name."

As a Catholic he was much misunderstood; at times he seems to have gone out of his way to provoke misunderstanding, and never does he seem to have taken obvious steps to avoid it.

When he brought historical arguments to correct religious excess, he was thought lukewarm in the Faith. He was constantly misrepresented at Rome by people who no doubt were perfectly sincere in their representations of him. Newman felt his unpopu-larity intensely. On entering the Church he found a different ethic from what he had been used to; and in finding there his spiritual home he had to endure a sort of social exile. "So many dead," he writes in 1848, "so many separated. My mother gone; my sisters nothing to me, or rather foreign to me; of my greatest friends, Froude, Wood, Bowden taken away; all of whom would now be, or be coming, on my side." Fifteen years later, in one of his low-spirited moods, he wrote in his journal, "O how forlorn and dreary has been my course since I have been a Catholic! here has been the contrast—as a Protestant, I felt my religion dreary, but not my life—but, as a Catholic, my life dreary, not my religion." Newman was, of course, aware that the Catholic Church had promised him the truth, not easy conditions of life, but this did not prevent him from circuitously reflecting, like Job, on his discomforts.

For a long time his talents were not appreciated; even converts who had previously looked up to him as to a remote personage, now presumed to level him down to a fallacious equality with themselves. So that, sometimes what seems like touchiness on Newman's part was no more than a decent sense of propriety. Thus, his resentment of Cardinal Barnabo. On the other hand, up to the time of the *Apologia,* he seems to have been singularly reticent in any attempt to give a true impression of himself among Catholics. It was almost as if the endurance of personal misunderstanding were a condition of his development. From his first stay in Rome after his reception into the Church, he appears to have had difficulty in making himself, his work and aims understood. "It is difficult to get into the mind of a person like me, especially considering so few speak English, and fewer still understand it spoken—and I can say so little in Italian," he wrote from Rome. But Newman, though he was over a year in Rome, did not take the obvious practical steps to solve his difficulty; he did not master Italian, not even French, which would have greatly helped him to give his Roman superiors some clue to his mind.

Newman had a temperamental reluctance to make the first move in any relationship; only when he had been first approached did he respond. This was partly the difficulty in the sad affair of the deferred bishopric. In his *Life* of Newman, Wilfrid Ward writes, " . . . when Manning spoke of the subject to the Roman authorities in 1860, it was made clear to him that Newman could have the bishopric if he wished for it. But Newman's temperament made it impossible for him to move a finger in the matter, and in a busy world no action was taken by others when the person most closely concerned made no sign." Newman's own words were, "For myself, I never asked anyone a single question from first to last on the subject, first of the delay and then of the abandonment of the intention."—An admirable restraint, but Newman might perhaps have unbent in this case, since he himself asserted that the bishopric would have helped to save the cause of the Irish University.

It is probable that Newman reserved the more extreme instances of his periodic depressions for his journals; in them we come into contact with an aspect of his inner life which is very different from that other aspect which shines forth from his intellectual writings. In his journals, an exaggerated bleakness alternates with his characteristic self-insight. "I have no friend at Rome," he wrote in 1860, "I have laboured in England, to be misrepresented, backbitten and scorned. I have laboured in Ireland, with a door ever shut in my face. I seem to have had many failures, and what I did well was not understood. I do not think I am saying this in any bitterness."

> This [he continues] has naturally made me shrink into myself, or rather it has made me think of turning more to God, if it has not actually turned me. It has made me feel that in the Blessed Sacrament is my great consolation, and that while I have Him who lives in the Church, the separate members of the Church, my Superiors, though they may claim my obedience, have no claim on my admiration, and offer nothing for my inward trust.

This passage may be compared with that in the *Apologia* where he recalls his boyhood's "mistrust of the reality of material phenomena," and his "thought of two and two only supreme and luminously self-evident beings, myself and my Creator." This motif of external mistrust and an intense personal relationship to God, is a constant factor among the many apparent inconsistencies which Newman's life presents.

Two things seem to have afflicted Newman during the greater part of his life as a Catholic. One was a sense of persecution, and the other was persecution. The two did not always coincide, and so it seems too frequently that Newman complains too much, and without sufficient cause; that he sees no-one's point of view but his own. On the other hand, he did have to contend with a great many indignities and injustices. His enemies were real enemies, not so much that they nurtured personal animosity toward him, but they—factions like those of Ward, Manning and

Faber—who saw no further than the present tense, frustrated his farther-sighted intentions. Ward preferred Newman as a person to Manning. Manning observed, partly in his own defence,

> That Newman has a morbid sensitiveness is well known. His relations with Faber, the late Cardinal, Father Coffin, the London Oratory, underwent the same change as his relations to me. I never referred to him in print except with affection and respect as a friend. If I have been opposed to him, it has only been that I must oppose either him or the Holy See.

Newman's complaint, "Whenever I have attempted to do anything for God, I find after a little while that my arms or my legs have a string round them," was certainly an exaggeration, as his important Catholic works prove. But he did have a trying time in Ireland; he was treated wrongly over the Bible affair and the Oxford scheme. He was not without justification for his sense of being surrounded by hostility.

Perhaps, too, the expense of spirit which he put into the inter-Catholic quarrels was not altogether fruitless. When he attacked his enemies indirectly in his *Letter to the Duke of Norfolk*, for instance, he gave his name, as it were, to a permanent series of axioms for the protection of other Catholic thinkers in the same predicament, as in his assertion:

> I think it a usurpation, too wicked to be comfortably dwelt upon, when individuals use their own private judgment, in the discussion of religious questions, not simply "abundare in suo sensu," but for the purpose of anathematizing the private judgment of others.

2

Newman greatly valued intimate friendships. He was isolated from the world, not only by his temperament, but inevitably by his intellectual superiority and originality. In 1859 his journal records: "My God, when shall I learn that I have so parted with the world, that, though I may wish to make friends with it, it will not make friends with me?" He adhered to his intimates, those who had sentimental associations with the past, and those who came near to understanding him. "No one knows but myself how great an infliction upon me it has been that you all have so simply treated me as *dead*," he wrote in 1862 to his old Littlemore curate, W. J. Copeland.

Although he refuted Pusey publicly, he defended him privately, not for his views, but for his revered and scholarly person. More than once, Newman wrote to Father Coleridge of *The Month* to deprecate some disrespectful tone which he had noted in an attack on Pusey.

The year before the death of his beloved friend, Keble, Newman visited him, and found that Pusey was a fellow guest: " . . . there was something awful," he writes, "in three men meeting in old age who had worked together in their best days. Vanity of vanities . . ."

Newman was blessed with an admirable Bishop of Birmingham. Dr. Ullathorne was a man with a humble background and wise ways. He supported and respected Newman, and his humility and forbearance in dealing with the great Oratorian is a striking factor throughout Newman biography. Manning remarked that Newman twisted Ullathorne round his little finger; perhaps he did, but the relationship throve on it, lasting to the end of their days.

Despite a few minor upheavals, the Oratory at Birmingham stood loyally by Newman, regarding his friends as theirs, his detractors as their own. When, for instance, Monsignor Talbot visited the Oratory in Newman's absence, we learn of his receiving a very cold reception. The beloved Ambrose St. John remained at Newman's side from their Littlemore days to the end of his life, and was never replaced in Newman's affections.

Most of his friendships, such as that with the Froude family, he maintained by correspondence. He made a habit of recording anniversaries of particular occasions in his own and his friends' lives, dating back to his childhood and university days. And the

deaths of his friends, as they occurred one by one leaving him
isolated by his advanced years, were constantly before him.
"Around my birthday," he writes to Henry Wilberforce in 1871,
"are grouped the deaths of many whom I have known and loved.
This year two on the same day—Lady Rogers and Mrs. Stewart
on the 16th. Besides I have the 12th, 13th, 14th, 15th, 19th, 21st,
22nd, 23rd, 24th, 25th, 28th, 29th—and, four times, two on the
same day. I have no such galaxy in any other part of the year.
I wonder what day I shall die on—one passes year by year over
one's death day, as one might pass over one's grave."

3

He had an obsession with time wasted, and always fancied
that his life as a Catholic was passing with nothing to show for it.
From Dublin he wrote to Ambrose St. John, "To the rising
generation, to the sons of those who knew me, or read what I
wrote 15 or 20 years ago, I am a mere page of history. I do not
live to them; they know nothing of me . . ."

He had difficulty in relaxing from his mental activities, even
when ordered to rest by his doctors. From the Oratory's country
house at Rednal he writes fretfully again to Father St. John,
"What teases me is the loss of time . . . My feeling is that I
have not yet fulfilled my mission and have work to do. This
haunts me."

And even after his major works had been completed, in his
seventy-fourth year, he notes in his journal, "I have so depressing
a feeling that I have done nothing through my long life . . ."
and, a few months later, "I have been startled on considering
that in the last 15 years I have only written two books, the
'Apologia' and the Essay on Assent—of which the former was
almost extempore. What have I been doing with my time?"

Sometimes, throughout the second half of his life, he was
oppressed by a sense that his energy as well as his time was
ebbing, and he frequently looks nostalgically to the period of
what seemed to him his greatest powers: "How I wish I had in

me the energy which I had when I began the Tracts for the Times!"

A memorable passage in a letter to his old friend Miss Holmes, gives an idea of Newman's wry self-image as early as 1860, "I have fallen off in flesh and shrunk up during the past year, and am like a grey grasshopper or the evaporating mist of the morning."

4

Newman approached practically everything from a personal point of view, not quite a 'subjective' one. "Myself and my Creator"—that is both the root and flower of his mentality. On this depends his originality of thought; he appeals to that in the human person which is both unique in form and essentially common to all. When, a few months after he entered the Catholic Church, he was approached for an account of the reasons for his conversion, he refused to state them in a hasty inclusive formula: "People shall not say 'We have now got his reasons, and know their worth.' No, you have not got them, you cannot get them, except at the cost of some portion of the trouble I have been at myself." As we know from various of his writings, Newman had no special reticence about the reasons for his conversion, but he knew that an individual commitment was necessary to the convert of true quality.

His approach to history, which played so important a part in his religious course was a personal one. Hence, the peculiarly biographical flavour of his historical essays. In an interesting letter of 1849, in which he answers an enquirer as to the truth of the Catholic Church he writes, " . . . there are other arguments to prove it; and to my mind the overbearingly convincing proof is this;—that, were St. Athanasius and St. Ambrose in London now, they would go to worship, not to St. Paul's Cathedral, but to Warwick Street or Moor Fields. This my own reading of history has made to me an axiom, and it converted me, though I cannot of course communicate the force of it to another."

Newman's writings are not a neat and well-rounded whole. He is inconsistent, and that because of his personal approach to things together with his great capacity for development. To such a man, the objects of his attention will appear to be developing, and observed from time to time, they will undergo a change.

He reacted to whatever was fixed in the opinions of those around him. In the Church of England his mind tended to narrowness, in the Church of Rome to breadth. Both tendencies led to unpopularity. A corrective influence is always unpopular. As a Catholic, he defended what was true in Anglican opinions and resisted what was excessive in Catholic ones. Hence, he appeared to have conflicting loyalties, to make inconsistent statements.

To the present writer Newman's inconsistencies do not seem to be a problem to be grappled with: circumstances account for them. Some temperaments are only true when they are inconsistent.

For instance, it is perhaps more mysterious than surprising that Newman should assert in one of his letters, "What is it to me what people think of me? I have ever acted on this plan, I never got the worst of it."—when it has seemed clear that he cared very touchily what people thought of him. What is to be made of his curious statements to the effect that he did not wish to set up again at Oxford, when it seems clear that he did? One cannot simply dismiss his conflicting statements by calling him equivocal, for the sincerity of his mind is impressive. But one can sometimes discern that tone of detachment in his personal writings (as when, having occasion to criticize the prominent Catholic laity, he writes, "I do it as I might criticize a piece of Latin composition.") which raises the question whether he was more detached from personal interests than he appeared. In so complex a person, it is impossible to say whether he really cared what people thought of him or not, whether he wanted to go to Oxford or not, for the greater probability is that he both cared and did not care, both desired and did not desire; and so with all his inconsistencies, large and small.

"It is my cross" he wrote to a friend, "to have false stories circulated about me, and to be suspected in consequence. I could not have a lighter one. I would not change it for any other." That is a claim which nothing else he wrote can refute.

6

"It was like coming into port after a rough sea; and my happiness on that score remains to this day without interruption." So Newman in his *Apologia* described his coming to the Catholic Church. Many would say, he had a fairly rough time in port. But half-way through his life as a Catholic he writes more fully and seriously to a Catholic friend, words which amplify and supplement those familiar ones in the *Apologia*, and which prove at least the sense in which he viewed his present trials:

> I have found in the Catholic Church abundance of courtesy, but very little sympathy, among persons in high place, except a few—but there is a depth and a power in the Catholic religion, a fulness of satisfaction in its creed, its theology, its rites, its sacraments, its discipline, a freedom yet a support also, before which the neglect or the misapprehension about oneself on the part of individual living persons, however exalted, is as so much dust when weighed in the balance.

His fellow-Oratorian, Father Neville, reports Newman's last words, near the end of his life, on the subject of his 'wrongs': "You must not suppose that these little affairs of mine will be on the *tapis* in the courts of the next world."

MURIEL SPARK.

57. TO THE REV. T. W. ALLIES

Littlemore.   *9th October, 1845*

My dear Allies,

I am to be received into what I believe to be the one Church and the one Communion of Saints this evening, if it is so ordained. Father Dominic, the Passionist, is here, and I have begun my confession to him. I suppose two friends will be received with me.

May I have only one-tenth part as much faith as I have intellectual conviction where the truth lies! I do not suppose any one can have had such combined reasons pouring in upon him that he is doing right. So far I am most blessed; but, alas! my heart is so hard, and I am taking things so much as a matter of course, that I have been quite frightened lest I should not have faith and contrition enough to gain the benefit of the Sacraments. Perhaps faith and reason are incompatible in one person, or nearly so.

Ever yours, most sincerely,
John H. Newman.

58. TO MISS MARIA ROSINA GIBERNE

Littlemore.   *28th January, 1846*

My dear Miss Giberne,

Your feelings at present must indeed be very much tried, and I sincerely thank you for letting me share them. Take your present trial, as you do, as a gracious means of bringing you under the more intimate protection of your true friends, those Saints and Angels unseen, who can do so much more for you with God, and in the course of life, than any mere child of man, however dear and excellent. You speak as if I were not in your case, for though I left Littlemore, I carried my friends with me, but alas! can you point to any one who has lost more in the way of friendship, whether by death or alienation, than I have? but even as regards friends of this world I have found that Divine Mercy wonderfully makes up my losses, as if "instead of thy fathers thou shalt have children" were fulfilled in individuals as well as to the Church. I am now engaged in looking over, sorting, burning my papers and letters, and have had pangs and uttered deep sighs, such as I have not at all yet (though I used before) since my reception into the Church. So many dead, so many separated. My mother gone; my sisters nothing to me, or rather foreign to me; of my greatest friends, Froude, Wood, Bowden taken away, all of whom would now be, or be coming, on my side. Other dear friends who *are* preserved in life *not* moving with me; Pusey strongly bent on an opposite course; Williams protesting against my conduct as rationalistic, and dying; Rogers and J. Mozley viewing it with utter repugnance. Of my friends of a dozen years ago whom have I now? and what did I know of my present friends a dozen years ago? Why, they were at school, or they were freshmen looking up to me, if they knew my name, as some immense and unapproachable don; and now they know nothing, can know nothing of my earlier life; things which to me are as yesterday are to them as dreams of the past; they do not know the names, the state of things, the occurrences, they have not the associations, which are part of my own world, in which I live. And yet I am very happy with them, and can truly say with St. Paul, "I have all and abound," —and, moreover, I have with them, what I never can have had with others, Catholic hopes and beliefs—Catholic objects. And so in your own case, depend on it, God's Mercy will make up to you all you lose, and you will be blessed, not indeed in the same way, but in a higher.

I am sorry I did not tell you any thing about the impressions I formed of things and persons in my wanderings. If any thing takes me to Cheltenham, I will give you an account of all I have seen. Everything has been as I could wish it to be. I have received most abundant cordial single-hearted kindness—and have found a great deal to admire—and everywhere the signs of an awful and real system. I was especially pleased with Ushaw College, near Durham, with the professors and above all the President, Dr. Newsham. The Bishops have been especially kind to me, and I think I have made the friendship of some of them, as far as it can be done in a day or two.

Ever your affect. friend,

John H. Newman.

59. TO SPENCER NORTHCOTE

Maryvale.   *February, 1846*

My dear Northcote,

It is unreasonable in anyone to object that the grounds a person gives for his conversion cannot be expressed in a formula, but require some little time and consideration to master; which seems to be your correspondent's complaint of my volume. If I could express them in a formula, they would not really be the more intelligible or comprehensible—indeed to show this as a general principle is the main object of the Essay. Catholicism is a deep matter—you cannot take it up in a teacup.

Any dogmatic or sententious proposition would too surely be misunderstood. If I said, for instance, "I have become a Catholic, because I must be either a Catholic or an infidel," men would cry out "So he has flung himself into the Catholic Church to escape infidelity," whereas I should only mean that Catholicism and Christianity had in my mind become identical, so that to give up the one was to give up the other.

I do not know how to do justice to my reasons for becoming a Catholic in ever so many words—but if I attempted to do so in few, and that in print, I should wantonly expose myself and my cause to the hasty and prejudiced criticisms of opponents. This

I will not do. People shall not say "We have now got his reasons, and know their worth." No, you have not got them, you cannot get them, except at the cost of some portion of the trouble I have been at myself. You cannot buy them for a crown piece—you cannot take them in your hand at your will, and toss them about. You must consent to *think*—and you must exercise such resignation to the Divine Hand which leads you, as to follow it any whither. I am not assuming that my reasons are sufficient or unanswerable, when I say this—but describing the way in which alone our intellect can be successfully exercised on the great subject in question, if the intellect is to be the instrument of conversion. Moral proofs are grown into, not learnt by heart.

I wish however to say something in answer to your friend's question—let me refer then to p. 138 of my Essay, where I state my conviction that were St. Athanasius and St. Ambrose now to come to Oxford, they would go to Mass at St. Clement's.

And in proof of this position, I should refer to Chs. IV and V, pp. 204—317, which your correspondent might read without troubling himself with the rest of the Essay. The argument of those chapters is this: that the general type of Christendom, and the relation of part with part, in early times and in the present is one and the same—that the Catholic Church and sects and heresies then, correspond to the Roman, Protestant, and other communions now—and in particular that the Anglican Church corresponds to the Semi-Arian body, or the Nestorian, or the Monophysite.

With kind remembrances to your circle, I am

Very sincerely yours,

John H. Newman.

60. TO J. D. DALGAIRNS

Milan.   *18th October, 1846*

You are always in my thoughts when I am at St. Carlo's shrine, who was a most wonderful saint, and died just at the age at which I have begun to live. But this is altogether a wonderful city—the city of St. Ambrose, St. Monica, St. Augustine, St. Athanasius, to say no more. Our parish Church belonged to the Jesuits and in it is preserved a cast of St. Ignatius's head taken after his death. The Church of St. Satyrus (St. Ambrose's brother) belonged to the Oratorians, and there is an altar to St. Philip. And St. Paul's was the favourite place of devotion of St. Carlo. But the memorials of St. Carlo are all about us—and to go back to early times, here is the Church from which St. Ambrose repelled the soldiers of the Arian, and where he and the people passed the night in prayer and psalmody. "Excubabat pia plebs in Ecclesia, mori parata cum Episcopo servo tuo"; I quote St. Augustine, as you may not have it at hand. We have just returned from the Duomo where there has been a great function including a (Pontifical?) high Mass in celebration of the Dedication of the Church by St. Carlo. The day is very wet, but the area of the Church was crowded from end to end . . .

We have missed Manzoni—but been besieged almost daily by his chaplain—Ghianda, whom we like very much indeed. He speaks Latin like a *native,* though he has given it up in his late conversations with us. Rosmini passed through Milan, sending me a civil message, with an explanation that he did not call since he could not speak Latin nor I Italian. This is not enough to explain his not calling. Ghianda has a great admiration for him, and Manzoni has also. I wish we had more to tell of him, but I cannot get at the bottom of his philosophy; I wish to believe it is all right, yet one has one's suspicions. I do not think we have got a bit further than this in our reflections and conclusions, to think that Dr. Wiseman was right in saying that we ought to be Oratorians . . . Altogether it seems rather the age for external secularism with the gentle inward bond of asceticism—and this is just Oratorianism. We have been asking Ghianda about the Dominicans, and *whether* they had preserved their traditions anywhere. He said he thought they had at Florence, and somewhere else. We asked what he meant—why that they were still Thomists &c. However, on further inquiry we found that the said Dominicans of Florence were manufacturers of scented water, &c. and had very choice wine in their cellar. He considered Lacordaire quite a new beginning, a sort of knight errant, and not a monk. However, as to our prospects, I repeat nothing can be known till we get to Rome.

I have asked St. John what else I have to say, and he says "Tell him you bully me!" This is true, but he deserves it. I am glad to tell you he is decidedly stronger. I have been making him take some quinine. The journey along the Valley before we came to the Simplon was very trying; and the weather now is not good. We have been so happy here for a month or five weeks, I quite dread the moving again—and if it is wet, so much the worse—but it does not do to anticipate evils.

61. TO HENRY WILBERFORCE

Collegio di Propaganda [*Rome*].   *13th December, 1846*

My dear Henry,

I am tempted to write to you again, since your kind message through the Ryders—and that the more because it is pleasant to think of an old friend in a far country. Nothing can exceed the kindness of the people with whom I am. Father Bresciano especially, the Rector, is a man of real delicacy as well as kindness, and he anticipates all our wants in the most acceptable way—he really enters surprisingly into our feelings; but after all there is nothing like an old friend. New friends cannot love one—if they would; they know nothing of one—but to one who has known another twenty years, his face and his name is a history; a long series of association is bound up with every word or deed which comes from, which has a meaning and an interpretation in those associations. And thus I feel that no one here can sympathize with me duly—for even those who think highly of me have the vaguest, most shadowy, fantastic notions attached to their idea of me, and feel a respect, not for me, but for some imagination of their own which bears my name. It would be sad indeed, if all this did not throw me back upon more directly religious thoughts than that of any creature—and indeed it does. Both what people here can do for me, and what they cannot, carries off the mind to Him who "has fed me all my life long until this day," whom I find protecting me most wonderfully under such new circumstances, just as He ever has before, and who can give me that sympathy which men cannot give. It is so wonderful to find myself here in Propaganda—it is a kind of dream—and yet so quiet, so safe, so happy—as if I had always been here—as if there had been no violent rupture or vicissitude in my course of life—nay more quiet and happy than before. I was happy at Oriel, happier at Littlemore, as happy or happier still at Maryvale—and happiest here. At least whether I can rightly compare different times or not, how happy is this very striking proof how I am blest. As we go about the Churches of Rome, St. John ever says of the last he sees, "Well, this is the most striking of all." This as yet has been the happiness of my own life—though of course I do not know what is before me, and may at length against my will be brought out into the world—but it does not seem likely. I say it does not seem likely, for I can't tell as yet what they will make of me here, or whether they will find me out. It is very difficult to get into the mind of a person like me, especially considering so few speak English, and fewer still understand it spoken—and I can say so little in Italian. Then again in a College one sees so few people out of doors. It is most difficult even to get to speak Italian, though I am in an Italian house; what with the time in chapel, the Latin spoken in lecture, and the brief vacations. I am living the greater part of my time to and with myself—with St. John in the room opposite. What can people know of me? Nor would it do good to go out—both because I am so slow at the language and because I am so bashful and silent in general society. Miss Giberne, who is here, tells me a saying of Rickards about me, that when my mouth was shut it seems as if it would never open, and when open as if it would never shut. So that I don't expect people will know me. The consequence will be, that, instead of returning with any special responsibilities upon me, any special work to do, I should on my return slink into some ready-formed plan of operation, and if I did not become a friar or Jesuit, I should go on humdrumming in some theological seminary or the like. It is one especial benefit in the Catholic Church that a person's usefulness does not depend on the accident of its being found out. There are so many ready-formed modes of usefulness, great institutions, and orders with great privileges and means of operation, that he has but to unite himself to one of them, and it is as if Pope and Cardinals took him up personally. I am always, I think, egotistical to you, but indeed I believe to no one else. So, since I am in for it, I will add, what (as far as I know) I have never told to anyone—that, before now, my prayers have been so earnest that I never might have dignity or station, that, as they have been heard as regards the English Church, I think they will be heard now also.

As yet the persons I have chiefly seen, besides the good Jesuits here, are those of the Gesu and the Roman College. They are all abundantly kind—and I think I shall gain a good deal from them—there are none however yet, who quite come up to our good priests at Milan, to one of whom in particular we got much attached. They are generally somewhat cut and dried here —(all I say to you is in confidence). One thing however has struck me here and everywhere, (though I am ashamed to introduce it with an "however"—ashamed to introduce it at all) the monstrous absurdity of supposing that the Catholic Priests are not absolute and utter believers in the divinity of their own system. They are believers so as to be bigots—their fault is that they generally cannot conceive how educated Englishmen can be Anglicans with a good conscience—but they have a profound confidence in the truth of Catholicism—indeed it would be shocking to entertain the question, except that it is so commonly asked in England . . .

Ever your affectionately,

J. H. N.

62. TO MRS. WILLIAM FROUDE

Maryvale, Perry Bar.   *3rd July, 1848*

My dear Mrs. Froude,

Do not suppose your letter disappointed me, or pained me, except as I was indeed pained to see how much pain it had given you to write it, as when you talk of fearing that we are parted for ever. And beside this, you actually confess to so much pain, that so far I too am very much pained, but not at all of anything you have said about your state of mind.

You do not do me justice, if you think I did not know and enter into that state of mind, before I read your letter. Nor am I now going to argue with you. Far from it, God's teaching is more powerful than man's; and to you and William more suitable. To Him I leave you securely and cheerfully. May He be over you, and William and your children, and bring you forward in His own way! Do what you so religiously propose to do. I mean, cultivate that great virtue, faith, which I acknowledge may be possessed in the Anglican Church; which, knowing your earnestness and sincerity, I will believe that you possess in it, if you tell me so.

This is not inconsistent with my holding that in *reality* there is "no medium between scepticism and Catholicism," and on the contrary it is quite consistent with my saying that, if you join us, it must be "to save your soul": sentiments, which I am surprised you are startled at, seing I have invariably expressed them, e.g. in the Essay on Development, in Loss and Gain, in all my private letters written three years since, to Dr. Pusey (in spite of his published letter about me, which for that reason pained, as misrepresenting, me) and, I cannot but think, at that time, or before, to you.

But to return. Your postscript suggests one remark. It seems you are going to "make yourself believe again" as in 1834: but recollect, though you can believe what you choose, you must believe what you ought. Now, assuming *duty* proved, still you cannot believe without 1. a *creed*. 2. an *authority* which will not mislead you. At least put these first *before you*, even if (as you imply) you do not think in your position you need *prove* them. E.g. the Catholic makes his act of faith 1. in the *Creed*, and the so called Creed of Pope Pius, and the other dogmatic teaching of the Roman Church—2. in the *authority* of the Roman Church. This at least is intelligible. You too should have your answers, if you are to bring your good intention to a right issue;—and, if I may add one remark, which I suppose you will allow, you should either have in your hand your whole Creed, or be able to ascertain any point of it, when necessary.

I have done. May all blessings be with you all. I shall remember you daily in the Mass.

Ever affectionately yours,

John H. Newman.

63. TO F. M. CAPES

The Oratory, Birmingham.   *8th December, 1849*

Thank you for your valuable letter. The subject, which you have named, jumps with much I have been thinking of, especially the introductory lectures on the Nature of the Proof—but I fear these would swell into a whole (uninteresting) set. Again, such a subject requires very delicate treatment. Your Italian divines, whom I sincerely wish to follow in dogmatics, are not in my mind the best of polemics—now "The proof of Christianity" is just the point on which polemics and dogmatics meet as on common ground. It is in the province of both, and I cannot altogether stand the Italian treatment of it, unless I mistake their words and they mine. They know nothing at all of heretics as realities—they live, at least in Rome, in a place whose boast is that it has never given birth to heresy, and they think proofs ought to be convincing which in fact are not. Hence they are accustomed to speak of the argument for Catholicism as a demonstration, and to see no force in objections to it and to admit no perplexity of intellect which is not directly and immediately wilful. This at least is their tendency in *fact*, even if I overstate their theory. They have not a dream what England is, and what is the power of fascination which the Anglican Church (e.g.) exerts in the case of many minds. F. Passaglia understood it a little better when he got to Westminster Abbey, and declared the chanting to be a great "scandalo"; and I suspect he was cowed by the vision of Oxford. At present they will not abide in Italy the use of terms which, if not the ideas also contained in them, are received with us. E.g. when you in your Papers on "Four Years' Experience" speak of the argument for Catholicism being "the greater probability," (do you not?) you say what would scandalise an Italian, and would be put down to my school. At least one Jesuit attacked me as a probabilist in doctrine, though I am not conscious of dreaming of being one; and certainly I should be afraid that I might say things which, though distinctly contained in de Lugo, are contrary to the tone of this day. I really do not think I differ in *idea*, and I have altered my *language* in consequence, but I don't feel clear that I should not offend those whom I wish to be on good terms with. As to you, I distinctly think you have expressed yourself incautiously, unless I have misunderstood you—but what *I* think of *you*, others may think of me. At all events, it would take time, and thought, to write carefully on such a subject, and I don't think I could do it by Lent.

I should like to know some time *argumentatively* why my suggestion about eternity having no succession produces no alleviation of your difficulty—I wish to know it as a fact, to guide me in the use of it. It tends to destroy the difficulty in my own case.

I could not make out whether you said my Sermons were "selling" or "telling"—I wish them to "tell," but I am very much more interested, I must own, in the sale.

64. TO F. M. CAPES

In Vigil. N. Dom. 1850

My dear Capes,

I don't look on the Church of England as important in contrast to *Dissent,* but as a bulwark against infidelity, which Dissent cannot be. Were the Church of England to fall *Methodism might remain* awhile. I can't tell, for I don't know it—but surely, on the whole, the various denominations exist under the shadow of the Establishment, out of which they spring, and, did it go, would go too: i.e. they would lose their organisation, and whatever faint intellectual basis they have at present. Infidelity would take possession of the bulk of the men, and the women, so they had something to worship, would not care whether it was an unknown tongue, or a book of Mormon, or a pudding sleeve gown. Infidel literature would be the fashion, and there would be a sort of fanatical contempt and hatred of all profession of belief in a definite revelation.

Perhaps it is absurd so talking, for the Established Church could not fall without a revolution—and, while it exists in any shape, it so far forth witnesses to a dogmatic and ritual religion, i.e. a revelation—but, in proportion as it is liberalized, it lets in infidelity upon the country, for there is nothing else to stand against infidelity. I can as little triumph then in the decline and fall of the Establishment as take part in the emancipation of the Jews—I cannot, *till* the Catholic Church is strong enough to take its place. I don't see that this is inconsistent with my laughing at it as in my Lectures or Loss and Gain, for such ridicule only disparages it in the eyes of Puseyites who *ought* to leave it, not in those of Erastians and Establishmentarians, who constitute its strength. Is this a refinement? I mean, I don't think anything I have written would tend even to make men such as Lord John or Sir R. Peel give up the Church of England . . .

Ever yours affectionately,

J. H. N.

P.S.—Thanks for your news—Manning is with Hope at Abbotsford—What does this mean?

65. TO HENRY WILBERFORCE

Oratory, Birmingham. *28th December, 1850*

My dear H.,

The difficulty of answering William Froude is first his vagueness, and next his difference from me in first principles. *I do not think he could resist intimacy*—but he keeps at arms' length. I have before this expostulated with him for not seeing me—his excuse to himself is "Oh, it is so painful to talk with J. H. N., to differ from him—I can't bear it—and I could not talk out to him all I felt." Yet I feel certain he could not envelope himself in generalities, if he fairly opened his mind to a Catholic whom he knew and loved. But he is not the only person who has winced from the conversation of Catholics.

As to the argument from the promise, it is but one part of a large question. Take his *"inexorable* logic"—now how unreal this term is, when you come to particularize. Supposing a man tells me that for certain he will call on me to-day or to-morrow, and does not come to-day, is it inexorable logic which makes me expect him to-morrow? (Who was the father of Zebedee's children? is it inexorable logic which makes me say Zebedee?) I mean, there are certain things inevitable, certain principles being granted. On the other hand it is doubtless quite possible to fall into the extravagance of dealing with moral proofs as if they were mathematical—which is really "inexorable logic." But the question is *to which* does our Catholic argument belong? the former kind of logic falsely called inexorable, or the latter? If to the former, it is a mere *name* fastened on a good argument.

People love to reason *till* they are beaten; then talk of inexorable logic—as others talk of sophistry, jesuitry, &c. I don't think the Puseyistic and Transcendentalist "inexorable logic" (for strangely enough Pusey and my brother Frank, Isaac Williams and Thackeray, agree here) a whit more respectable than the "sophistry" of Luther on the Galatians, and the "Jesuitism" of the *Record* or *Christian Observer*.

Give a dog an ill name and hang him—our Anglo-Catholic friends enjoyed my logic while it attacked the Evangelicals, Hampden, &c., &c., but when it went *too far*, then it was inexorable, and I deteriorated.

As to the articles in the *Guardian*, it astonishes me they are by Rogers—how so clever a man can argue so weakly! But besides they are but *negative*. W. F. should be asked *what* he believes— what he has *positive* in his religion—to say that the Roman Church is wrong does not make the Anglican right. And this is what I think so unfair in his argument—that they dare not, won't, say, *what* they believe and *why*—they fence off. I said to dear W. F. about two years ago *"What* do you believe? and *why?"* and I have got, and believe he can give, no answer. The unfairness of this, unfairness, I mean, to himself, trifling with awful matters, is to me *incomprehensible*. The inexorable logic topos may parry my attack, but how can it satisfy himself? his "remaining where he is" does not *ipso facto* give him a creed.

For instance, let me say, as Rogers and others, I suppose, will say—"I need not hold Scripture inspired or more than a human document—but *I see* contained, brought out, in it, a superhuman character. Did I find that character in Hume's England, or in Livy, *n'importe*—here is a fact and a supernatural one—a real person, more than man—bearing on Him the tokens of coming from God—*Him* I believe, without an implicit submission to *Scripture* as proved infallible."

Well—I admit this is a view—but I want to see what you *mean* by it—or how far you carry it—so I must ask you some questions, not to puzzle you, not to confute you, but really to get at *what you mean* fully, and thus to see what your view is worth.

You mean, that our Lord's words and works, and history, as making up His character, are intrinsically supernatural, and recommend themselves as such to our moral instincts. Well then *do you believe* those words and works and history? i.e. do you accept them as true? Our friend looks suspicious, and begins in his heart to suspect I am one of the inexorable logicians. He wants to know more what I am driving at, before he answers.

I proceed—of course there must be something *practical* in your recognition of our Lord—He is not a mere beautiful picture—but a master, a teacher—else He is nothing. When then you say "Our Lord is enough for us," you mean that you have a Teacher from Heaven, and His teaching, revealed to you through the medium of Scripture. Well then, my question is, do you make His words and works and history therein contained, a rule to you, a rule of faith and conduct? Our friend at last is obliged to assent.

(1) Then I want to know, do you submit yourself to *all* His words and works and His whole history, or do you admit some things and not others, and if so, why?

(2) Is His history with His words and works, as a *whole,* clear enough to teach you definitely what to believe and what to do?

Here at length I shall be sure to be accused of inexorable logic—yet surely these two considerations are the necessary and immediate result of turning my mind to the subject. Is there no such fault as what the Provost used to call "inaccuracy of mind"? W. F. is an engineer—would he ever dream of assenting to any speculator who offered him a Patent, without applying his mind to see how the machinery worked? Theories are looked hard at by a clear headed man, and the flaw is then seen at once. To use general terms and glowing words is only fit for women and for Sewell of Exeter. It is to Sewellise, or to Mauricise.

Now I would say that the greater part of our Lord's teaching is *not* clear—and where it is clearest, it is most startling to the imagination. Perhaps the clearest doctrine of all laid down is that of Eternal Punishment. (Is this doctrine to be received as a sole dogmatic truth, like some promontory coming clear out of a thick sea fog?)

On the other hand, can anyone without trifling call the Sermon on the Mount, the institution and doctrine of the two Sacraments, the Discourse before the Passion, the institution of the Church, Matt. xvi.—intelligible without a comment? I do not mean that they have not our sense—but could we be sure of it? *Why* do we not take the precepts about turning the face to the smiter, &c., literally? &c., &c. Are we, or are we not, to take "This is My Body"—John vi., literally? In corroboration, does He not expressly refer us to a further teaching, that of the Paraclete?

Well then on the whole, *what* is our creed? does anyone mean to say he finds the Anglican creed, and nothing more or less, in our Saviour's teaching? Does our friend, thus taught, believe in the Athanasian creed, in the Atonement, in Original Sin, in the Real Presence, in Sacramental influence, in &c., &c.? Surely I have a right to ask him *what* he believes.

He won't tell; I know he won't—but he will talk of my inexorable logic. But he has to answer God, not me—it is not a question of polemics, but of personal duty.

I have brought out what I mean, not at all to my own satisfaction—but I have set it down to illustrate what I meant by saying "take him off *generals*—bring him down to particulars—bring him to book."

All I can say is, (not alluding to dear W. F.) I have no sympathy in such a state of mind—nor ever had—it is to me simply incomprehensible. I could not feed on words, without ideas. It is sheer Sewellism.

As to Mr. B. he is so unreal as to be simply ludicrous.

As to both of them, I should say to them, Pray for grace and light—pray to view things *really*. I have very great doubts, if either of them prays unreservedly to be led into the truth; if they say, "O my God, I am in darkness—but I wish to be led into the truth—deny me not the truth *at any sacrifice*—I will go through all things for it." E.g. *you* were anxious and miserable—if they are so too, I am hopeful about them. As to dear W. F. he is continually in my prayers, but I wish he seemed to take things less easily.

Ambrose and I laughed heartily at your Preacher. He said

"Sarved him right"—and I smiled grimly. Carissime, you have from time immemorial loved me, *and* distrusted me, especially during the last year. You have *gone* to bad Preachers—enjoy them.

Ever yours affectionately,

J. H. N.

66.   TO SISTER IMELDA POOLE

Edgbaston.   *28th November, 1852*

When I got up to London on Friday (the 19th) I found to my great disgust that the lawyers had had a consultation the evening before, and were for attempting a new trial; a second was to be held the next day (the 20th) at which I was to be present. They put the matter into my hands, and I suspect fancied I should be eager for it; but were thrown on their backs by finding I was simply against it. I did not observe this at the time, but, since they deferred to me, I thought I had it all my own way, and congratulated myself when the consultation was over, that the idea of a new trial was at an end. I got ready my speech, and packed up my portmanteau ready for prison, if so be—knowing I should be carried thither from court. Also my friends in King William Street packed up an altar and vestments and Father St. John, who was with me, got leave from the Cardinal for my saying Mass in prison.

All Sunday I had friends calling on me—everything was arranged. Meanwhile all Sunday Badeley was importuning me for a new trial; but I made no account of this, as I thought the matter simply in my hands, (as it was technically, but I mean, morally).

When we got into Court on Monday the 22nd, Sir A. Cockburn (my leading counsel) leant over the back of my bench, for I sat under him, and said, "Well, new trial or not?" I thought he asked for form's sake, and that he knew quite well there was to be none; so I answered briefly "Not." Then I heard him grumbling behind me, and began to suspect that he and the rest had *got up* their speeches and their tactics with a view to moving for a new trial. He then spoke to me a second time to the effect that he had looked at the evidence, and could make something of it. I repeated "No." Then Serjeant Wilkins, another of my counsel, attacked me. Money was no object, he said, he would pledge himself to go about begging from Protestants—he would take no fees himself. I said, "No." I found he had been up half the night getting up the evidence.

Presently the judges came in, and Cockburn leant over again. "You have now," he said, "a last chance, Yes or No?" I answered "No," and he went out of Court. I had sitting near me Serjeant Bellasis, who was the only lawyer (he was not one of my counsel) who had agreed with me in opposing a new trial. I said to him, "Well, it's all over, is it not?" He said, "Yes."

Cockburn when he went out of Court spoke to Mr. Badeley, who, as you know, has been my most zealous and active counsel from the first. "We can make nothing of Dr. Newman," he said, "you must persuade him." He came accordingly to Serjeant Bellasis. Now Serjeant Bellasis had all along said, "I agree with you quite, in opposing the idea of a new trial—but, when it comes to the point, if they persist, you must yield." The Cardinal too, who, with the Bishop of Southwark, had confirmed my own view of the matter, had ended by saying, "Well, if your lawyers persist you must obey them as you would physicians." At this moment then, Badeley came to Serjeant Bellasis and said, "Dr. Newman must give way, all his five counsel are for a new trial." On this Serjeant Bellasis, who was sitting next me, turned round to me, and said, "You cannot resist longer—you must give in." I said, "Is there no one else to ask? What a terrible thing to decide upon by myself." We looked round—there was no one. "Well, but," I said, "'tis too late. You told me so just now." He answered "It is not too late." Then I said "I give in—let them move for a new trial."

Accordingly when the notes of the trial had all been read, a tiresome matter of three hours and a half, Cockburn got up.

Lord Campbell thought he was going to speak, in *mitigation of damages,* and affecting (if I may use the word) consideration for me, he said, "Sir Alexander, Dr. Newman's affidavit—don't omit his affidavit." "My lord," he answered, "I am giving reasons for granting us a Rule for a new trial." I did not look at the poor old man, but had I any resentment against him, alas at that moment, and in the rest of the proceedings, it would have been gratified to the very full. He changed colour, shook, and his voice trembled. A military friend who was at my elbow said his head quivered as though he had been shot in the ear. Serjeant Bellasis said to me, "Do you see how Campbell is agitated?" And, I repeat, for the rest of the time (two or three hours) he had to endure a lengthened attack upon him face to face, from Sir Alexander Cockburn, who thrust at his conduct in the most determined pitiless way in the survey of the whole trial. Nor is it the only attack he will have to stand. The opposite counsel reply in January, and then we rejoin—and my other lawyers have one after another to rise, and to inflict the same castigation upon him.

It is generally considered that the whole affair is at an end. *I* should say so, except from my knowledge of the special hatred my opponents bear me, which has been present to my mind from the first. Next the course of Providence all through has been so dark, that we never have been able to guess at what was coming. When I went up to town last week, no one even then could guess anything. The future was as dark up to the 22nd, as it had been throughout. No one could conjecture what the punishment would be. The lawyers all in the dark, asked Sir A. Cockburn at the consultation—he would not hazard any guess. I have affidavits from Sir B. Brodie, Mr. Babington, and Dr. Evans that a prison would have most serious effects upon my health. I swore in my own affidavit, that I believed from what I was told, that it would shorten my life—yet they could not bring themselves to say absolutely that I should *not* be sent to prison. This being the case, there may still be quite a new turn of things in January.

However, if the Rule for a new trial is granted me, the great probability is, that the whole matter will *end*. Because in that case the four judges will have decided that the verdict was *against the evidence,* in other words that I ought not to have been so condemned. People say that Achilli *cannot* recommence proceedings with such a recorded judgment against him.

Again, I believe he will be incidentally found guilty of perjury.

Again, he owes his lawyers 1,100*l.*, which he had meant *me* to pay, and they may be unwilling to go on without security for the money—and his friends may not like to recommence, when they shall have already committed themselves to so large a sum.

If I were simply to beat him, he would have all *my* expenses. But, if he *does* begin a new trial, then I have two courses.

If I cannot get money, or cannot get the witnesses, I should make affidavit that this is the case—and submit—when lawyers say no *punishment* could ensue after such an exposure as will have taken place.

But if I *can* get the witnesses, the expense will be comparatively small. For I can bring them to a day, and I shall know just *whose* evidence is worth bringing.

If on the other hand the judges in January do *not* allow me a fresh trial (every one thinks they *will*) then I shall be brought up for judgment as I was last Monday—but with this advantage that we shall have done what we *could,* and that my counsel will have been able to attack Campbell and expose the verdict;—which they say, must lessen the sentence.

Pray for me and believe me,

Yours affectionately in Christ,

John H. Newman.

67. TO HENRY WILBERFORCE

[July, 1853]

I have seen our house at Ham once in 1813, in the holidays, when my father, brother, and myself rode there from Norwood—

ringing and no one came; and how at last he ventured to attempt and open the hall door without leave, and found himself inside the house, and made a noise in vain—and how, when his patience was exhausted, he advanced further in and went up some steps and looked about him, and still found no one at all—all along thinking it the house of the true Bishop, and a very fine one too. And how at last he ventured to knock at a room door, and how at length out came a scullery-maid and assured him that the master was in London; whereupon, gradually, the true state of the case unfolded itself to his mind, and he began to think that had that Superintendent been at home, a servant would have answered the bell and he would have sent in his card or cartel with his own name upon it for the inspection of the said Superintendent.

4. And the fourth chapter of the work will go on to relate how the Bishop of Ossory pleasantly suggested, when he heard of the above, that the carman's mistake was caused by a certain shepherd's plaid which the author had upon his shoulders, by reason of which he (the author) might be mistaken for a Protestant parson. And this remark will introduce the history of the said plaid, and how the author went to Father Stanislas Flanagan's friend, Mr. Geoghegan in Sackville Street, and asked for a clerical wrapper, on which the said plaid was shown him, and he objecting to it as not clerical, the shopman on the contrary assured him it was. Whereupon in his simplicity he bought the said plaid and took it with him on his travels and left behind him his good Propaganda cloak; and how now he does not know what to do, for he is wandering over the wide world in a fantastic dress like a Merry Andrew, yet with a Roman collar on.

5. And the fifth chapter will narrate his misadventure at Waterford—how he went to the Ursuline convent there and the Acting Superior determined he should see all the young ladies of the school, to the number of seventy, all dressed in blue, with medals on—some blue, some green, some red—and how he found he had to make them a speech and how he puzzled and fussed himself what on earth he should say impromptu to a

parcel of school-girls; and how, in his distress, he *did* make what he considered his best speech; and how, when it was ended, the Mother school-mistress did not know he had made it. or even begun it, and still asked for his speech. And how he would not, because he could not, make a second speech; and how, to make it up, he asked for a holiday for the girls; and how the Mother school-mistress flatly refused him, by reason (as he verily believes) because she would not recognise and accept his speech, and wanted another, and thought she had dressed up her girls for nothing; and how he nevertheless drank her raspberry vinegar, which much resembles a nun's anger, being a sweet acid, and how he thought to himself, it being his birthday, that he was full old to be forgiven if he could not at a moment act the spiritual jack pudding to a girls' school.

This is as much as I have to send you. Would you kindly add your own criticisms and those of the two Fathers?

Love to all.

Ever yours affectionately,

J. H. N.

69. TO MRS. WILLIAM FROUDE

5th May, 1854

My dear Mrs. Froude,

I have been to England for a day and found your letter, and brought it with me here where I have just arrived and now sit down to thank you for it and the former one.

Be sure I shan't forget you and Wm. please God. I shall for some time give my Friday's mass (excepting the 26th inst) to that intention.

Do not fancy you can put me in a painful position to dear Wm. I don't mind differing with him. I don't mind giving you advice in which he would not concur. But I wish to be sure I tell him so when I do it. He is so true and tender, but I leave you safely to him. But I can disguise from him what I think and feel about you.

As to your reference to my letters, of course I may forget about myself—but just consider, since you have them with you, whether I am not right in saying, that I never was in doubt what *my duty was*. I doubted what was true, but I used to say "To join the church of Rome would be against my conscience. I *could not* do it." I don't say this was not a false conscience, but a conscience it *was*, and it is ever right to go according to one's conscience, though a false one.

Moreover, it is a Catholic principle that no one can be in doubt what he ought to *do* (i.e. without fault). We are often left "speculatively" doubtful, and use the theological word, never "practically." Shortly before my reception, when my book was partly printed, I saw I *ought* to be a Catholic, and I did not then wait till I had finished the printing, but left the book unfinished, as it stands.

When my dear friend Bowden lay dead, I wept bitterly over his body, saying he had gone, and left me without light; this was the same feeling as far as I recollect. I don't think I was remaining a Protestant, thinking I ought *not* to remain, but with a sense of duty that I *ought* to remain *till* I got clear light.

I am not defending myself, but I am writing with reference to you, my dear Mrs. Froude. See then whether your doubt be merely speculative. Can you say "I am certain I ought now and here, at this time and place, to remain a Protestant"? Are you sure that, whatever remaining *speculative* doubts or difficulties you may have, you have not a secret feeling that you ought to be a Catholic? I am not attempting to answer this question *for* you, but I really cannot help having an opinion on the subject.

I hope I make this clear, but am somewhat anxious lest I should not.

Ever yours affectionately,

J. H. N.

70. TO MISS E. M. FROUDE

6 Harcourt Street, Dublin.　　　　　　　*9th July, 1855*

My dearest Isy,

I am very glad to have your present. A penwiper is always useful. It lies on the table, and one can't help looking at it. I have one in use, made for me by a dear aunt, now dead, whom I knew from a little child, as I was once. When I take it up, I always think of her, and I assure you I shall think of you, when I see yours. I have another at Birmingham given me by Mrs. Phillipps of Torquay, in the shape of a bell.

This day is the anniversary of one of the few times I have seen a dear brother of mine for 22 years. He returned from Persia, I from Sicily, where I nearly died, the same day. I saw him once 15 years ago, and now I have not seen him for 9 years.

My dear Isy, when I think of your brother, I will think of you. I heard a report he was to go and fight the Russians. I have another godson, called Edward Bouverie Pusey, who is a sailor, already fighting the Russians either in the Baltic or at Sebastopol.

Ever yours affectionately,

John H. Newman

of the Oratory.

P.S. You will have a hard matter to read this letter.

71. TO MRS. WILLIAM FROUDE

The Oratory, Hagley Road, Birmingham.　　　*20th May, 1856*

My dear Mrs. Froude,

May God reward you, as He will, for all your trials, and your resolute struggle under them. As to your answers to William's objections, no one could make better. As to the expression of them in words, every one must feel how difficult this is. He beyond others will and must, because his great difficulty, or rather obstacle, in writing to me was, that he could not do himself justice upon paper.

If you had acted hastily, impetuously, doggedly, without listening to others, that might have been a fair objection to you; but *you* surely are the best judge of your own reasons, and you have tested them by a long course of years.

The absolute certainty of faith in the truth of what the Church conveys to you from God, is the reward, through divine grace, of those souls who, before receiving it, have exercised their mental powers to the best; and you must throw yourself, in regard to it, on the Power, Love, and Faithfulness of Him who calls you.

You need not believe any thing that the Pope says, except when he speaks ex cathedrâ. His chance sayings need not be better than another man's, nor his measures in detail. I believe there were great corruptions all over Europe, before the rise of Protestantism; but I am very doubtful if much can be proved against the Pope's measures.

Since you distinctly ask me, I have no right to keep from giving you my distinct judgment, that you are bound to join the Church at once.

> Ever yours affectionately,
> with much anxiety for you,
> John H. Newman.

God support you.

72. TO WILLIAM FROUDE

18th January, 1860

My dear William,

It is a cause of great sadness to me, when I look back at my life, to consider how my time has been frittered away, and how much I might have done had I pursued one subject. Had not each year brough its own duties, I should have turned to the subject which I spoke of long ago but it is not one to be taken up by halves, and now, how many years have I?

As to your question whether, when I say that I feel the view of the subject which you put out a sophism, I mean that it is so in reference to the pursuit of Truth, generally, or only in reference to the pursuit of "religious truth." Speaking under the correction of my fuller thought I should say

(1) that I not only do not mean that there is anything sophistical in the principles on which non-religious truth is pursued at present, but that theologians (who ought to know in Arte sua) all affirm that Christianity is proved by the same rigorous scientific processes by which it is proved that we have an Indian Empire or that the earth goes around the sun. I mean the proof is in this same line or order, for of course it is difficult to say whether we have more or less right, or neither more nor less to be certain that India belongs to the English (Empire) than that the earth goes around the sun.

(2) But the scientific proof of Christianity is not the popular, practical, personal evidence on which a given individual believes in it. And here I think it is where your question really comes in. I should differ from you, if I understand you, in thinking that there is a popular and personal way of arriving at certainty in Christianity as logical as that which is arrived at by scientific methods in subjects non-religious. I was struck how table turning was put down—by the sort of argument indeed which I originally heard you used in conversation—in the world at large in a few days by the authority of a great name, Faraday, presenting to the public one argument which was received on its plausibility by the man, or on his word without trial.

I consider the proof (grounds) on which a given individual believes in Christianity are of this character or order. But they are so far more cogent as to lead legitimately not only to opinion or passive acceptance but to certainty as cogent as scientific proof. Nay I go further, I think that is a sophism in (considering) the certainty of secular science so far superior to the certainty, or persuasion as you would call it, of the personal evidence for Christianity. I suspect that when all scientific proof, even for the existence of India, is examined microscopically there will be found hiatus in the logical sequence so considerable as to lend to the question "are there no broad, just principles of knowledge which will protect us from scepticism in all reasoning about things external to us, both scientific and popular?" As to what you say about a person, I don't think we should disagree in principle when the subject was fully worked out.

I have heavy trials and discouragements in the midst of enormous mercies, but should I be led to pursue the subject of this letter (which would be by very slow marches) I should ask your leave to put various points before you, as iron girders are sent to the trying house.

I have a husky cough which makes me almost anxious, as being somewhat new, and so resolved not to go.

Ever yours affectionately,

J. H. N.

73. TO SIR JOHN ACTON

The Oratory, Birmingham.   *5th July, 1861*

My dear Sir John,

I don't like writing in a hurry when I ought to write with care—but then I don't like to delay. So I must do my best.

I did not mean to differ from you (nor do I) in any principle, but in a fact. The *Rambler* certainly does seem to me ever nibbling at theological questions. It seems to me in its discussions to come under the jurisdiction of the ecclesiastical power; and, therefore, I think the ecclesiastical power ought to be deferred to.

If it advocated homeopathy or the broad guage—and the Bishops of England said anything in discouragement of such conduct, I do not see how it could be bound to defer to the Bishops.

If it said that the classics ought to be taught to laymen, and the Bishops said that Prudentius was far better poetry than

189

Virgil, and, in order to the cultivation of poetical taste, insisted on the *Rambler* being silent in its praises of Virgil, I do not see that the *Rambler* need be silent.

But this is not the fact. The Bishops have a direct jurisdiction in the education of the clergy for the ministry—they act under an Ecumenical Council. To discuss the question of the education of the clergy does seem to be entering on a question under their jurisdiction. This the *Rambler* has done. It has not itself given judgment, but it has discussed at length, through its correspondents, the question. I cannot tell you how this discussion has annoyed me, not only for the sake of the *Rambler*, but in itself.

The Articles on Campion again—no one surely can say that a Life of Campion was *obliged* to come out with the statement or insinuation that St. Pius preferred to maintain untenable claims to retaining England in the Church; no reader surely but was surprised that it came into the narration. Such matters should not be dealt a back-handed blow—it was not a history of St. Pius or of his times—even then, a Saint surely is not to be approached as a common man. If the Ecclesiastical Power makes Saints, it requires that they, as well as their images, should receive the 'debitum honorem et venerationem.' The historical character of St. Pius, as it seems to me, was treated very much as if, in showing a church, the sacristan were to take an axe and knock off a piece of the altar, and then, when called to account, were to say that the altar was about to be removed as it was in the way, and he was only, by his act, beginning the intended reforms.

Rednal, July 6th—Then again, in the article on Ward's philosophy, I think the reviewer spoke of the highest ecclesiastical courts of the Church having for two centuries impeded in Italy the advance of science or something of the kind. Now, however true this may be, was it necessary to say it thus? and was it not anyhow an *attack* upon the said courts? I don't see that those courts went beyond their *powers* in the bare fact of their impeding science. They thought science interfered with religion, and no one can say that they had not a *prima facie* case in their favour. And they had the community (I suppose) with them. But whether this be so or not, is not the point. What I would insist on is that it is not wonderful, if a writer in the *Rambler* attacks those courts, the representatives of those courts will attack him, —and, (without saying that the *prima facie* view of the matter in the eyes of the public will be in their favour, if he is writing *ex professo* on the subject and they come in his way) yet I think if a writer, reviewing Ward, has a sudden side blow at them, the good sense of the public will side with *them,* if they in turn inflict some severe stroke upon their assailant.

I am saying all this by way of explaining what I meant by saying that the *Rambler* now is in a false position if authority speaks against it. It has been sufficiently theological and ecclesiastical to impress the world with the idea that it comes under an ecclesiastical censor, and if it caught it for tilting against Inquisitors, Ecumenical Councils, and Saints, the world would be apt to say: "serve him right!" This is how it appears to me.

And further, I must, though it will pain you, speak out. I *despair* of Simpson being other than he is. He will always be clever, amusing, brilliant, and *suggestive.* He will always be flicking his whip at Bishops, cutting them in tender places, throwing stones at Sacred Congregations, and, as he rides along the high road, discharging peashooters at Cardinals who happen by bad luck to look out of the window. I fear I must say I despair of any periodical in which he has a part. I grieve to say it, but I have not said it till the whole world says it. I have, I assure you, defended him to others, and it is not many weeks, I may almost say days, since I was accused of "solidarity with the *Rambler.*" But what is the good of going on hoping against hope to the loss of union among ourselves, and the injuring of great interests? For me, I am bound to state my convictions when I have them; and I have them now.

You will act with true sincerity of intention and with full deliberation, whatever conclusion you come to about the *Rambler,* but I don't think Protestants ought to say that an independent organ of opinion is silenced, but one that loved to assail, and to go out of his way to assail, what was authoritative and venerable.

Ever yours most sincerely,
John H. Newman.

74. TO FATHER HENRY BITTLESTONE

Cambridge.   *29th July, 1861*

My dear Henry,

Knowing your disputatious power, I am not sure you will not be able to deny that I *am* in Cambridge, in spite of the post-mark—but you must let me assume that I am there, and it shall be a reserved point to discuss when I see you again.

On Friday, after seeing Badeley, whose torments seem to have been extraordinary, we caught the train to Hampton Court, where we slept. Of course I am not going to write descriptions, but I will say that we were both enchanted with the place, and thought how great her Majesty must be to have palaces such as to enable her to chuck Wolsey's building to her servants and pensioners.

Well—I thought we should enjoy our incognito, and so we did during good part of 24 hours—but at length we fell on Platner, who is so mighty in words, that I simply fell—and Wm,[1] making an excuse that just now I was unable to talk, picked me up and carried me off.

Forthwith we fled; whither was a secondary question. We rowed to Kingston—the weather has been, and is, sometimes lovely sometimes splendid. Then, after dining, we set off for Richmond through Ham. Thence at once by train to London, musing all the way where we should find ourselves at night fall. On getting to Waterloo station we made for King's Cross, and by half past nine p.m. behold us at Cambridge.

I have been here once before, for a quarter of a day, in 1832.

[1] Father William Neville.

Then, I recollect my allegiance to Oxford was shaken by the extreme beauty of this place. I had forgotten this—but a second sight has revived the impression. Certainly it is exquisitely beautiful.

We weathered Mr. L. though we were so near capsizing, as to be asked by him to change our place, because we were in the way of his confessional—and, as there was but one person, a stranger, at the Bull in the Coffee Room, we have been quite comfortable.

He has a strange distrait manner, and I took him for some enthusiastic parson, say a Drummondite or the like. I said but a few words to him, but he seemed absent—but, as he fidgetted about, and went in and out of the room, read the Bible, then sat where he could see me say office, and certainly followed our movements, we migrated to the other end of the room.

This was no annoyance to us; but what did annoy us was, that, when we went into King's Chapel to hear the chanting and see the place, a little man at once fastened his eyes on us, whom William instantly jaloused as having been at the Oratory. William, who acts as a sort of guardian angel or Homeric god, instantly enveloped me in darkness, rustling with his wings, and flapping about with a vigour which for the time was very successful. But alas, all through the day, wherever we were, this little man haunted us. He seemed to take no meals, to say no prayers, to know our times for these exercises with a preter-natural exactness. William was ever saying, whether we were here or there, in garden or in cloister—"Don't look that way—turn this way—there's the little man again." His anxiety led him to make matters worse, for he boldly approximated him to make sure of the individual, but with too little caution, for the little man caught his hand and asked him how he was. However, his guardship kept me out of harm's way, and we dined peacefully at six. There was then no further danger—we lounged out at seven and were tempted, by the merest accident, to turn aside into Peterhouse. We were not two seconds in the Court, when William cried out, "There's the little man—don't look." But it would not do—he pounced upon his prey, and William turned quite red, whipping his finger as if he had been stung. He most civilly asked us, if we should like to see the Munich painted glass in the Chapel, and went at once for the Porter. Then he vanished—but William is now out paying him a call with my card; and I should certainly have done the same, but that I am far from well this morning, very weak, because I have not had any sleep (from distress, it is not so much as pain) since 3. I heard 3 strike and every hour till I got up.

I have been hardly able to speak, certainly not to converse, with our fellow-occupant in the Coffee Room, who has left for the North just now—having never seen Cambridge before, and, like ourselves, having been down for the Sunday. He began talking this morning about Cambridge, which I agreed with him was most beautiful. He said he had been into the University Church for the evening service—and, after a word or two between us, he suddenly said "I think I have seen *you* in the pulpit of St. Mary's Oxford some thirty years ago." Well, I answered rather bluntly, "how *could* you know me? for my friends, who have seen me only half that time ago, don't know me, they think me so much changed."

This led to some conversation, when at length we got to the Essays and Reviews. After which I started, *proprio motu,* a new subject, that of the movement for the alteration of the Liturgy. He said that was a religious movement, very different in spirit from the others. I agreed, but I said I had been much struck with the effect, which I heard was produced by a book written by a lawyer, a Mr. Fisher, whom the Bps had noticed in their charges. His book, they said, was a logical, candid work; but it was remov-the veil, from the eyes of a number of evangelicals, shewing them that they could not honestly use the baptismal service, and demanding in consequence its alteration. I said I thought this a remarkable movement and would gather strength. So we shook hands and parted.

I came down again, and he was not gone. It seemed to me rude not to have asked his name—So I said to him, "Since you know me, pray do not let us part without my having the satisfaction of knowing with whom I have been conversing."

He looked nervous, and distrait—and then said "I am the Mr. Fisher, of whom you have been talking."

Ever yours affectionately,

J. H. N.

75. TO EDWARD BELLASIS

The Oratory, Birmingham.   *20th August, 1861*

My dear Bellasis,

I am at Rednal tho' I have dated above from habit. This is so nice a place, that I am trying to stay here, if I can.

Your letter did me a great deal of good. The fable of the Diggings is very apposite. If I have been digging a field with my own ideas and my own hopes, and, though they have failed, have been preparing ground for the sowing, the showers, and the harvest, of divine grace, I have done a work so far, though not the various definite works which I have proposed to myself. I ought to be most thankful to be so employed. I was not unmindful of God's mercy to myself and others, in making us Catholics, when I wrote, but I looked on this, as *His* work, as it was, not mine—however a digging, though it is but turmoil, confusion, and unsettlement, is a co-operation.

But I cannot in a few words express to you what the matter is with what I may call the *physical* texture of my soul. It is not a matter of reason, nor of grace—but, just as the body wearies under continual toil, so does the mind. I should *illustrate* the trial which I mean, tho' it might not be to the letter, if I said I had received no piece of personal good news for thirty years and more. I question whether I have had any success, except getting a scholarship at Trinity when I was 17, and a fellowship of Oriel at 21. In one year (about 1830) I used to say laughingly I had been put out of five places; of course this was only a way of speaking, but there was truth in it, three of them I recollect—

the Tutorship at Oriel, then Whitehall Preachership, and the Secretaryship of the Church Missionary Society; I was voted out of the list. Of course I deserved it, and never complained, but I say it is a matter not of reason, but of psycho-physical effect. So it has been with me all through life. I think I never have been praised for anything I did, except once, for my lectures on Catholicism in England by the Bishop and Catholics of Birmingham—and at the time of that praise the Achilli proceedings, arising out of those very Lectures, had begun, or at least were in distinct prospect.

The case is the same of late years. Whenever I have attempted to do anything for God, I find after a little while that my arms or my legs have a string round them—and perhaps I sprain myself in the effort to move them in spite of it.

Thank you for your friendly wish to see me at Ramsgate. I cannot conceive a pleasanter or more sunny sight, in this sunny weather, than to see you with your wife and family during your vacation.

Ever yours most sincerely,

John H. Newman.

76.   TO FATHER WILLIAM NEVILLE

27th March, 1862

My dear William,

You may send the following "Heads of a Discourse" to Patterson.

Yours ever affectionately,

J. H. Newman.

For Patterson.

Seven reasons for not writing more books.

I do not write

(1) because in matters of controversy I am a *miles emeritus, rude donatus.*

(2) because no one serves on Parliamentary Committees after he is sixty.

(3) because Rigaud's steam engine which was hard to start was hard to stop.

(4) because Hannibal's elephants never could learn the goose-step.

(5) because Garribaldi's chaplains in ordinary never do write.

(6) because books that do not sell do not pay.

(7) because just now I am teaching little boys nonsense verses.

"Nos indamnatos, homines Romanos, miserunt in carcerem; et nunc occulte not ejiciunt? Non ita; sed veniant, et ipsi nos ejiciant."

77. TO THE EDITOR OF *The Globe*

The Oratory, Birmingham.   *28th June,* [*1862*]

Sir,

A friend has sent me word of a paragraph about me, which appeared in your paper of yesterday, to the effect that "I have left, or am about to leave, my Oratory at Brompton, of which I have been for several years the head, as a preliminary, in the expectation of my private friends, to my return to the Church of England."

I consider that you have transferred this statement into your columns from those of a contemporary in order to give me the opportunity of denying it, if I am able to do so. Accordingly, I lose not an hour in addressing these lines to you, which I shall be obliged by your giving at once to the public.

The paragraph is utterly unfounded in every portion of it.

1. For the last thirteen years I have been head of the Birmingham Oratory. I am head still; and I have no reason to suppose I shall cease to be head unless advancing years should incapacitate me for the duties of my station.

2. On the other hand, from the time I founded the London Oratory, now at Brompton, twelve years ago, I have had no

jurisdiction over it whatever; and so far from being its head, it so happens that I have not been within its walls for the last seven years.

3. I have not had one moment's wavering of trust in the Catholic Church ever since I was received into her fold. I hold, and ever have held, that her Sovereign Pontiff is the centre of unity and the Vicar of Christ; and I ever have had, and have still, an unclouded faith in her creed in all its articles; a supreme satisfaction in her worship, discipline, and teaching; and an eager longing and a hope against hope that the many dear friends whom I have left in Protestantism may be partakers of my happiness.

4. This being my state of mind, to add, as I hereby go on to do, that I have no intention, and never had any intention, of leaving the Catholic Church and becoming a Protestant again, would be superfluous, except that Protestants are always on the look-out for some loophole or evasion in a Catholic's statement of fact. Therefore, in order to give them full satisfaction, if I can, I do hereby profess *ex animo*, with an absolute internal assent and consent, that Protestantism is the dreariest of possible religions; that the thought of the Anglican service makes me shiver, and the thought of the Thirty-nine Articles makes me shudder. Return to the Church of England! No! "The net is broken, and we are delivered." I should be a consummate fool (to use a mild term) if in my old age I left "the land flowing with milk and honey" for the city of confusion and the house of bondage.

> I am, Sir,
> Your obedient servant,
> John. H. Newman.

78. TO FATHER AMBROSE ST. JOHN

[*October*], *1862*

. . . I have ever been brought through—I said I should when

the Achilli matter began; but here my own anticipation *then* of what was likely to happen *now* appals me. It appals me to think that I should so rightly have guessed what was to take place at the end of another ten years. I then said that, as when I was 20 I was cut off from the rising talent of the University by my failure in the Schools, as, when 30, I was cut off from distinction in the governing body by being deprived of my tutorship, as, when 40, I was virtually cast out of the Church of England by the affair of No. 90, as, when 50, I was cast out of what may be called society by the disgrace of the Achilli sentence, so, when I should arrive at 60 years, I should be cast out of the good books of Catholics and especially of ecclesiastical authorities. This appals me in this way—viz. what is to happen if I live to be seventy? Am I to lose all of you and to be left desolate? or is our house to be burned to the ground? or am I to be smitten with some afflicting disorder? These are the questions which come before me, and don't be angry with me for mentioning them, for it is a great relief to me to speak and a pain to be silent. Well, I suppose it is all intended to keep me from being too happy. How happy should I be if let alone—how fond of living! On the other hand certainly, I have been carried marvellously through all those troubles which have come to me hitherto, and so I believe I shall be to the end . . .

Now be kind enough to say a Hail Mary for me instead of quarrelling with me for saying all this, and believe me.

Ever yours most affectionately,

J. H. N.

P.S.—So Brodie is gone and Dr. English, and our Provost's eldest son whom we used to see riding on a pony at Littlemore.

79.   TO SISTER MARY GABRIEL

7th April, 1863

. . . I am engaged just now in receiving one of the Froudes—a boy of sixteen who arrived here yesterday from School. My dear friend, his father, who is not a Catholic has seen his children one after another, (this is the fourth) received into the Church; and he has borne it so gently, so meekly, so tenderly, (though it has given him a sense of desolation more cruel to bear) that I do trust God's mercy has the same gift in store for himself. Please give him your prayers, and ask your Sisters to do the like. It is the infallibility of the Church which is his stumbling stone. He would confess that her authority is probable, but he cannot receive her absolute infallibility, and since she claims (as he thinks) what she has not, therefore the claim itself is a proof against her. What a good Catholic he would make, if the grace of God touched his heart. Get our Lady to ask for him—what a joyful day it would be!

Ever yours affectionately in Christ,

John H. Newman

of the Oratory.

80. TO MISS E. BOWLES

19th May, 1863

Don't think about *me*. God uses his instruments as he will. "Hunc humiliat et hunc exaltat." To myself I feel as full of thought and life as ever I was—but a certain invisible chain impedes me, or bar stops me, when I attempt to do anything, —and the only reason why I do not *enjoy* the happiness of being out of conflict is because I feel to myself I could do much in it. But in fact I could not do much in it. I should come into collision with everyone I met—I should be treading on everyone's toes. From the very first an effort has been successfully made to separate all converts from me, and they are the only persons who would be likely to move aside of me without jostling . . . I know what the Cardinal said to Father Faber, and what Father Faber said to the world, viz.; "That I had put myself on the shelf, and there was no help for it."

But now to go to the root of the matter. This country is under Propaganda . . . If I know myself, no one can have been more loyal to the Holy See than I am. I love the Pope personally into the bargain. But Propaganda is a quasi-military power, extraordinary, for missionary countries, rough and ready. It does not understand an intellectual movement. It likes quick results, scalps from beaten foes by the hundred. Our Bishop once, on his return from Rome, said pointedly to me what I am sure came as a quasi-message from Propaganda, that at Rome "they liked good news."

True, the words were said with an implied antithesis—for I had lately been to Rome to complain. I suppose the issue of the Achilli matter must have made them despise me at Rome—but, whatever the cause of it was, two years after, Propaganda, without saying a word to me, appointed three Bishops to examine and report to it whether the Rule of the Birmingham Oratory could be, on a certain point, suspended to advantage . . . Our Fathers prevailed on me to go to Rome about it. When I got there I found to my great relief and gratitude that, at the last moment, the dear Pope, when the matter necessarily came before him, simply asked: "Has Dr. Newman been consulted?" and would not give his assent to the act. Then, when I saw him, he asked me why I wished to get him to make me head or general of the two Oratories, of which not even a dream had come into our minds here, more than that of making you a Father General of us;—showing what hidden tales against me were going on. When we saw Mgr. Barnabo, he was very cross, and asked me why I had come to Rome, when, if I had remained quiet at home, the Pope would, as it turned out, have acted for us. When Monsell went to Rome shortly after, he came back with the remark that I had no friend at Rome. It was true;—but what had I *done*? *this* I had not done, and there was the rub, I had not preached sermons, made speeches, fussed about, and reported all my proceedings to Propaganda. I had been working away very hard in Ireland at the University, and saying nothing about it.

Well, immediately my Dublin engagement was over, at the Cardinal's and our Bishop's direct solicitation, I interposed in the *Rambler* matter, and found myself in consequence, to my surprise and disgust, compelled to take the editorship on myself. I not only made the best of it, but I really determined to make it my *work*. All those questions of the day which make so much noise now—Faith and Reason, Inspiration, &c., &c.—would have been, according to my ability, worked out or fairly opened. Of course I required elbow-room—but this was impossible. Our good Bishop, who has ever acted as a true friend, came after the publication of the first number, and advised me to give up the editorship. He said I had caused dissatisfaction. I only edited two numbers; but I wrote enough to cause one of our Bishops formally to denounce one of my articles to Propaganda. What did Propaganda know of the niceties of the English language? yet a message came (not a formal one) asking explanations . . . As what was said to me was very indirect and required no answer, I kept silence, and the whole matter was hushed up. I suppose so, for I have heard no more of it, but I suppose it might (*pel bisogno*) be revived in time.

Don't you see that this, if nothing else, puts a great obex to my writing? This age of the Church is peculiar—in former times, primitive or medieval, there was not the extreme centralization which now is in use. If the private theologian said anything free, another answered him. If the controversy grew, then it went to a Bishop, a theological faculty, or to some foreign University. The Holy See was but the Court of ultimate appeal. *Now,* if I, as a private priest, put anything into print, Propaganda answers me at once. How can I fight with such a chain on my arm? It is like the Persians driven to fight under the lash. There was true private judgment in the primitive and medieval schools—there are no schools now, no private judgment (in the religious sense of the phrase) no freedom, that is, of opinion. That is, no exercise of the intellect. No, the system goes on by the tradition of the intellect of former times. This is a way of things which, in God's own time, will work its own cure, or necessity; nor need we fret under a state of things, much as we may feel it, which is incomparably less painful than the state of the Church before Hildebrand, and again in the fifteenth century.

I am only speaking of it in its bearing on myself. There was some talk, when the Bishop put in his plea against me, of calling me to Rome. Call me to Rome—what does that mean? It means to sever an old man from his home, to subject him to intercourse with persons whose languages are strange to him—to food, and to fashions, which are almost starvation on one hand, and involve restless days and nights on the other—it means to oblige him to dance attendance on Propaganda week after week, and month after month—it means his death. (It was the punishment on Dr. Baines, 1840—41, to keep him at the door of Propaganda for a year).

This is the prospect which I cannot but feel probable, did I say anything, which one Bishop in England chose to speak against and report. Others have been killed before me. Lucas went of his own accord indeed—but when he got there, oh! how much did he, as a loyal son of the Church and the Holy See as ever was, what did he suffer because Dr. Cullen was against him? He wandered (as Dr. Cullen *said* in a letter he published in a sort of triumph), he wandered from church to church without a friend, and hardly got an audience from the Pope. And I too should go from St. Philip to Our Lady, and to St. Peter and St. Paul, and to St. Laurence and to St. Cecilia, and, if it happened to me, as to Lucas, should come back to die.

We are not better than our Fathers. Think of St. Joseph Calasanctius, or of Blessed Paul of the Cross, or of St. Alfonso— or of my own St. Philip, how they were misunderstood by the authorities at Rome. The Cardinal Vicar called Philip, to his face and in public an ambitious party man, and suspended his faculties. It is by bearing these things that we gain merit, but has one a right to *bring it on one*?

81. TO THE REV. J. KEBLE

The Oratory, Birmingham.   *15th August, 1863*

My dearest Keble,

I returned from abroad last night, and, among the letters on my table waiting my arrival, found yours. I answer it before any of the others.

Thank you very much for it, and for the books which accompany it, which I value first for your dear sake, next for their venerable and excellent subject. I am pleased too that you should tell me about your wife and brother—but how odd it seems to me that you should speak of yourself and of him as old! Did you ever read Mrs. Sheridan's Tale of Nourjahad? such I think is the name. I have not read it since a boy. I am like one of the Seven Sleepers awakened when you so write to me, considering all my recollection of Hursley and Bisley, which remain photographed on my mind, are of twenty-five years ago, or thirty. I cannot think of little Tom but as of the boy I carried pick-a-back when he was tired in getting up from the steep valley to the table land of Bisley. And I recollect your father and your dear sister and your wife as you cannot recollect them—at least the latter two—for in my case their images are undimmed by the changes which years bring upon us all. My great delight is to take up your Poetry Lectures—I only love them too well, considering my age, and that their subject is not simply a religious one. But what do *you* mean by saying that you are "as if dying"? I have heard nothing of your being unwell; and I trust you will live long, and every year more and more to the glory of God.

I have not been abroad for pleasure till now, since I went with dear Hurrell. I went to St. Germains near Paris to see the Wilberforces. Then my dear and faithful friend who went with me—Ambrose St. John—insisted I should cut across to Treves, the place of sojourn of St. Athanasius, St. Ambrose, and St. Jerome. Then I went down the Moselle and up the Rhine, which was all new to me; and we came back by Aix la Chapelle. I had a bad accident there, with (thank God and my Guardian Angel) no harm whatever. I had a bag in one hand and cloaks in the other, and turning round sharp at the top of a staircase, was sent down two flights headlong—but thank God I got nothing but a slight strain of the arm. Since then I have been stopping at Ostend to recruit.

I have said all this, knowing it will interest you. Never have I doubted for one moment your affection for me, never have I been hurt at your silence. I interpreted it easily—it was not the silence of others. It was not the silence of men, nor the forgetfulness of men, who can recollect about me and talk about me enough, when there is something to be said to my disparagement. You are always with me a thought of reverence and love, and there is nothing I love better than you, and Isaac, and Copeland, and many others I could name, except Him Whom I ought to love best of all and supremely. May He Himself, Who is the over-abundant compensation for all losses, give me His own Presence, and then I shall want nothing and desiderate nothing, but none *but* He, *can* make up for the loss of those old familiar faces which haunt me continually.

Ever yours most affectionately,
John H. Newman.

82. TO FATHER AMBROSE ST. JOHN

[*Rednal*].   *30th August, 1863*

My letter has been stopped—first by my great day-long doings in the Library. I have been dusting, arranging, and re-arranging to an heroic degree, though I have not yet done all. And next Frederick Rogers paid me a visit, and was the whole of yesterday with me. It is 20 years since we met. When he first saw me, he burst into tears, and would not let go my hands—then his first words were: "How altered you are!" The lapse of so long a time brings itself in no other way so vividly. In memory, actions and doings of years ago appear like yesterday, and indeed in the course of the day he was led to cry out: "Oh, how like you!" and quoted parallel remarks of mine on occasions when we had been together, but, in the countenance, the silent course of years speaks unmistakably and all at once. We talked exceedingly freely on all subjects—my *own* difficulty is to keep from speaking *too* freely. It pleased me to find that he had no scepticism and had not gone back, apparently, one hair's breadth—but, I fear, neither has he advanced. It was a sad pleasure to me to find how very closely we agreed on a number of matters which have happened since we met. It was almost like two clocks keeping time.

83.   TO THE REV. R. W. CHURCH

The Oratory, Birmingham.   *23rd April, 1864*

Private.

My dear Church,

Copeland encourages me to write to you. I am in one of the most painful trials in which I have ever been in my life and I think you can help me.

It has always been on my mind that perhaps some day I should be called on to defend my honesty while in the Church of England. Of course there have been endless hits against me in newspapers, reviews and pamphlets—but, even though the names of the writers have come out and have belonged to great men, they have been anonymous publications—or else a sentence or two on some particular point has been the whole. But I have considered that, if anyone with his name made an elaborate charge on me, I was bound to speak. When Maurice in the *Times* a year ago attacked me, I answered him at once.

But I have thought it very unlikely that anyone would do so—and then, I am so indolent that, unless there is an actual necessity, I do nothing. In consequence now, when the call comes on me, I am quite unprepared to meet it. I know well that Kingsley is a furious foolish fellow—but he has a name—nor is it anything at all to me that men think I got the victory in the Correspondence several months ago—that was a contest of ability —but now he comes out with a pamphlet bringing together a hodge podge of charges against me all about dishonesty. Now friends who know me say: "Let him alone—no one credits him," but it is not so. This very town of Birmingham, of course, knows nothing of me, and his pamphlet on its appearance produced an effect. The evangelical party has always spoken ill of me, and the pamphlet seems to justify them. The Roman Catholic party does not know me;—the fathers of our school boys, the priests, &c., &c., whom I cannot afford to let think badly of me. Therefore, thus publicly challenged, I must speak, and, unless I speak strongly, men won't believe me in earnest.

But now I have little more to trust to than my memory. There are matters in which no one can help me, viz. those which have gone on in my own mind, but there is also a great abundance of public facts, or again, facts witnessed by persons close to me, which I may have forgotten. I fear of making mistakes in dates, though I have a good memory for them, and still more of making bold generalizations without suspicion that they are not to the letter tenable.

Now you were so much with me from 1840 to 1843 or even 1845, that it has struck me that you could (if you saw in proof what I shall write about those years) correct any fault of fact which you found in my statement. Also, you might have letters of mine to throw light on my state of mind, and this by means of contemporaneous authority. And these are the two matters I request of you as regards the years in question.

The worst is, I am so hampered for time. Longman thought I ought not to delay, so I began, and, therefore, of necessity in numbers. What I have to send you is not yet written. It won't be much in point of length.

I need hardly say that I shall keep secret anything you do for me, and the fact of my having applied to you.

Yours affectionately,
John H. Newman.

84. TO MONSIGNOR TALBOT

The Oratory, Birmingham.   *25th July, 1864*

Dear Monsignore Talbot,

I have received your letter, inviting me to preach next Lent
in your Church at Rome to "an audience of Protestants more
educated than could ever be the case in England."

However, Birmingham people have souls; and I have neither
taste nor talent for the sort of work which you cut out for me.
And I beg to decline your offer.

I am, yours truly,
John H. Newman.

85. TO WILLIAM FROUDE

The Oratory Birmingham.   *28th July, 1864*

My dear William,

Though I was seriously distressed that you should suffer so
much, there was nothing in your letter for anyone to take offence
at. And I was rather amazed at Eddy[1] myself. His letters to you
have in great measure cleared the matter up, tho' I am still
expecting a letter from him and cannot write absolutely, any
more than you could to him, without knowing more of his
feelings and wishes—and I half fear I have shown my state of
mind to him, and that that is the reason why he does not write.

The reasons which he gives to you were news to me, though
I see at once they are the real ones. I suppose he could not all
at once bring these out to me—and I cannot but feel great
sympathy and pity for a poor boy wishing to flee the world
because it is so sweet—and I am sure you do too.

Nothing can shew both the naturalness and the confusion of
his idea better, than the way he has mixed up, as I think, two
things quite distinct—the religious state and the ecclesiastical

[1] Edmund, son of William Froude.

state. His one object is to leave secular pursuits, and he does not care how. When he spoke to me, I understood him to be desiring the ecclesiastical state, and to be aiming at orders, the priesthood. To that effect I wrote to you. In his letter from Elmsliegh, he writes to me about a *religious* order—as if it were the same thing. His mother writes to me about his wish for the *priesthood*—and to you he writes (somewhere) of the ecclesiastical *or* religious state, (or some such words). In truth his one object is to leave the world . . .

I have just heard from your wife to say that Eddy is going to write to me. I suppose he hardly knows what to say, and, if his letter does not come before evening, I shall write to him. The notion of his going to try his vocation as a regular *at once*, is to me simply preposterous—and I never will give my consent to it It would, in a year perhaps, determine his calling for life. As time went on, he might bitterly regret what he had done, and find that he must put the regret from him because he was under a vow. His life might be miserable. Of course it *might* turn out very well—and so it may turn out well if a child engaged himself to be married; but we must go by our best judgment. Nor could I trust the Religious fathers, under whom he put himself for trial and decision, unless I knew them most intimately—because of course they would be biassed as well as he, and, unless they were men of great caution and experience, would consider the devoutness and religiousness of youth the sufficient token of a vocation for themselves.

The notion then of his trying a religious vocation at once, I should quite put aside. As to an ecclesiastical vocation, if I understand his mother's expressions in the letter just come, I don't think he contemplates that, as distinct from the other—but I cannot make out. However, I look at it very differently. First, it seems to me in many cases the first step *towards* a religious vocation—therefore in admitting the idea of it in his case, I am saving myself from the danger of quenching his desire for a religious vocation, if it really comes from God. He would be proceeding by steps, not per saltum. 2. The listening to the idea determines nothing *at once*—for the irrevocable engagement to the ecclesiastical profession is not incurred by minor orders, but by the subdiaconate—which he could not receive before he is 21, and need not of course then—and so there is no reason, even if he *had* a calling to the priesthood that he should not go to Oxford.

In saying all this I am speaking as his director, and I should give (if I could safely) this advice, viz. go on just as if no thoughts had come across you—go on with your secular studies—go to Oxford or Cambridge if papa wishes, and see where you find yourself when you have taken your degree. If *then*, you deliberately consider that God wishes you to be a Priest, nay or a religious, I have nothing to say against it—or rather, I thank God.

And for yourself, my dear William, I think you would be in the position of many a parent besides yourself, who wishes his son to succeed him in his Bank, or a fine profitable business, and he *will* go into a profession or into the army—or who wants his son to marry a certain lady, and he *will* fix his affections on some one else. I do not think you would have any right to complain, *because* Eddy would be a *man*. And as to his pledging himself by a vow, so does every Anglican Clergyman on his ordination, and it is attended with serious civil disabilities—as they find full well when they (Angl. Clerg.) become Catholics; moreover, when a man is old enough to vow to love for ever a certain woman, I think he is old enough to vow celibacy.

There is only one difficulty which I should find on my side in *insisting* on Eddy going to the University (i.e., if *you* wished it) and it is what you speak of yourself when you allude to his being "placed in a perpetual conflict with himself." *As time went on*, I might find that it was the lesser of two evils for him to make up his mind about the Priesthood or Religious Order sooner than the date I have mentioned.

You must recollect that he is quite at *liberty*, if he *chooses*, to leave *me* and to take Fr. Suffield for his director. I think he *ought* not to do so—and, if he remains with me, I shall insist on his having no communication with Fr. Suffield. A soul cannot have two physicians at once. He never ought to have consulted Fr. Suffield on the point. I shall tell him so—but he is so distressed just now, that I must not wound him. Please do not hint this to him.

Thank you for letting me see the correspondence, which I return. I think his letters very good ones—and yours a very good one, and I trust and pray that, where everyone wishes what is right, everything will go well; though (if I am right in thinking he will not ultimately depart from at least his *ecclesiastical* direction) there must be in the event pain to you.

Ever yours most affectionately,

John H. Newman.

86. TO FATHER COLERIDGE, S.J.

30th December, 1864

. . . Paralysis has this of awfulness, that it is so sudden. I wonder, when those anticipations came on Keble in past time, whether they were founded on symptoms, or antecedent probability; for I have long feared paralysis myself. I have asked medical men, and they have been unable to assign any necessary premonitory symptoms; nay, the very vigorousness and self-possession (as they seem) of mind and body, which ought to argue health, are often the proper precursors of an attack. This makes one suspicious of one's own freedom from ailments. Whately died of paralysis—so did Walter Scott—so (I think) Southey—and, though I cannot recollect, I have observed the like in other cases of literary men. Was not Swift's end of that nature? I wonder, in old times, what people died of. We read, "After this, it was told Joseph that his father was sick." "And the days of David drew nigh that he should die." What were they sick—what did they die of? And so of the great Fathers. St. Athanasius died past 70—was his paralytic seizure? We cannot imitate the martyrs in their deaths, but I sometimes feel it would be a comfort if we could associate ourselves with the great Confessor Saints in their illness and decline. Pope St. Gregory had the gout. St. Basil had a liver complaint, but St. Gregory Nazianzen? St. Ambrose? St. Augustine and St. Martin died of fevers proper to old age. But my paper is out.

87.   TO FATHER WHITTY, S.J.

The Oratory, Birmingham.   *19th March, 1865*

My dear Father Whitty,

I thank you very much for your most kind letter; and thank you heartily for your prayers, which I value very much. It is very kind in you to be anxious about me, but, thank God, you have no need. Of course it is a constant source of sadness to me that I have done so little for Him during a long twenty years; but then I think, and with some comfort, that I have ever tried to act as *others* told me, and if I have not done more it has been because I have not been put to do more, or have been stopped when I attempted more.

The Cardinal brought me from Littlemore to Oscott; he sent me to Rome; he stationed and left me in Birmingham. When the Holy Father wished me to begin the Dublin Catholic University I did so at once. When the Synod of Oscott gave me to do the new translation of Scripture I began it without a word. When the Cardinal asked me to interfere in the matter of the *Rambler* I took on myself, to my sore disgust, a great trouble and trial. Lastly, when my Bishop, *proprio motu,* asked me to undertake the mission of Oxford, I at once committed myself to a very expensive purchase of land and began, as he wished me, to collect money for a church. In all these matters I think (in spite of many incidental mistakes) I should, on the whole, have done a work, had I been allowed or aided to go on with them; but it has been God's Blessed Will that I should have been stopped.

If I could get out of my mind the notion, that I *could* do

something and am *not* doing it, nothing could be happier, more peaceful, or more to my taste, than the life I lead.

Though I have left the notice of the Catechism to the end of the letter, be sure I value it in itself as coming from you. The Pope will be very glad to hear the author of it.

Ever yours affectionately,

John H. Newman.

88. (*Unpublished*) TO FATHER COLERIDGE, S.J.

The Oratory, Birmingham.   *8th May, 1865*

My dear Fr. Coleridge,

You will find by this morning's post that I have anticipated your wish, as contained in the letter I have just received. In my last I mentioned to you the Quarterly, Frazers, and the English-man's Magazine, as three periodicals which expressed the standard of lightness and heaviness in my own idea of a Magazine for Catholic usefulness. They do not differ very much from the Cornhill, which has as many (I allow) as *two* stories, which is too much, but has also, (at least had, when I used to see it) a scientific article, an economical, one of contemporary history or politics, and one of talk or chat. The two novels are, I suppose, one ethical (as Thackeray's or Trolloppe's) the other sensational. With the latter at least, a Catholic Magazine might dispense.

I know what a difficulty a Priest has in writing or editing literature which is not theological. I feel it very much myself. I have been too long in the groove, to say nothing else, to write any thing which [has] no theological meaning, but still I can't help saying now, as I did to Fr. Gallway, that it is not theology that Catholics want, but literature treated as Catholic authors cannot help treating it. You mentioned my Lectures on the Turks—I should not like a review to introduce theology more than they do. It is *secular* history written by a Catholic. I do not know how you feel on the subject, but it seems to me that

the Classics open an important field for a Catholic Magazine—
one popular with large classes of the community, one which the
Society has ever excelled in, and one which is congenial to at
least your antecedents. For instance, see how Keble (with whatever deficiencies in consequence of his Anglicanism) has christian-
ized their study in his Prelections. It seems to me that those
Prelections might be cogged from, and make an interesting series
of Papers—e.g. On right and wrong modes of reading the Classics
—according to the story of the two combatants and the gold and
silver shield—or "Eyes and no eyes." The French Revolution, at
least the Girondists, afford a specimen of the wrong reading of
them—M. de Roland—Charlotte Corday, &c., &c. Speaking without book, I should say that Plutarch's Lives did the mischief—
as constituting a sort of "Lives of the Saints," and he was one
of the new Platonic or Eclectic school—quite different from
honest old Herodotus or Pindar, who tell their evil and the evil
of their times, as it was.

Then again Education seems to me both an interesting and
fruitful topic. There are those Reports of the Public Schools
&c., &c., which supply abundant matter and suggest many
questions, unless you feel, as a member of the Society, that it is
not open to you to consider views different from those which,
I believe, are identified with your system.

I quite apprehend that wise rule of your Society to let every
one, who is entrusted with an office, to work in his own way.
As to the exception of politics, the only question I should
raise upon it, is, "What *is* politics?" or rather "What is *not*
politics?" If it means that, e.g. you are not to support Gladstone,
or not to side with Confederates against Federals, it is quite
intelligible—but does the prohibition extend to principles? may
you not show a preference for responsible government, for a
constitution, for Magna Charta, for a state conscience, for
established religion, if you choose to do so? May you not show
a kind feeling to the Bey of Tunis, or to legitimacy, or to a
paternal government, or to good administration? You ought to
know where the line must be drawn; else, all subjects come

into politics, as all subjects come into religion.

You should pay your contributors—as I doubt not you mean to do. With money you may command talent—without, there will be little effort and less punctuality—i.e. unless your writers are your own Fathers—but, when obedience is away, money is the main spring.

If you think it worth while, I am quite ready to go on for some months with the Saints of the Desert.

Very sincerely yours in Christ,

John H. Newman

of the Oratory.

P.S. You know Isaac Williams is gone.

89. TO DR. H. E. MANNING

31st May, 1865

My dear Archbishop,

On hearing of your appointment I said Mass for you without delay. I will readily attend your consecration—on one condition which I will state presently. As I come as your friend, not as a Father of the Birmingham Oratory, I do not propose to bring any other Father with me. I am sure you will allow me to escape any dinner or other meeting, as such public manifestations are so much out of my way. Nor do they come into the object of your asking me; which is, as you have said, to have my prayers at the function itself.

The condition I make is this:—A year or two back I heard you were doing your best to get me made a bishop *in partibus*. I heard this from two or three quarters, and I don't see how I can be mistaken. If so, your feeling towards me is not unlikely to make you attempt the same thing now. I risk the chance of your telling me that you have no such intention, to entreat you not to entertain it. If such an honour were offered to me, I should persistently decline it, very positively, and I do not wish to pain the Holy Father, who has always been so kind to me, if such pain can be avoided. Your allowing me then to come to your consecration, I shall take as a pledge that you will have nothing to do with any such attempts.

J. H. N.

90. TO FATHER AMBROSE ST. JOHN

Buckland Grange, Ryde.   *13th September, 1865*

Here I am, very comfortable, and if I had my dear fiddle with me, I might sing and play, "recubans sub tegmine fagi," in full content. Scarcely had I left Birmingham when it struck me that, since Pusey was to be at Keble's that evening, he would, no manner of doubt, get into my train at Oxford and travel down with me. But he did not. I determined to go to Keble's next morning to see him.

So I did. I slept at the Railway Hotel at Southampton Dock, a very reasonable house, and good too, (they are building an Imperial Hotel), and yesterday morning (Tuesday) retraced my steps to Bishopstoke, left my portmanteau there, and went over to Hursley. I had forgotten the country, and was not prepared for its woodland beauty. Keble was at the door; he did not know me, nor I him. How mysterious that first sight of friends is! for, when I came to contemplate him, it was the old face and manner, but the first effect or impression was different.

His wife had been taken ill in the night, and at the first moment *he*, I think, and certainly *I*, wished myself away. Then he said: "Have you missed my letter?" meaning, "Pusey is here, and I wrote to stop your coming." He then said: "I must go and prepare Pusey." He did so, and then took me into the room where Pusey was.

I went in rapidly, and it is strange how action overcomes pain. Pusey, being passive, was evidently shrinking back into the corner of the room, as I should have done, had he rushed in upon me. He could not help contemplating the look of me narrowly and long. "Ah," I thought, "you are thinking how old I am grown, and I see myself in you—though you, I do think, are more altered than I." Indeed, the alteration in him startled, I will add pained and grieved, me. I should have known him anywhere; his face is not changed, but it is as if you looked at him through a prodigious magnifier. I recollect him short and small, with a round head and smallish features, flaxen curly hair; huddled up together from his shoulders downward, and walking fast. This as a young man; but comparing him even as he was when I had last seen him in 1846, when he was slow in his motions and staid in his figure, there was a wonderful change in him. His head and features are half as large again; his chest is very broad, and he is altogether large, and (don't say all this to anyone) he has a strange condescending way when he speaks. His voice is the same; were my eyes shut, I should not be sensible of any alteration.

As we three sat together at one table, I had a painful thought, not acute pain, but heavy. There were three old men, who had worked together vigorously in their prime. This is what they have come to—poor human nature! After twenty years they meet together round a table, but without a common cause or free outspoken thought; kind indeed, but subdued and antagonistic in their language to each other, and all of them with broken prospects, yet each viewing in his own way the world in which those prospects lay.

Pusey is full of his book (the "Eirenicon"), which is all but published, against Manning, and full of his speech on the relations of physical science with the Bible, which he is to deliver at the Church Congress at Norwich; full of polemics and hope. Keble is quite different; he is as delightful as ever, and it *seemed* to me as if he felt a sympathy and intimacy with me which he did not show towards Pusey. I judge by the way and tone he spoke to me of him. I took an early dinner with them; and, when the bell chimed at 4 o'clock for service, I got into my gig, and so from Bishopstoke to Ryde, getting here between 7 and 8.

91. TO W. G. WARD

The Oratory, Birmingham.   *18th February, 1866*

My dear Ward,

I thank you very much for the present of your volume, and for your kind letter, but far more, of course, for your prayers. I do not feel our differences to be such a trouble as you do; for such differences always have been, always will be, in the Church; and Christians would have ceased to have spiritual and intellectual life if such differences did not exist. It is part of their militant state. No human power can hinder it; nor, if it attempted it, could do more than make a solitude and call it peace. And thus thinking that man cannot hinder it, however much he try, I have no great anxiety or trouble. Man cannot, and God will not. He means such differences to be an exercise of charity. Of course I wish as much as possible to agree with all my friends; but if, in spite of my utmost efforts, they go beyond me or come short of me, I can't help it, and take it easy.

As to writing a volume on the Pope's infallibility, it never so much as entered into my thought. I am a controversialist, not a theologian, and I should have nothing to say about it. I have ever thought it likely to be true, never thought it certain. I think, too, its definition inexpedient and unlikely; but I should have no difficulty in accepting it were it made. And I don't think my reason will ever go forward or backward in the matter.

If I wrote another pamphlet about Pusey, I should be obliged to have a few sentences to the effect that the Pope's infallibility was not a point of faith—that would be all.

> Ever yours affectionately in Christ,
> > John H. Newman
> > Of the Oratory.

92. *(Unpublished)* TO FATHER COLERIDGE, S.J.

The Oratory, Birmingham.   *24th October, 1866*

My dear Fr. Coleridge,

The worst effect that could happen from any letter of mine to you, would be your giving up controversial writing, for I do not know any one who would write with greater taste and self restraint, to say nothing of higher qualities, than yourself.

Of course I take a different view of Pusey from what you do, but for argument's sake I will allow that, as you say, he shuffles desperately—also, I take the very ground that you do, viz. that his word is taken as law by numbers when it should not be. Also, of course I think and desire, that for the sake of those numbers, and moreover (which it strikes me you do not so much consider) for the *sake of himself*, what he says incorrectly, should be set right, and brought home to him as requiring such right-setting.

And now, it is because I wish you so much to continue to write as controversialist in the Month, and hope you will, that I bore you about this matter. If I was sure you were giving up that office, I would not say another word.

Well then, I think anything like *abuse* is just as likely to effect your object with Pusey himself and his admirers, as the wind was likely, in contest with the sun, to blow off the traveller's coat. As to the quartern-loaf τόπος, if there is one thing more than another likely to shock and alienate those whom we wish to convert, it is to ridicule their objects of worship. It is wounding them in their most sacred point. They may have a false conscience, but, if they are obeying it, it is laughing at them for being religious. For myself, I can recollect myself firmly believing that what your friend calls a piece of quartern loaf was, not only that, but the body of Christ—and, to my own *consciousness* I as truly believed it and as simply adored it, as I do now the Blessed Sacrament on Catholic Altars. And what I did then, I know many Anglicans do now. Moreover, as the writer confessed by saying that it was "probably" nothing more than bread, it is possibly, or even not improbably something more—or at least, though *I* may not think so, I cannot condemn another who does. Now, I cannot see how laughing at a worship which has nothing laughable in it, and, which if not well founded, has no *intrinsic* incredibility, but is invalidated by purely historical considerations and ritual facts—how such a polemic has any tendency whatever, to weaken the worshipper's belief in its truth and obligation. On the other hand I see that it would offend him just as much as the blasphemous bills upon the Dublin walls against Transubstantiation disgust and anger the Catholics who pass by. Such ridicule is not the weapon of those who desire to save souls. It repels and hardens.

And now to go on to Pusey. In like manner, abuse of him will neither convert him nor any of his followers. I received an Oxford undergraduate the other day—he was speaking of Pusey, and took occasion to say how young men revered him—chiefly for his very austere life, and his great meekness in controversy. He said that they could not bear to hear him spoken against. I do not call exposing a man's mistakes "speaking against him," nor do I suppose *any* one would. But if, instead of exposing those errors in detail, and as matters of fact, in simple grave language, a controversialist *began* by saying "This man is absurd —he shuffles—he misrepresents—he is keeping men from the truth—" every word of it might be true, but I should say he was calling names, and indulging in abuse. For by abuse I mean accusation without proof—or condemnation before proof—and such a process of putting the cart before the horse defeats itself, and has no tendency to convince and persuade those whom it concerns.

I have not yet had an opportunity of reading Fr. Harper's book—I expect great instruction and pleasure in doing so; and I look with special interest at what comes from him from simple gratitude to him for some both kind and very seasonable letters I have had from him;—but I cannot deny I have been distressed at the tone he takes about Pusey, and for this plain reason, because I think he defeats his object by adopting it. What the

Guardian said of his work illustrates what I mean. It dismissed a learned and (I am sure) convincing work with the remark "We need only say that this book is written in the controversial style of the 16th and 17th centuries," or words to that effect. This was a convenient, for it was a telling way, of getting rid of a formidable opponent. It was a very good excuse to its readers for not going into his arguments. It was just in the same way that Marshall's important work on Christian Missions was got rid of. His acrimony against Protestants was made the excuse of tossing it aside.

Excuse all this and believe me,

Ever yours most sincerely in Christ,

John H. Newman.

P.S. I have no *English* of my notes. They are in French in the French edition.[1]

93. TO SIR JUSTIN SHEIL

The Oratory, Birmingham.   *22nd March, 1867*

My dear Sir Justin,

A diplomatist and a man of high commands as you have been will allow me, without being thought to take a liberty with you, to ask your confidence while I freely tell you my position as regards our Oratory undertaking.

Two or three years ago, when it was settled by our Bishop that I was to go there, it was on the strict condition that the Oratory took no part in the education of the place. I drew up a circular in which I said merely: "that I went for the sake of the religious instruction of the Catholic youth there"; and to my surprise the late Cardinal was so angry even with my recognising the fact of their being at Oxford in any way, that he sent the news of it to Rome, though I had not actually issued the paper, and it has created a prejudice against me ever since. Accordingly in the

[1] of the *Apologia*.

circular I sent you the other day, I could not put in a word about Catholic youth being at Oxford; and the intention of the present Archbishop is, if he can, to stamp them out from the place. However, this has not been enough—a further step has been taken, for last Monday I got a letter from Propaganda saying that they had heard that I had in my School here some youths preparing for Oxford, and solemnly ordering me neither directly nor indirectly to do anything to promote young men going there.

You are too well acquainted with a soldier's duties, not to know that it is impossible for me to disobey the orders of my commanders in the Church Militant. So, what I must do as regards the School is, to my great sorrow, to relinquish those who go to Oxford for a short time before they go there, *if* I should find they need, in addition to the general instruction we give them here, any *special* preparation for the University.

Now before proceeding, I will tell you my own opinion on the matter. I differ from you decidedly in this, viz., that, if I had my will, I would have a large Catholic University, as I hoped might have been set up in Dublin when I went there. But I hold this to be a speculative perfection which cannot be carried out in practice—and then comes the question what is to be done under the *circumstances*. Secondly then, I say that Oxford is a very dangerous place to faith and morals. This I grant, but then I say that *all places are dangerous*—the world is dangerous. I do not believe that Oxford is more dangerous than Woolwich, than the army, than London—and I think you cannot keep men under glass cases. Therefore I am on the whole not against young men going to Oxford; though at the same time there are those whom, from their special circumstances, of idleness, extravagance, &c. &c., I certainly should not advise to go there.

Such is my opinion, and it will surprise you to hear that, be it good or be it bad, no one in authority has ever asked for it through the discussion of the last two or three years.

And now let me go on to the practical question of the moment. From that and other articles in the *Westminster Gazette,* and from the letters which have come to me from Propaganda, I am sure that more stringent measures are intended, to hinder young Catholics going to Oxford, and I think they can only be prevented by the laity. What I should like you to do then is not to withdraw your name from our subscription list, but to join with other contributors, as you have a right to do, in letting me know formally your own opinion on the subject. And for myself I can only say that, if I find the sense of the contributors is against my going to Oxford without their being let alone in sending their sons there, I will not take their money, as I should be doing so under false pretences.

My dear Sir Justin,

Sincerely yours,

John H. Newman.

94. TO FATHER COLERIDGE, S.J.

The Oratory, Birmingham.   *26th April, 1867*

My dear Father Coleridge,

. . . When last Christmas I found the words "conditionate et provisorie" in the letter (of Cardinal Barnabo) to our Bishop, (though I had no suspicion at all of a secret instruction such as there really was contained in it) I told the Bishop formally my suspicions . . . You may fancy how he felt what I said, being conscious, as he was, of the secret instruction—and so he said that I had better wait till he went to Rome in May, and I have waited, except that I have begun to collect the money. Also I was going to commence my *personal* work at Oxford on the second Sunday after Easter, intending to preach every Sunday through the term, which, had I carried it out, would have led to a certainty to the Bishop's "blanda et suavis revocatio"; and thus, as it turns out, even though Mr. Martin had not written a word, things would have come to a crisis. The reason determining me to go to Oxford at once, in spite of the Bishop's advice at Christmas (though he fully came into the plan of the Oratory going to Oxford at Easter), when I after a while proposed it, was the delay that was likely to take place in beginning the Church, and all my friends kept saying: "You must do *something* directly to clench on your part Propaganda's permission to go, or the Archbishop will be getting the permission reversed." When then I found it impossible to make a demonstration in bricks and mortar (which for myself I had, in consequence of the suspicions felt, deprecated) nothing remained but to make a demonstration by actually preaching at Oxford—and this was to my view of the matter far more acceptable because a counter order from Propaganda would have been serious, had we begun to build, but would have been of no consequence at all, had we done nothing more than preach in the Chapel at St. Clement's.

However, as it has turned out, I am stopped both before building and preaching.

It is perfectly true, as you say, that both sides have not been heard at Rome. The questions you speak of circulated in December 1864, were too painful to speak about. For myself, up to this date no one has asked my opinion, and then those who might, by asking, have known it, have encouraged or suffered all sorts of reports as to what my opinion is, instead of coming to me for it.

It is my cross to have false stories circulated about me, and to be suspected in consequence. I could not have a lighter one. I would not change it for any other. Ten years ago I was accused to the Pope of many things (nothing to do with doctrine). I went off to Rome at an enormous inconvenience, and had two interviews with the Holy Father, *tête-à-tête*. He was most kind, and acquitted me. But hardly was my back turned but my enemies (for so I must call them) *practically* got the upper hand. Our Bishop seems to think no great good comes of seeing the Pope, if it is only *once* seeing him. What chance have I against persons who are day by day at his elbow? . . .

For twenty years I have honestly and sensitively done my best to fulfil the letter and spirit of the directions of the Holy See and Propaganda, and I never have obtained the confidence of anyone at Rome. Only last year Cardinal Reisach came to England. I had known him in Rome. He never let me know he was in England. He came to see Oscott, and I did not know it. He went to my ground at Oxford, but he was committed, not to me, but to the charge of Father Coffin . . .

I have lost my desire to gain the good will of those who thus look on me. I have abundant consolation in the unanimous sympathy of those around me. I trust I shall ever give a hearty obedience to Rome, but I never expect in my lifetime any recognition of it.

Yours most sincerely,
John H. Newman.

95. TO FATHER AMBROSE ST. JOHN

3rd May, 1867

Your welcome letter, notifying your arrival at Rome, got here on Wednesday at noon.

I have just had a letter from Father Perrone, so very kind that you must call on him and thank him. He says he always defends me. Also Father Cardella said Mass for me on St. Leo's day. Thank him too.

Ignatius's Pamphlet is just out, but we do not hear anything about it yet.

If it ever comes to this, that you can venture to speak to Barnabo on the secret instruction, you must say that people gave money to the Church on the *express condition,* as the main point, that I should reside a great deal in Oxford. Hence his precious instruction made me unwittingly collect money on false pretences. Far as it was from the intentions of the Most Eminent Prince, he co-operated in a fraud. Distil this "blande suaviterque" into his ears.

A. B. has been here. He says I should have had an address

from the clergy, but Manning and Patterson stopped it on the plea that it would be thought at Rome to be dictating. He speaks of the clique having had two blows—(1) my leave to found an Oxford Oratory; (2) Mr. Martin's letter. Heavy blows both. C. D. reeling under the first, went to Oakeley and blew up Propaganda. Ward writes to Dr. Ives that what they have to oppose in England, as their great mischief, is Father Newman. He has written to Monsell that there are "vital" differences between us. Is not this Evangelical "vital religion" all over? and is he not dividing Catholics into nominal Christians and vital Christians as much as an Evangelical could do in the Church of England? A. B. says that Vaughan is sent by Ward to Rome— he has now got back . . . Ward says that he loves me so, that he should like to pass an eternity with me, but that whenever he sees Manning he makes him creep—(I have not his exact words)—yet that Manning has the truth and I have not. A. B. thinks that Manning will throw Ward over—that is, next time . . .

96. TO FATHER AMBROSE ST. JOHN

Wednesday night, 8th May, 1867

I am *not a bit* softened about Barnabo. He has not at all explained the "blanda et suavis revocatio" which was to be *concealed* from me *till* I attempted to go to Oxford—*not at all*. And to plead the Bishop's cause before him is an indignity both *in* you and *to* the Bishop. But I don't see how it can be helped —I have allowed your defence of the Bishop and do allow it. There is nothing else that *can* be done. Neve and Palmer wishing it, but the judge is the culprit.

I doubt not Barnabo and Capalti call you and me "pover' uomo" behind our backs, as they do the Bishop. The idea of a Diocesan Bishop having toiled . . . as he has, to be so treated! As for me, I am not a Bishop, and I have not aimed at pleasing them except as a duty to God—at least for many years.

As I am writing I recapitulate the *Rambler* affair. I won't write a *defence* of the passage in the *Rambler* till I know more clearly what I am accused of, either in Catholic doctrine injured, or sentences and phrases used by me. But *you* can write to Barnabo the *facts*—viz. that the Bishop told me that Barnabo was hurt at the passage, and (I *suppose* getting it translated!) showed it the Pope and said to the Bishop that the *Pope* too was hurt, but that *neither you nor I at that time could make out with what*. That at the Bishop's wish I wrote to Cardinal Wiseman, *then in Rome*, the letter I sent you yesterday, to say that I would make any statement *they wished* and explain my passage *according* to it, if they would but tell me what they wanted—that both the Bishop and I expected an answer to that letter, that no answer ever came; that, at the end of six months or so, Manning said or wrote to me to say: "By the bye that matter of the *Rambler* is all at an end"—which I thought, and think now, came from Cardinal Wiseman and was meant to convey to me that I need do no more in the matter. I think I have said all this yesterday, but as I wrote quickly to save the post, lest I should have omitted anything, I repeat it here. Don't offer for me that I *now* will make explanations, *unless* they wish to revive an old matter.

97. TO FATHER COLERIDGE, S.J.

The Oratory, Birmingham.   *30th August, 1867*

My dear Father Coleridge,

Thank you for your affectionate letter. There are a hundred reasons why I was bound to bring the Oxford matter to an end.

For three years complete it has involved me in endless correspondence, conversation, controversy, and bother, taking up my time and thoughts. I felt it was *wrong* thus to fritter away any longer such remaining time as God gives me. It has been my Cross for years and years that I have gone on "operose nihil agendo."

There was the *Rambler* matter. The Cardinal and our Bishop

urged me to interfere with the conductors—and thanked me when I consented. It involved me in endless trouble and work. The correspondence is a huge heap. I have been obliged to arrange and complete it with notes and collateral papers, that I may ultimately be shown to have acted a good part. This was the work of four or five years, and what came of it?

I seem to be similarly circumstanced as regards the Dublin University matters from 1852 to 1858. Letters and papers without end and about nothing—and those not yet sorted and arranged.

I do believe my first thought has ever been "what does God wish me to do?" so I can't really be sorry or repine—but I have very few persons on earth to thank—and I have felt no call, after so many rebuffs, to go on with this Oxford undertaking, and I am come to the conclusion that, if Propaganda wants me for any purpose, it must be so good as to ask me—and I shall wait to be asked—i.e. (as I anticipate) "ad Graecas calendas."

See what a time it has taken to tell you reason one. I will mention only one other, which is abundantly clear, (if it ever were doubtful) from the answers I have had to my late circular. The money was given to *me* personally—the subscribers wanted to see *me* in Oxford (I am talking of the majority of them)—they would not give their money for an Oxford mission merely. When the Propaganda decided that I was not personally to be there, it would have been a misappropriation of their money to spend it merely in an Oxford Church. I inclose one of my circulars.

Yours affectionately,
John H. Newman.

98. TO SIR JOHN T. COLERIDGE

Rednall.   *17th September, 1868*

Dear Sir John Coleridge,

I must begin by apologizing for my delay in acknowledging

your letter of the 10th. Owing to accidental circumstances my time has not been my own; and now, when at length I write, I fear I shall disappoint you in the answer which alone I can give to your question. It almost seems to me as if you were so kind as to wish me to write such an account of my visit to Mr. Keble as might appear in your "Memoir;" but, as I think you will see, my memory is too weak to allow of my putting on paper any particulars of it which are worth preserving. It was remarkable, certainly, that three friends—he, Dr. Pusey, and myself—who had been so intimately united for so many years, and then for so many years had been separated, at least one of them from the other two, should meet together just once again; and, for the first and last time, dine together simply by themselves. And the more remarkable, because not only by chance they met all three together, but there were positive chances against their meeting.

Keble had wished me to come to him, but the illness of his wife, which took them to Bournemouth, obliged him to put me off. On their return to Hursley, I wrote to him on the subject of my visit, and fixed a day for it. Afterwards, hearing from Pusey that he, too, was going to Hursley on the very day I had named, I wrote to Keble to put off my visit. I told him, as I think, my reason. I had not seen either of them for twenty years, and to see both of them at once would be more, I feared, than I could bear. Accordingly, I told him I should go from Birmingham to friends in the Isle of Wight, in the first place, and thence some day go over to Hursley. This was on September 12, 1865. But when I had got into the Birmingham train for Reading, I felt it was like cowardice to shrink from the meeting, and I changed my mind again. In spite of my having put off my visit to him, I slept at Southampton, and made my appearance at Hursley next morning without being expected. Keble was at his door speaking to a friend. He did not know me, and asked my name. What was more wonderful, since I had purposely come to his house, I did not know him, and I feared to ask who it was. I gave him my card without speaking. When at length we found out each other, he said, with that tender flurry of manner which I recollected so well, that his wife had been seized with an attack of her complaint that morning, and that he could not receive me as he should have wished to do, nor, indeed, had he expected me; "for Pusey," he whispered, "is in the house, as you are aware."

Then he brought me into his study and embraced me most affectionately, and said he would go and prepare Pusey, and send him to me.

I think I got there in the forenoon, and remained with him four or five hours, dining at one or two. He was in and out of the room all the time I was with him, attending on his wife, and I was left with Pusey. I recollect very little of the conversation that passed at dinner. Pusey was full of the question of the inspiration of Holy Scripture, and Keble expressed his joy that it was a common cause, in which I could not substantially differ from them; and he caught at such words of mine as seemed to show agreement. Mr. Gladstone's rejection at Oxford was talked of, and I said that I really thought that had I been still a member of the University I must have voted against him, because he was giving up the Irish Establishment. On this, Keble gave me one of his remarkable looks, so earnest and so sweet, came close to me, and whispered in my ear (I cannot recollect the exact words, but I took them to be) "And is not that just?" It left the impression on my mind that he had no great sympathy with the Establishment in Ireland as an Establishment, and was favourable to the Church of the Irish.

Just before my time for going, Pusey went to read the Evening Service in church, and I was left in the open air with Keble by himself. He said he would write to me in the Isle of Wight as soon as his wife got better, and then I should come over and have a day with him. We walked a little way, and stood looking in silence at the church and churchyard, so beautiful and calm. The he began to converse with more than his old tone of intimacy, as if we had never been parted, and soon I was obliged to go.

I remained in the island till I had his promised letter. It was to the effect that his wife's illness had increased, and he must give up the hopes of my coming to him. Thus, unless I had gone on that day, when I was so very near not going, I should not have seen him at all.

He wrote me many notes about this time; in one of them he made a reference to the lines in "Macbeth" : —

> When shall we three meet again?
> When the hurley-burley's done,
> When the battle's lost and won.

This is all I can recollect of a visit of which almost the sole vivid memory which remains with me is the image of Keble himself.

I am, dear Sir John Coleridge,
Yours faithfully,
John H. Newman.

99.   TO DR. ULLATHORNE

28th January, 1870

Private.

I thank your Lordship very heartily for your most interesting and seasonable letter. Such letters (if they could be circulated) would do much to re-assure the many minds which are at present disturbed when they look towards Rome. Rome ought to be a name to lighten the heart at all times, and a Council's proper office is, when some great heresy or other evil impends, to inspire the faithful with hope and confidence. But now we have the greatest meeting which has ever been, and that in Rome, infusing into us by the accredited organs of Rome (such as the *Civilta,* the *Armonia,* the *Univers,* and the *Tablet*) little else than fear and dismay. Where we are all at rest and have no doubts, and, at least practically, not to say doctrinally, hold the Holy Father to be infallible, suddenly there is thunder in the clear sky, and we are told to prepare for something, we know not what, to try our faith, we know not how. No impending danger is to be averted, but a great difficulty is to be created. Is this the proper work for an Ecumenical Council? As to myself personally, please God, I do not expect any trial at all, but I cannot help suffering with the various souls that are suffering. I look with anxiety at the prospect of having to defend decisions which may not be difficult to my private judgment, but may be most difficult to defend logically in the face of historical facts. What have we done to be treated as the Faithful never were treated before? When has definition of doctrine *de fide* been a luxury of devotion and not a stern painful necessity? Why should an aggressive and insolent faction be allowed to make the hearts of the just to mourn whom the Lord hath not made sorrowful? Why can't we be let alone when we have pursued peace and thought no evil? I assure you, my dear Lord, some of the truest minds are driven one way and another, and do not know where to rest their feet; one day determining to give up all theology as a bad job and recklessly to believe henceforth almost that the Pope is impeccable; at another tempted to believe all the worst that a book like Janus says; at another doubting about the capacity possessed by Bishops drawn from all corners of the earth to judge what is fitting for European society, and then again angry with the Holy See for listening to the flattery of a clique of Jesuits, Redemptorists and Converts. Then again think of the score of Pontifical scandals in the history of eighteen centuries which have partly been poured out, and partly are still to come out. What Murphy inflicted upon us in one way, M. Veuillot is indirectly bringing on us in another. And then again the blight which is falling upon the multitude of Anglican ritualists, who themselves perhaps, or at least their leaders, may never become Catholics, but who are leavening the various English parties and denominations (far beyond their own range) with principles and sentiments tending towards their ultimate adoption into the Catholic Church.

With these thoughts before me, I am continually asking

myself whether I ought not to make my feelings public; but all I do is to pray those great early Doctors of the Church whose intercession would decide the matter—Augustine and the rest— to avert so great a calamity. If it is God's Will that the Pope's Infallibility should be defined, then it is His Blessed Will to throw back the times and the moments of that triumph He has destined for His Kingdom; and I shall feel I have but to bow my head to His Adorable Inscrutable Providence. You have not touched on the subject yourself, but I think you will allow me to express to you feelings which for the most part I keep to myself . . .

John H. Newman.

100.   TO FATHER WALFORD, S.J.

The Oratory.   *19th May, 1870*

My dear Fr. Walford,

Thank you for your affectionate letter. It is very pleasant to us to find you remember our Novena, and again that you take an interest in my new book, which was very difficult to write, yet without being easy to read.

1. Difficulties such as your nephew's are, as you know, not uncommon. It is a delicate thing to answer them without knowing something of the objector, for what is apposite for one is unsuitable for another. As to the wonderful revival of religion in the Established Church, I certainly think it comes from God. If so, it must tend, as it visibly does tend, to the Church's benefit. One cannot conceive the generation which is brought up under it, when they come to maturity and to power, resting satisfied with the Anglican system. If their fathers, the present generation, yearn for unity and for communion with St. Peter, much more will their children. There is nothing to prove that the present race of Catholicizing Anglicans is in bad faith; and there is much to show on the other hand that they are in good faith. It is

possible indeed that the next generation may go off into Liberalism, as Hale and Chillingworth, the disciples of Laud. But I rather hope that Holy Church will arrest and win them over by her beauty and sanctity, her gentleness, serenity, and grandeur. Anyhow, we need not say that Anglicans at this time cast out devils through Beelzebub; rather they are like the man of whom our Lord said, "Forbid him not," &c.

2. As to your nephew's fears about the definition of the Pope's Inf., while they are but fears, they are not arguments, because he says he has no expectation that they will ever be fulfilled.

Very sincerely yours in Christ,

John H. Newman.

101. TO FATHER COLERIDGE, S.J.

The Oratory.   *5th February, 1871*

My dear Fr. Coleridge,

I began to read Fr. Harper's papers,[1] but they were (to my ignorance of theology and philosophy) so obscure, and (to my own knowledge of my real meaning) so hopelessly misrepresentations of the book, that I soon gave it over. As to my answering, I think I never answered any critique on any writing of mine, in my life. My "Essay on Development" was assailed by Dr. Brownson on one side, and Mr. Archer Butler on the other, at great length. Brownson, I believe, thought me a Pantheist—and sent me his work to Rome, by some American Bishop. Mr. Butler has been lauded by his people as having smashed me. Now at the end of twenty years, I am told from Rome that I am guilty of the late Definition by my work on Development, so orthodox has it been found in principle, and on the other side Bampton Lectures have been preached, I believe, allowing that principle. The *Guardian* acknowledges my principle as necessary, and the Scotch editors of Dorner's great work on our Lord's Person, cautioning of course the world against *me*, admit that develop-

[1] A criticism of the *Grammar of Assent*.

ment of doctrine is an historical fact. I shall not live another 20 years, but, as I waited patiently, as regards my former work, for "Time to be the Father of Truth," so now I leave the judgment between Fr. Harper and me to the sure future.

Father Mazio said of my "Development," "I do not know how it is, but so it is, that all these startling things, Mr. Newman brings them round at the end to a good conclusion," and so now the *Quarterly* (if I recollect) talks in a kind sense of my surprises, and the *Edinburgh* of my audacity. I do not mean myself to surprise people or to be audacious, but somehow, now at the end of life, I have from experience a confidence in myself, and, (though with little of St. Cyprian's sanctity, but with more of truth, as I trust, in my cause) I am led to take myself some portion of the praise given him in Keble's line, and to "trust the lore of my own loyal heart." I trust to having some portion of an "inductive sense," founded in right instincts.

My book is to show that a right moral state of mind germinates or even generates good intellectual principles. This proposition rejoices the *Quarterly*, as if it was a true principle—it shocks the *Edinburgh*, as if Pascal and others were much more philosophical in saying that religion or religiousness is not ultimately based on reason. And the *Guardian* says that whether this view will or will not hold is the problem now before the intellectual world, which coming years is to decide. Let those, who think I ought to be answered, those Catholics, first master the great difficulty, the great problem, and then, if they don't like my way of meeting it find another. Syllogizing won't meet it.

You see then I have not the very shadow of a reason *against* Fr. Harper's future papers, as I think they will all go ultimately, after I am gone, to the credit of my work.

While I say this, of course I am sensible it may be full of defects, and certainly characterized by incompleteness and crudeness, but it is something to have started a problem, and mapped in part a country, if I have done nothing more.

Yours most sincerely,
John H. Newman.

102. TO THE EDITOR OF *The Times*

September, 1872

Sir,

You have lately, in your article on the Massacre of S. Bartholomew's Day, thrown down a challenge to us on a most serious subject. I have no claim to speak for my brethren; but I speak in default of better men.

No Pope can make evil good. No Pope has any power over those moral principles which God has imprinted on our hearts and consciences. If any Pope has, with his eyes open, approved treachery or cruelty, let those defend that Pope who can. If any Pope at any time has had his mind so occupied with the desirableness of the Church's triumph over her enemies as to be dead to the treacherous and savage acts by which that triumph was achieved, let those who feel disposed say in such conduct he acted up to his high office of maintaining justice and showing mercy.

Craft and cruelty, and whatever is base and wicked, have a sure Nemesis, and eventually strike the heads of those who are guilty of them. Whether in matter of fact Pope Gregory XIII. had a share in the guilt of the S. Bartholomew Massacre must be proved to me before I believe it. It is commonly said in his defence that he had an untrue, one-sided account of the matter presented to him, and acted on misinformation. This involves a question of fact, which historians must decide. But even if they decide against the Pope, his Infallibility is in no respect compromised. Infallibility is not Impeccability. Even Caiaphas prophesied, and Gregory XIII. was not quite a Caiaphas.

I am, Sir, your obedient servant,

John H. Newman.

103. TO THE EDITOR OF *The Guardian*

September, 1872

Sir,

I cannot allow such language as Mr. Capes uses of me in yesterday's *Guardian* to pass unnoticed, nor can I doubt that you will admit my answer to it. I thank him for having put into print what doubtless has often been said behind my back; I do not thank him for the odious words which he has made the vehicle of it.

I will not dirty my ink by repeating them; but the substance, mildly stated, is this—that I have all along considered the doctrine of the Pope's Infallibility to be contradicted by the facts of Church history, and that, though convinced of this, I have in consequence of the Vatican Council forced myself to do a thing that I never, never fancied would befall me when I became a Catholic—viz., forced myself by some unintelligible quibbles to fancy myself believing what really after all in my heart I could not and did not believe. And that this operation and its result had given me a considerable amount of pain.

I could say much, and quote much from what I have written, in comment upon this nasty view of me. But, not to take up too much of your room. I will, in order to pluck it up "by the very roots" (to use his own expression), quote one out of various passages, in which, long before the Vatican Council was dreamed of, at least by me, I enunciated absolutely the doctrine of the Pope's Infallibility. It is in my "Discourses on University Education," delivered in Dublin in 1852. It runs as follows: —

"Deeply do I feel, ever will I protest, *for I can appeal to the ample testimony of history to bear me out,* that, in questions of right and wrong, there is nothing really strong in the whole world, nothing decisive and operative, but the voice of him to whom have been committed the keys of the kingdom and the oversight of Christ's flock. That voice is now, as ever it has been, a real authority, *infallible* when it teaches, prosperous when it

THE LETTERS OF JOHN HENRY NEWMAN

commands, ever taking the lead wisely and distinctly in its own province, adding certainty to what is probable and persuasion to what is certain. Before it speaks, the most saintly may mistake; and after it has spoken, the most gifted must obey . . . If there ever was a power on earth who had an eye for the times, who has confined himself to the practicable, and has been happy in his anticipations, whose words have been deeds, and whose commands prophecies, such is he in the history of ages who sits on from generation to generation in the chair of the Apostles as the Vicar of Christ and Doctor of His Church . . . Has he failed in his successes up to this hour? Did he, in our fathers' day, fail in his struggle with Joseph of Germany and his confederates; with Napoleon—a greater name—and his dependent kings; that, though in another kind of fight, he should fail in ours? What grey hairs are on the head of Judah, whose youth is renewed like the eagle's, whose feet are like the feet of harts, and underneath the everlasting arms?"—pp. 22—28.

This passage I suffered Father Cardella in 1867 or 1868 to reprint in a volume which he published at Rome. My reason for selecting it, as I told him, was this—because in an abridged reprint of the discourses in 1859 I had omitted it, as well as other large portions of the volume, as of only temporary interest, and irrelevant to the subject of University education.

I could quote to the same purpose passages from my "Essay on Development," 1845; "Loss and Gain," 1847; "Discourses to Mixed Congregations," 1849; "Position of Catholics," 1851; "Church of the Fathers," 1857.

I underwent, then, no change of mind as regards the truth of the doctrine of the Pope's Infallibility in consequence of the Council. It is true I was deeply, though not personally, pained both by the fact and by the circumstances of the definition; and, when it was in contemplation, I wrote a most confidential letter, which was surreptitiously gained and published, but of which I have not a word to retract. The feelings of surprise and concern expressed in that letter have nothing to do with a screwing one's conscience to profess what one does not believe, which is Mr.

Capes's pleasant account of me. He ought to know me better.
John H. Newman.

104. TO DEAN CHURCH

28th December, 1872

My dear Dean,

On the contrary, it was simply a bran new coat,[1] which I never put on till I went on that visit to you—and which I did not wear twice even at Abbotsford—I thought it due to London. Indeed, all my visiting clothes are new, for I do not wear them here, and I am almost tempted, like a footman of my Father's when I was a boy, who had a legacy of clothes, to leave home, as he his place, in order to have an opportunity of wearing them. *They* (the clothes) must wish it, I am sure—for they wear out a weary time themselves in a dark closet, except on such occasions, few and far between.

Don't fancy when I talked of a "bore," that I had any other than that *general* feeling, which I ever have, that giving away one of my books is an impertinence, like talking of the shop. I used to say at Oxford that lawyers and doctors ever talked of the shop—but parsons never—now I find priests do—I suppose that, where there is *science,* there is the tendency to be wrapped up in the profession. An English clergyman is primarily a gentleman—a doctor, a lawyer, and so a priest is primarily a professional man. In like manner the military calling has been abroad a profession, accordingly they never go in mufti, but always in full military fig, talking as it were, *always* of the shop. Now I have a great dislike of this shoppism personally. Richmond told some one that, when he took my portrait, I was the only person he could not draw out.

---

[1] The following news paragraph had appeared :

"St. Paul's Catheral. A few weeks since one of the vergers of the Cathedral accosted a poorly clad, threadbare looking individual who stood scanning the alterations of the sacred edifice with ' Now then move on, we don't want any of your sort here ! ' It was Dr. Newman ! "

Now have I not really been talking of the shop enough for a whole twelvemonth, having talked of my dear self? But you see I have a motive—viz. lest you should dream you have trod on my toes, and so elicited from me the complaint that you have been bored by me.

Ever your affectionately,
John H. Newman.

105. TO LORD BLACHFORD (FREDERICK ROGERS)

The Oratory.   *11th April, 1875*

My dear Blachford,

. . . As to my pamphlet,[1] what you say of its success agrees, to my surprise as well as my pleasure, with what I hear from others. What surprises me most is its success among my own people. I had for a long time been urged by my friends to write —but I persisted in saying that I would not go out of my way to do so. When Gladstone wrote, I saw it was now or never, and I had so vivid an apprehension that I should get into a great trouble and rouse a great controversy round me, that I was most unwilling to take up my pen. I had made a compact with myself, that, if I did write, I would bring out my whole mind, and specially speak out on the subject of what I had in a private letter called an "insolent and aggressive faction"—so that I wrote and printed, I may say, in much distress of mind. Yet nothing happened such as I had feared. For instance, Ward is unsaying in print some of his extravagances, and a priest who with others has looked at me with suspicion and is a good specimen of his class, writes to me, "I hope everybody will read and re-read it. . . . I may also congratulate you that you have carried with you the Catholic mind of England, and made us feel but one pulse of Ultramontane sympathy beating in our body—May God give you length of days &c." In Ireland Cardinal Cullen spoke of me in the warmest terms in his Lent Pastoral, read in all the

[1] *Letter to the Duke of Norfolk.*

churches of his diocese, and my friend Dr. Russell of Maynooth, who had been frightened at the possible effect of some of my pages, wrote to me, after being present at a great gathering of bishops and priests from all parts of Ireland, on occasion of Archbishop Leahy's funeral, that I had nothing to fear, for there was but one unanimous voice there, and that was in my favour.

Of course as time goes on "the clouds may return after the rain"—but anyhow I have cause for great thankfulness—and I trust that now I may be allowed to die in peace. Old age is very cowardly—at least so I find it to be . .

106. TO DR. ULLATHORNE

The Oratory.   *18th December, 1877*

My dear Lord,

I have just received a great compliment, perhaps the greatest I have ever received, and I don't like not to tell you of it one of the first.

My old College, Trinity College, where I was an undergraduate from the age of 16 to 21, till I gained a Fellowship at Oriel, has made me an Honorary Fellow of their Society. Of course it involves no duties, rights or conditions, not even that of belonging to the University, certainly not that of having a vote as Master of Arts, but it is a mark of extreme kindness to me from men I have never seen, and it is the only instance of their exercising their power since it was given them.

Trinity College has been the one and only seat of my affections at Oxford, and to see once more, before I am taken away, what I never thought I should see again, the place where I began the battle of life, with my good angel by my side, is a prospect almost too much for me to bear.

I have been considering for these two days, since the offer came to me, whether there would be any inconsistency in my accepting it, but it is so pure a compliment in its very title that

I do not see that I need fear its being interpreted by the world as anything else.

Begging your Lordship's blessing, I am your obedient and affectionate servant in Christ.

John H. Newman.

P.S.—The Pope made me a D.D., but I don't call an act of the Pope's a *"compliment."*

107. TO MR. GREENHILL

The Oratory.   *18th January, 1879*

My dear Mr. Greenhill,

You flatter me by your question[1]; but I think it was Keble who, when asked it in his own case, answered that poets were not bound to be critics, or to give a sense to what they had written; and though I am not, like him, a poet, at least I may plead that I am not bound to *remember* my own meaning, whatever it was, at the end of almost fifty years.

Anyhow there must be a statute of limitation for writers of verse, or it would be quite a tyranny if, in an art which is the expression not of truth but of imagination and sentiment, one were obliged to be ready for examination on the transient state of mind which came upon one when home-sick, or sea-sick, or in any other way sensitive or excited.

Yours most truly,

John H. Newman.

108. TO DR. ULLATHORNE

The Oratory, Birmingham.

2nd February, Feast of the Purification, 1879

My Right Rev. Father,

I trust that his Holiness, and the most eminent Cardinal Nina

[1] Concerning the two last lines of *Lead Kindly Light.*

will not think me a thoroughly discourteous and unfeeling man, who is not touched by the commendation of superiors, or a sense of gratitude, or the splendour of dignity, when I say to you, my Bishop, who know me so well, that I regard as altogether above me the great honour which the Holy Father proposes with wonderful kindness to confer on one so insignificant, an honour quite transcendent and unparalleled, than which his Holiness has none greater to bestow.

For I am, indeed, old and distrustful of myself; I have lived now thirty years *in nidulo meo* in my much loved Oratory, sheltered and happy, and would therefore entreat his Holiness not to take me from St. Philip, my Father and Patron.

By the love and reverence with which a long succession of Popes have regarded and trusted St. Philip, I pray and entreat his Holiness in compassion of my diffidence of mind, in consideration of my feeble health, my nearly eighty years, the retired course of my life from my youth, my ignorance of foreign languages, and my lack of experience in business, to let me die where I have so long lived. Since I know now and henceforth that his Holiness thinks kindly of me, what more can I desire?

Right Rev. Father,
Your most devoted,
John H. Newman.

109. TO THE DUKE OF NORFOLK

The Oratory.   *20th February, 1879*

My dear Duke,

I have heard from various quarters of the affectionate interest you have taken in the application to Rome about me, and I write to thank you and to express my great pleasure at it.

As to the statement of my refusing a Cardinal's Hat, which is in the papers, you must not believe it—for this reason:

Of course, it implies that an offer has been made me, and I have sent an answer to it. Now I have ever understood that it is a point of propriety and honour to consider such communications sacred. The statement therefore cannot come from me. Nor could it come from Rome, for it was made public before my answer got to Rome.

It could only come, then, from some one who not only read my letter, but, instead of leaving to the Pope to interpret it, took upon himself to put an interpretation upon it, and published that interpretation to the world.

A private letter, addressed to Roman Authorities, is interpreted on its way and published in the English papers. How is it possible than any one can have done this?

And besides, I am quite sure that, if so high an honour was offered me, I should not answer it by a blunt refusal.

Yours affectionately,
John H. Newman.

110. TO "A NON-CATHOLIC FRIEND"

28th February, 1879

Everything has two sides. Of course my accepting would disappoint these men, but declining would disappoint those. And just now for the same reasons would their feelings be contrary, viz., because my accepting would show the closest adherence of my mind to the Church of Rome, and my declining would seem an evidence of secret distance from her. Both sides would say: "You see, he is not a Catholic in heart."

Now this has ailed me this thirty years; men won't believe me. This act would force them to do so. So that to a man in my mental position your argument tells the contrary way to what you anticipate.

But again, as to what you kindly call my "post of deep moral value," this must be viewed relatively to Unitarians, Theists and Sceptics, on the one side, and Catholics and Anglicans on the other. I wish to be of religious service, such as I can, to both parties—but, if I must choose between Theists and Catholics, "blood is thicker than water." You forget that I believe the Catholic religion to be true, and you do not. It is not that I am insensible to and ungrateful for the good opinion of Theists, but Catholics are my brothers, and I am bound to consult for them first

J. H. N.

111. TO CARDINAL MANNING

The Oratory.   *4th March, 1879*

Dear Cardinal Manning,

I hardly should have thought it became me, since no letter has been addressed to me, to write to anyone at Rome myself, on the gracious message of the Holy Father about me.

Since, however, the Bishop of Birmingham recommends me to do so, I hereby beg to say that with much gratitude and with true devotion to His Holiness, I am made acquainted with and accept the permission he proposes to me in his condescending goodness to keep place within the walls of my Oratory at Birmingham.

I am, sincerely yours, kissing the Sacred Purple,

John H. Newman.

112. TO CARDINAL MANNING

The Oratory.   *5th March, 1879*

Dear Cardinal Manning,

Wishing to guard against all possible mistake I trouble you with this second letter.

As soon as the Holy Father condescends to make it known to me that he means to confer on me the high dignity of Cardinal, I shall write to Rome to signify my obedience and glad acceptance of the honour without any delay.

I write this thinking that the impression which existed some fortnight since, that I had declined it, may still prevail.

Yours very sincerely,

John H. Newman.

P.S. This second letter is occasioned by something that came to my knowledge since my letter of yesterday.

113. TO SISTER MARIA PIA (MISS MARIA GIBERNE)

Birmingham.   *3rd July, 1882*

I did not forget you on the Visitation, but said Mass for you on two other days instead, because I heard that William George Ward was dying. How it was that his serious state of health was not known generally before, I cannot tell, but they say that it is a simple break up. His principal complaint is that of which Fr. Joseph Gordon died, and that was three years upon him.

It will be still some time before Palmer's Journal will issue from the Press. I shall send it to you. It seems to me very interesting—but 40 years is more than a generation and I can't prophesy how it will strike most people. The Czar does not appear in it, though afterwards he had Palmer to dine with him. I think the book shows the impossibility of a union of Greece with Anglicans, and of Greece with Rome. As for the Russian ecclesiastics, he found that they had all but given up the idea of unity, or of the Catholicity of the Church. So far, they were behind the Anglicans, who at least profess belief in one Catholic Church.

I am very well as far as health goes—but I am more and more infirm. I am dim sighted, deaf, lame, and have a difficulty in talking and writing. And my memory is very bad.

I fear the enemies of the Church are all but effecting its absolute fall in France. The first and second generation after us will have a dreadful time of it. Satan is almost unloosed. May we all be housed safely before that day!

Are you not 80 now?

114. TO LORD BRAYE

Birmingham.   *29th October, 1882*

My dear Lord Braye,

I thank you for your most touching letter, which I think I quite understand and in which I deeply sympathise. First, however, let me say a word about myself . . . I am thankful to say that I am at present quite free from any complaint, as far as I know, but I am over eighty, and it is with difficulty that I walk, eat, read, write or talk. My breath is short and my brain works slow, and, like other old men, I am so much the creature of hours, rooms, and of routine generally, that to go from home is almost like tearing off my skin, and I suffer from it afterwards. On the other hand, except in failure of memory, and continual little mistakes in the use of words, and confusion in the use of names, I am not conscious that my mind is weaker than it was.

Now this is sadly egotistical; but I want you to understand why it is that I do not accept your most kind invitations, any more than I have Lord Denbigh's. I decline both with real pain; and thank you both. But I have real reasons, which friends sometimes will not believe, for they come and see me and say: "How well you are looking!"

Now what can I say in answer to your letter? First, that your case is mine. It is for years beyond numbering—in one view of the matter for these fifty years—that I have been crying out: "I have laboured in vain; I have spent my strength without cause, and in vain; wherefore my judgment is with the Lord and my work with my God." Now at the end of my days, when the next world is close upon me, I am recognised at last at Rome. Don't suppose I am dreaming of complaint; just the contrary. The Prophet's words, which expressed my keen pain, brought, because they were his words, my consolation. It is the rule of God's Providence that we should succeed by failure; and my moral is, as addressed to you: "Doubt not that He will use you —be brave—have faith in His love for you—His everlasting

247

love—and love Him from the certainty that He loves you."

I cannot write more today, and since it is easier thus to write, than to answer your direct questions, I think it better to write to you at once than to keep silence. May the best blessings from above come down upon you—and they will.

I am, my dear Lord Braye,

Yours (may I say?) affectionately,

John H. Card. Newman.

115.   TO DEAN CHURCH

12th April, 1885

My dear Dean,

Thank you for your impressive Easter Sermon.

It is 63 years today since I was elected at Oriel; the turning day of my life.

Yours affectionately,

J. H. Card. Newman.

116.   TO DEAN CHURCH

25th March, 1886

My dear Dean,

Many thanks. I am going up to the Duchess [of Norfolk's] Requiem Mass on Monday. How I am to get thro' it, I can't tell. I hope I shall not be using your house as an Infirmary—I am, not ill, but so weak and sleepy.

Ever yours affectionately,

John H. Card. Newman.

INDEX

INDEX